Other books by John W. Jones

The Burnout Syndrome:
Current Research, Theory, and Interventions

Preemployment Honesty Testing:
Current Research and Future Directions

Applying Psychology in Business:
The Handbook for Managers and Human Resource Professionals

High-Speed
MANAGEMENT

John W. Jones

High-Speed MANAGEMENT

Time-Based Strategies for Managers and Organizations

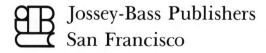
Jossey-Bass Publishers
San Francisco

For sales outside the United States, contact Maxwell Macmillan International Publishing Group, 866 Third Avenue, New York, New York 10022.

Manufactured in the United States of America

The paper used in this book is acid-free and meets the State of California requirements for recycled paper (50 percent recycled waste, including 10 percent postconsumer waste), which are the strictest guidelines for recycled paper currently in use in the United States.

Library of Congress Cataloging-in-Publication Data

Jones, John W. (John Walter), date.
   High-speed management : time-based strategies for managers and organizations / John W. Jones.
     p. cm. — (The Jossey-Bass management series)
   Includes bibliographical references and index.
   ISBN 1-55542-489-9
   1. Time management. 2. Industrial management—United States.
3. Competition—United States. 4. Competition, International.
I. Title. II. Series.
HD69.T54J66 1993
658.4'093—dc20
                                          92-27755
                                             CIP

FIRST EDITION
HB Printing   10 9 8 7 6 5 4 3 2 1   *Code 9289*

The Jossey-Bass Management Series

Consulting Editors
Organizations and Management

Warren Bennis
University of Southern California

Richard O. Mason
Southern Methodist University

Ian I. Mitroff
University of Southern California

CONTENTS

ix

Part Two: Organizational Strategies

PREFACE

High-speed management (HSM) is becoming one of the major competitive strategies of the 1990s. Time-based managers (hereafter referred to as HSM managers) work smarter and more productively than their slower-responding counterparts because HSM allows managers to quickly conceptualize, develop, market, distribute, support, and update new products and services for targeted groups of customers. HSM is especially useful to companies whose managers are expected to succeed in both the national and the international market.

High-Speed Management is a second-generation book that presents time-based competitive strategies. First-generation books have already built the case that speed will be one of the major corporate battlegrounds of the future. However, most of these books are either too philosophical, lacking in practical strategies and solutions, or too narrow in their focus (for example, they may focus only on speeding up the manufacturing process). Also, first-generation books typically focus on what the entire organization should do differently, while this book focuses on the fundamental changes required of both individual managers *and* entire organizations.

Audience

This book should appeal to accomplished business managers who want to gain a competitive advantage by working faster, smarter, and more efficiently than others. These managers will learn how to (1) become highly effective HSM managers, and (2) assist their companies to become more competitive by implementing organization-level HSM strategies. The book should prove relevant for senior executives who want to base their company's future on a new, more competitive style of management. Management consultants and corporate trainers also should benefit from *High-Speed Management*, since it provides practical strategies that can easily be taught to managers who want to transform themselves into skilled practitioners of time-based management. Even MBA students should find the text useful. All these audiences will find comfort in the knowledge that the HSM strategies reviewed here are based on sound scientific principles and credible case studies. Even if readers find that only a few of the HSM strategies are useful in their situation, they can dramatically improve their competitive posture for the 1990s and beyond.

Overview of the Contents

This book begins with an introduction that describes how time-based strategies are rapidly reshaping both national and global competition. HSM strategies provide managers with a competitive advantage, allowing them to beat competitors to market with new products and services more systematically. In addition, companies that reach markets the fastest can charge a premium until their slower competition catches up. Speed-based companies can also gain market share, since they will encounter few, if any, competitors offering similar products and services.

Part One consists of seven chapters that describe specific HSM strategies for the *individual manager*. These chapters teach managers a wide variety of time-based management skills — including effective time-management practices, quick strategic decision-making skills, and computer-assisted negotiations — that will make them faster, more efficient performers. Part One also teaches managers how to anticipate future business trends, how to succeed in the Information Age, and how to cope with the demands of time-based management without becoming burned out.

In Chapter One, prospective HSM managers learn that they must master the essential skills of management (such as planning, organizing, motivating, and communicating) before they attempt to master high-speed management. In Chapter Two, a variety of time-management skills are presented to help managers save time and increase their overall productivity. Chapter Three teaches prospective HSM managers that they must be able to predict, plan for, even invent the future if they want to consistently beat out their competitors. In Chapter Four, prospective HSM managers learn how to make quicker, more accurate business decisions while avoiding "analysis paralysis."

Chapter Five teaches aspiring HSM managers how to resolve conflicts quickly and successfully by using a variety of strategic negotiating skills. HSM managers must know how to use both cooperative and competitive negotiating tactics to reach profitable agreements. In Chapter Six, prospective HSM managers learn how to locate relevant business information quickly, and how to develop effective speed-reading, speed-learning, and critical-thinking skills; this chapter also explains the importance of becoming computer literate in order to gain an electronic edge over competitors. Chapter Seven illustrates that by keeping physically fit and managing stress, HSM managers can outperform over-stressed and depressed managers. The chapter also explains how to avoid the potential pitfalls and dangers of time-based management, including job burnout, work addiction, substance abuse, and coronary-prone behavior.

Part Two includes nine chapters that cover a variety of high-speed *organizational strategies* that can be used by management teams to transform their departments, divisions, and entire companies into speed-based enterprises. These strategies include maintaining an intelligence system on competitors, hiring and training fast and efficient workers, accelerating product releases, closing sales quickly, maintaining a satisfied customer base, and monitoring the company's financial health.

Chapter Eight points out how companies can use professionally developed personnel selection systems to hire a dependable, skilled, and productive workforce that will optimally support and quickly advance an HSM culture. Chapter Nine discusses the premise that companies must be aware of their competitors' strategies in order to consistently outdistance those competitors in the marketplace. Chapter Ten teaches management teams how to consistently and significantly reduce the time between product conceptualization and product availability.

Chapter Eleven discusses how companies can quickly document and satisfy the needs of a targeted group of customers and thereby take the driver's seat in acquiring, expanding, and retaining meaningful market share. Chapter Twelve shows companies how to use time-based sales strategies and computerization to speed up the process of qualifying leads, closing sales, and cross-selling the customer base. Chapter Thirteen points out the benefits of staying very close to customers at all times in order to meet their identified and unidentified needs continually. Specific strategies are offered for quickly identifying and successfully resolving any problems clients might be experiencing. It is much more profitable to keep well-established clients than to locate, cultivate, and win over new ones.

Chapter Fourteen encourages management teams to monitor and analyze important financial statements and ratios vigilantly, so that corrective actions can be taken whenever needed, to increase revenues, contain costs, and increase earnings. This chapter also presents strategies for quickly increasing the profitability of a company's investments, including strong credit policies, inventory management procedures, and payroll control plans. By keeping financial score at all times, HSM managers are better able to seize new profit-making opportunities. The case studies in Chapter Fifteen describe the top fifteen companies in the United States and abroad that best execute the principles of high-speed management.

Finally, the book's concluding chapter provides practical suggestions on how to become an HSM manager or organization. This chapter recommends some initial steps that prospective HSM managers can take to transform their management style, along with ways entire companies can begin to develop a speed-based culture. General Motors is presented as an example of a company that could benefit from implementing HSM strategies.

Acknowledgments

I would like to thank William Terris for his encouragement on this project and other projects throughout my career, and William Hicks at Jossey-Bass for realizing the need for a second-generation book on time-based management strategies. To Verona Haffenden I owe thanks for her support in preparing this manuscript. I would like to express my gratitude and love to my wife, Catalina Soto, for her enthusiastic interest in the project. I also want to thank my mother, Anita Jones, for her continuous support of my scholastic pursuits. And finally, this book is dedicated to the memory of my father, Walter Jones, the first HSM manager I learned from.

Arlington Heights, Illinois   John W. Jones
September 1992   *Industrial and Organizational*
                                                        Psychologist

To my father,
WALTER T. JONES, JR.,
who introduced me to the
joys and challenges of business

THE AUTHOR

John W. Jones is vice president of research and service at London House/Science Research Associates, a management consulting firm and publisher of personnel tests in Rosemont, Illinois. He is a licensed psychologist in Illinois and was awarded the Diplomate in Industrial and Organizational Psychology by the American Board of Professional Psychology. Jones is a member of the American Psychological Association and the Society for Industrial and Organizational Psychology. He is the editor-in-chief of the *Journal of Business and Psychology* and the associate editor of the *American Journal of Health Promotion*. He received his Ph.D. (1980) in psychology from De Paul University in Chicago, Illinois, and his Certificate in Business Administration (1991) in entrepreneurial studies from the School of Business Administration, University of Illinois, Chicago, where he specialized in marketing and operations management.

High-Speed
MANAGEMENT

Speed as a Competitive Resource

This book was written for managers interested in learning high-speed management (HSM) strategies. Traditional managers assume they have plenty of time to weigh their options, generate multiple alternatives, think through different business scenarios, and produce lengthy staff reports justifying their decisions and plans of action. The traditional manager's ultimate goal is to work on lower-risk projects and stay within budget at all costs. The results are predictable: sluggish companies, reduced competitiveness, disgruntled employees, customer dissatisfaction, and eventual decline of market share.

HSM managers offer a new style of leadership. They know that time is money, and they see time as a competitive resource, not an obstacle. They realize that there is no single time-based

1

strategy, no "silver bullet" that can be applied successfully across the board. However, they do recognize that there are a number of time-based strategies that, when used in concert, can yield strong competitive advantage. For example, HSM managers feel that niche marketing is critical in quickly understanding and meeting a targeted group of customers' needs for specific products and services. HSM managers know the importance of continuously innovating and upgrading their products and services to keep them from falling out of favor with customers. They realize they must adopt the computer technology that gives their staffs the most current proven tools to perform their jobs in an accurate, comprehensive, and efficient manner. Most importantly, HSM managers realize they must create a corporate culture in which rapid innovation, speed to market, and quick adaptation to change come naturally.

Companies in the 1990s are under increasing pressure to reduce the time-to-market lag if they are to succeed in the everchanging marketplace. They must use time-based management techniques such as quick decision making, concurrent engineering, process simplification, rapid innovation, just-in-time manufacturing, and automation to continuously reduce the time between product definition and product availability. HSM managers must work continuously to streamline and simplify business units and practices. One way of accomplishing this is by reducing the number of intermediaries, thereby eliminating organizational layers. HSM managers provide challenging time-to-market goals that their staffs strive to meet and exceed. HSM managers provide the information systems needed for immediate, rapid, and accurate communication of all relevant business information. They realize that change, innovation, and improvement are ongoing processes, and that they can never accept the status quo. Markets based on fashion styles (such as women's apparel) have always been under this type of time pressure. However, in today's business climate nearly all industries are feeling the need to compete in time.

Glimpses of High Speed Management

To date, few corporations can be characterized as 100 percent HSM organizations. This is probably because the HSM philosophy and the accompanying management strategies are still in their infancy. Examples of advanced HSM enterprises include Federal Express, Domino's Pizza, and Citicorp. Federal Express pioneered overnight delivery in the airfreight industry, while Domino's became the second largest pizza chain in the country by delivering their pizzas in thirty minutes or less, guaranteed!

Citicorp completely adopted a time-based management philosophy to differentiate itself from the competition. It was one of the first banks to offer user-friendly and convenient automated teller machines (ATMs), which allow customers to make withdrawals and deposits twenty-four hours a day. Customers can even use ATMs to invest in money market funds or to purchase certificates of deposit. Citicorp also uses a time-based strategy when selling mortgage loans. Other banks typically take thirty to sixty days to process a loan. Loan decisions at these slow-response banks go through complex, time-consuming channels while buyers and sellers anxiously wait for a decision. At Citicorp, the number of approval steps was reduced so that a decision typically could be reached within fifteen days. Citicorp's mortgage business doubled within a year after implementing this time-based strategy.

Other companies, such as H&R Block, Motorola, and Lens Crafters, continually strive to build their corporate strategies around speed. In 1990, H&R Block rolled out its new Rapid Refund electronic tax-filing program, to gain competitive advantage and to differentiate itself from its competition. With this program customers were willing to pay an additional $25 to have their tax returns electronically delivered directly to the Internal Revenue Service's computer. Nearly three million customers utilized this high-speed service. For an additional charge, tax filers expecting refunds could get them in days from H&R Block, instead of waiting weeks or months to get them from the IRS. Tom Bloch, CEO of H&R Block, reported that the quick-refund program has had a very positive and immediate impact on their major competition — the millions of do-it-yourselfers who, Bloch estimates, still account for 50 percent of all tax filings.

Business units at Motorola have eliminated delays in the

design, production, and sales of their electronic pagers. For example, Motorola's sales staff use laptop computers to identify and record the unique product features a customer requests for a customized pager. The salesperson then uses a modem to transmit the design data to the Motorola factory in Florida. Production can start literally within minutes after the order is received. Disciplined managers at Motorola accept no excuses for missed deadlines. Completed pagers are ready to be shipped within hours, and the final product can be in the customer's hands as early as the next day. Time-based strategies such as these are used to meet deadlines consistently, speed up order taking, and finalize sales quickly.

Lens Crafters is a time-based company that has revolutionized the eyecare industry. Corrective lenses used to be produced and stocked in a central location far removed from the customers, who each went to their own eye doctor to get a prescription for the lenses. Getting an appointment with their doctor often took weeks. Customers would then go to a retail store to select their frames. The frames had to be fitted with lenses that took weeks or longer to deliver from the central location. Needless to say, the traditional approach was very time-consuming.

Lens Crafters retail stores integrated the design, production, and delivery of eyeglasses under one roof. It usually takes only one hour for a pair of eyeglasses to be completed. Moreover, Lens Crafters' customers can now get their eyes checked at the same retail store, usually in fifteen minutes or less. No wonder Lens Crafters is one of the most profitable divisions of the U.S. Shoe Corporation.

Only a few companies have attempted to fully adopt time-based management strategies. Yet there are numerous examples of business units within larger corporations that use HSM principles for competitive gain. For example, business units at AT&T have reduced the amount of time it takes to design and manufacture new phone products—from approximately two years to one year. AT&T managers accomplished this by using multidisciplinary teams of experts, concurrent engineering principles, and extremely tough deadlines. Similarly, General Electric

Company slashed the amount of time it takes to design and produce new circuit-breaker boxes — from three weeks to three days. This was accomplished by reducing management layers to speed up decision making, streamlining manufacturing processes, and establishing interdisciplinary work teams with the authority to set and meet aggressive deadlines.

Emerging Gurus of Time-Based Management

In their book *Competing Against Time: How Time-Based Competition Is Reshaping Global Markets*, George Stalk, Jr., and Thomas Houts have documented a number of benefits of time-based management. For example, HSM managers who reduce the time required to fill customer needs can charge from 20 to 100 percent more than the average industry price for the faster response time. Premium prices can be charged for faster service as well as for quickly bringing new products to market. For instance, Hertz launched its Number One Club Gold Program and found that members were willing to pay an additional $50 per year to be able to make a reservation by phone, go directly from the plane to the Hertz shuttle bus, and then bypass the registration desk by getting dropped off directly at their car, with the keys in the trunk and the rental agreement hanging from the mirror.

Market share should also increase because time-based companies that are capable of satisfying their customers' needs the fastest should win business from their slower-responding competitors. In addition, inventories should shrink since large inventory stockpiles will not be necessary to ensure quick delivery. Instead of stocking up on a product, the fastest producers can make and ship an order shortly after the order is placed.

Stanley Davis: Any Time

Stanley Davis wrote *Future Perfect* in 1987 to provide managers with a visionary analysis of the future, so that they would sense the importance of anticipating events and begin to create the time-based organizations needed to thrive in future decades. Tom Peters, management guru of the 1980s and coauthor of *In*

Search of Excellence, rated *Future Perfect* the "book of the decade." Davis points out in his chapter "Any Time" that, in business, everything is measured in the time dimension:

> Few major corporations can be counted by cen-
> turies, careers are measured by decades, and prod-
> ucts by years. Accounts are generally payable
> monthly, people often work nine to five, coffee
> breaks are fifteen minutes, push-button phones
> save you seven seconds dialing time, and lasers
> work in nanoseconds (one billionth of a second).
> (1987, p. 12)

Davis points out that in the business world, the concept of time is undergoing a radical transition. During the industrial age, for example, the 9-to-5 concept of time was based on a regularly occurring internal event that was most relevant to the producing company. In the postindustrial age, the time focus is more on the consumer. That is, today's managers need to think about offering 24-hour customer service, 7 days a week and 365 days a year. In addition, postindustrial-age managers must con-tinually shorten the time interval between identifying the cus-tomer's need and the successful fulfillment of that need.

Davis also believes that every manager should measure the elapsed time of every step from product conceptualization to product consumption and then continuously work to reduce all critical time intervals. Davis reports that marginal reductions in time (10–20 percent) generally can be accomplished by sim-ply improving efficiency. However, major reductions (50–100 percent or more) typically require reconceptualization of the entire production, distribution, and/or delivery systems.

As a futurist, Davis offers the vision of *zero-based time.* The ultimate goal of this abstract and futuristic concept is the complete elimination of customer waiting. When customers need a product or service, it should be available immediately. Davis encourages managers to continually think about how they can create products and services in "real time" that can be delivered instantaneously. This contextual shift alone — of seeing the product in design, development, production, and consumed all at the same time — will begin to speed up processes.

Davis wants managers to see time as a resource rather than a restraint. He sees time joining the ranks of price, quality, and service in determining market successes. Davis offers the following advice to managers who are serious about using time in this new context — as a competitive resource:

- Consumers need to receive products and services instantaneously, according to *their* time frame and preference.
- Producers who deliver products and services faster than their competitors will have a very strong competitive advantage.
- The long-term goal is to reduce to zero the lag time between the identification and the fulfillment of the customers' needs.

Robert Tucker: The Speed Imperative

In his book *Managing the Future*, Robert Tucker isolates ten driving forces of change that are confronting managers in the 1990s, including using technology for competitive advantage, providing high-quality products and services, and gaining and retaining market share by offering outstanding customer service. However, Tucker's number one driving force for the 1990s is exploiting the benefits of speed. He feels that customers will welcome time-based management because speed is part of contemporary American culture.

> Americans have always valued efficiency. We are the nation that invented fast food, one-hour dry cleaning, and instant coffee. . . . Saving people time can become a competitive advantage if you exploit it. To put it simply, customers gravitate to businesses that value their time. Therefore, speed — speed of transaction, speed of repair, speed in responding

to new demands — is a factor in the customer's decision of whom to patronize. (1991, p. 30)

Tucker points out that the speed imperative, as he refers to
it, has rocketed certain future-oriented companies to the top,
while crushing companies that have ignored it. As mentioned
earlier, Domino's Pizza built an entire business around speed.
Domino's Pizza has carved out a competitive niche by making
speed of delivery — rather than the quality of its pizza — the
keystone of its success. This strategy has helped fuel Domino's
rise to being the second largest pizza chain in America.

Tucker shows how other speed-based companies have anticipated and capitalized on customers' needs for greater convenience and speed. For instance, Federal Express revolutionized
the parcel industry with its overnight delivery guarantee. One-
hour photo minilabs such as Moto Photo and Fox Photo took
market share from Eastman Kodak when Kodak did not shorten
its film processing turnaround time. Tucker emphasizes that
these entrepreneurial minilabs took business from the traditional film developers despite the fact that the minilabs are
more expensive than the traditional photo-finishers (6 percent
higher on average). The minilabs succeeded by reducing the
fulfillment "float time" and by changing forever the customer's
perception of waiting time.

Tucker concludes that speed clearly is transforming entire
industries, creating new winners and losers every day. He feels
the speed imperative will continue to influence industries and
markets throughout the 1990s. He offers the following eight-step
program for exploiting the speed imperative:

1. *Assess importance of speed.* Determine whether speed is critical
   to your business or industry. Determine whether your customers value speed.
2. *Reduce float time.* Challenge all time-based assumptions at
   your company. Realize that the future lies in reducing the
   float time between customers' purchase decisions and a
   company's satisfaction of those requests. Document all the
   important request-through-fulfillment cycles your custom-

ers experience, and pick out the most time-consuming areas for immediate reduction.

3. *Involve the customer.* Survey customers to determine where and how delays affect their satisfaction with your business. Next, identify ways speed can increase their satisfaction and ultimately their purchasing behavior. Get employees, managers, and customers involved in brainstorming ways to speed up business processes, services, and transactions.

4. *Measure results.* Always measure the amount of time between request and fulfillment. This will make management and employees more responsive to the time issue. Two important categories in business that need to be measured are manufacturing speed and speed to the customer. Management must set clear expectations and standards for speed in these two areas, and then assess how their employees measure up against those standards.

5. *Promote efforts.* Let customers know that you are making improvements that allow for faster product development, faster service, and so on. The speed imperative should be mentioned in marketing and promotional efforts to gain competitive advantage wherever possible.

6. *Charge for speed.* Realize that most customers are willing to pay more for products that are developed fast and serviced quickly. Determine if the cost of reducing or eliminating bottlenecks in the request-through-fulfillment cycle can be passed on to customers.

7. *Reward speed.* Reward employees who develop and support a time-based corporate culture. Employees must realize that speed is more than a value-added fad. It must be perceived as an essential dimension of every product or service the company offers.

8. *Guarantee speed.* Finally, customers must feel confident that speed-based companies will consistently deliver on their time guarantees. Domino's Pizza guarantees timely delivery, as does Federal Express. Wells Fargo Bank pays customers if they have to wait in line for more than five minutes. This motivates Wells Fargo employees to always work in a highly

efficient manner, and to immediately open up service lines when needed. (Adapted from Tucker, 1991)

Tom Peters: Time-Obsessed Competition

Tom Peters published *Thriving on Chaos: Handbook for a Management Revolution* in 1987. A number of time-based management philosophies, principles, and tactics were described in his pioneering text, including niche marketing, simplifying organizational structure, no-nonsense delegation, and pursuing fast-paced innovation. In a 1990 *Management Review* article, "Time-Obsessed Competition," Peters continued to analyze companies that are competing in the time dimension. Peters believes that time-based competition will be one of the primary corporate battlegrounds in the 1990s.

In his 1990 article, Peters provided a list of "must-dos" for companies planning to compete in time. His list differs from Tucker's because he thinks most companies will need to undergo a "corporate revolution" if they want to be successful in their efforts. Some of his major recommendations include:

1. *Decentralize and share information.* All corporate computers need to be linked up so that all critical information is available to everyone in the organization on a "real time" basis. In addition, customers and vendors need to be electronically linked up to the company. With all parties accessing and basing their decisions on a shared data base, faster operations and quicker decisions can occur.
2. *Flatten the organizational structure.* Peters firmly believes that in a time-competitive world, a company cannot survive with a six- to eight-layer organizational structure. Vertical companies with too many layers tend to have excessive meetings; they pass too many memos up and down the hierarchy and information gets bottlenecked in the middle. The time-obsessed company seeks a flat organizational structure. Peters compares the flat structure of the future to a network, or spider web, while the multilayered bureaucracies of the past resemble pyramids.

3. *Redesign all business processes.* The most effective method of cycle-time reduction is the wholesale redesign of all relevant business processes. Unnecessary and trivial delays in these processes need to be eliminated at once. Moreover, once a process is more quickly completed, a manager must start all over to figure out how another cycle-time reduction can be achieved. The HSM manager can never rest on his past successes!

4. *Measure time improvement.* Like Tucker, Peters is keenly aware that what gets measured gets done. He feels that "time consumption" should be the critical management factor that gets measured. Peters went as far as suggesting that speed is one of the most important measurements throughout the company, and that measures of quality, service, and profitability should come second.

5. *Empower employees.* Quite simply, a company cannot expect quick decisions to be made by front line workers unless those workers have the authority, the managerial backing, and the empowerment to make such decisions. Employees must be trusted and encouraged to do whatever it takes to support a time-based corporate culture. To compete in time, front line employees must be allowed to transcend restrictive job descriptions and reporting structures. They must also be encouraged to access and act on "real time" information, regardless of where and from whom they get the information.

Peters is continually fine-tuning his conceptualization of time-based management. He wrote a 1991 *Industry Week* article, "Beyond Speed: We're All in the Fad-and-Fashion Business." In this article he argues that all products should increasingly be viewed as "fashions" that will quickly be replaced by newer, more stylish ones. Computer chips, motorcycles, and even audio-visual equipment will be fashionable only about as long as the latest-style suit or dress. Managers must accept the fact that copycat products can appear very quickly. Once their company launches a clever new product, it might be only a matter of days, weeks, or months before rival companies release similar products. Therefore, Peters feels that time-based managers must be able to think about creating and destroying a new product all at the same time. This seems like a contradiction, but Peters explains the need for management to develop such a strategy:

> A system to deal with fads and fashions in chemicals, running shoes, or computers must be constructed. Spanking new corporate capabilities must be acquired. But at the same time, destroying that system, being the redefiner before a subsequent redefiner redefines you out of business, is equally important—no more, no less important than the design of the original scheme. . . . The [manager's] primary task then is to create *systems* and destroy them—at once. Build *structures* and dismantle them—at once. (1991, p. 26)

Time-Based Strategies

Time-based management is as much a philosophy as it is a collection of unique management skills and strategies. Management philosophers and consultants such as Stewart Davis, Robert Tucker, and Tom Peters are trying to motivate managers to initiate a time-based management revolution. Yet they offer very few practical strategies for how the typical manager can begin to think and act in a "time-obsessed" manner, and how the typical manager can initiate organizational interventions to gradually transform a slow-responding company into a fast-paced organization. This book picks up where the books I have discussed in this introduction leave off.

Part One

MANAGERIAL STRATEGIES

Chapter One

Master the Basics

Prospective HSM managers should master basic management skills and orientations *before* they try to conquer time-based management strategies. Melany Baehr, a noted industrial psychologist from the University of Chicago, used a job analysis questionnaire to identify the following sixteen essential managerial skills (see Baehr, 1992):

- Setting organizational objectives
- Financial planning and review
- Improving work procedures and practices
- Interdepartmental coordination
- Developing and implementing technical ideas
- Judgment and decision making

15

- Developing group cooperation and teamwork
- Coping with difficulties and emergencies
- Promoting safety attitudes and practices
- Communications
- Developing employee potential
- Supervisory practices
- Self-development and improvement
- Personnel practices
- Promoting community-organization relations
- Handling outside contacts

Important Management Skills

This section elaborates on some of the skills traditionally re-
garded as critical for success that all prospective HSM managers
should master first.

Leadership

HSM managers need to work hard to earn the title "leader" from
their subordinates, peers, and superiors. HSM managers must
commit themselves to the mission of their organizations and
be able to foster that same kind of commitment in their followers through their inspiration, motivation, and vision. Some
of the key characteristics of successful — and unsuccessful —
leaders are:

A strong leader	A weak leader
Is an excellent listener	Is compelled to talk
Is easily accessible	Is hard to locate
Makes firm decisions	Avoids decision making
Promotes staff	Is self-promoting
Simplifies processes/ projects	Complicates processes/ projects
Is optimistic and encouraging	Is pessimistic and discouraging

Gives credit and praise	Takes credit and seeks praise
Strategically confronts problems	Anxiously avoids problems
Takes responsibility	Blames others
Hires strong employees	Seeks weak subordinates
Is an active manager	Is a passive manager
Is proactive	Is reactive
Is open to change	Seeks the status quo
Takes risks	Follows rules
Has a broad business focus	Has a narrow business focus

A successful leader typically loves his work and therefore serves as an inspirational role model to his employees. He stays on top of current trends and developments in his industry, and he shares relevant information with his peers and subordinates. Most importantly, he shares a clear vision of his goals with his staff. Warren Bennis, in his classic text *On Becoming a Leader*, describes the importance of vision in leadership:

> The first basic ingredient of leadership is a *guiding vision*. The leader has a clear idea of what he wants to do — professionally and personally — and the strength to persist in the face of setbacks, even failures. Unless you know where you're going, and why, you cannot possibly get there. (1989, pp. 39–40)

Planning

There are many levels of planning, ranging from strategic planning to operational planning. This extremely important managerial function involves establishing relevant and obtainable goals, objectives, priorities, and strategies. It requires making accurate decisions about the allocation of resources, the assignment of responsibilities, and the scheduling of essential activities. Effective planning means deciding what to do, how to do it, who will do it, and when it will be completed. HSM managers must definitely master the planning process before they attempt to master time-based strategies such as faster product develop-

ment. The following summary outlines a classic approach to
strategic planning:

Phase I: Analytic Phase

1. *Environmental analysis.* Identifying and studying key external
    factors and determining the impact of those factors on the
    firm's current and future operations and success. External
    factors include technological, political, legal, social, demo-
    graphic, and economic changes, and competitors and
    suppliers.
2. *Internal analysis.* Assessing the key internal strengths and
    weaknesses of the firm in the following areas: financial, sales
    and marketing, organizational, technical, and human re-
    sources. Markets served and products offered are also
    scrutinized.
3. *Distinctive competencies.* Identifying resources and other fac-
    tors or considerations — such as reputation, quality, service,
    special niches, flexibility, location, personnel, and so
    forth — that provide a company with a meaningful edge over
    its competitors.
4. *Distinctive weaknesses.* Identifying areas of vulnerability (such
    as low-quality products) where the competition has a com-
    petitive edge. These areas need to be minimized or
    eliminated.

Phase II: Action Phase

1. *Mission statement.* Preparing a very concise statement of the
    general nature and direction of the company, that offers a
    clear description of the business, the company's basic phi-
    losophy and values, and the strategic direction of the
    company.
2. *Strategic posture.* Creating an overall plan of action in re-
    sponse to all identified opportunities and threats, thus
    providing a general indication of how the corporate mis-
    sion will be achieved. Types of strategic postures include
    expansive growth, niche marketing, product innovation,
    and so forth.

3. *Goal setting.* Setting goals based on the Phase I analysis. Goals are used as planning and control tools for the overall business and for the functional areas. Goals are phrased as outcomes; they are challenging and measurable. Goals are communicated to all relevant parties; specific action steps are listed to achieve each goal.
4. *Specific strategies.* Creating plans of action detailing how managers within specific functional areas (for example, marketing and finance) will go about achieving near-term goals.
5. *Writing the plan.* Putting the plan on paper. This is important because a company is more committed to a written plan. The written plan will guide nearly all management decisions and employee actions.
6. *Implementing the plan.* Communicating the written plan to key people in the company. All managers and employees must be held highly accountable for sticking to the plan while completing all action steps in a timely manner.
7. *Monitoring and revising the plan.* Usually a planning coordinator monitors the entire implementation of the plan and keeps senior executives apprised of all successes and failures. The plan is updated on a regular basis as new threats and opportunities are identified.

Motivating

Successful managers are excellent motivators. Motivational strategies include influence techniques to generate enthusiasm for one's work and commitment to one's job. Successful managers are supportive, encouraging, inspiring, and persuasive. Other motivational styles include leading by example, making inspirational appeals, and using logic to convince others. The most successful managers are able to clearly and succinctly articulate a compelling vision that appeals to the values of their employees and also generates enthusiasm and commitment for cooperative activity.

Rewarding

This managerial practice involves offering tangible or intangible rewards for successful performance at work. Tangible rewards for subordinates include pay increases, bonuses, promotions, better work schedules, or special assignments. Intangible rewards include such things as giving praise, expressing personal appreciation, awarding certificates, giving public recognition, or holding a special ceremony to honor a person's contributions. Fairly and appropriately rewarding employees is a managerial practice that improves manager-employee relationships. Rewards are also used to strengthen an employee's job satisfaction and commitment to the organization. HSM managers must use reward strategies to ensure that their staffs successfully support a speed-based management culture.

Team Building

Effective managers are able to inspire the best efforts of specialized work teams in order to meet their company's goals. Successful managers realize that certain common characteristics need to be present if their work teams are to succeed. Successful team members share and understand the group's goals, objectives, and mission; accept and respect one another; and derive satisfaction and reward from the group's achievements. (Team recognition and reward should take the place of personal recognition and reward.) Team members participate in open communications and decision making. They use group problem-solving techniques to minimize conflicts and strive to cooperate with one another in a relaxed manner. Finally, team members possess the knowledge, skills, and abilities to complete assignments with minimum redundancy in talent.

Listening

In this time of rapid change and increased job pressures, strong managers must be excellent listeners. Employees need to be listened to as they share their ideas and vent their frustrations.

This is more important than ever in time-based companies, where managers can never use the excuse that they are too busy to listen to their employees. Research shows that good listeners hold the high-level positions in a company and are promoted more often than less effective listeners. Weak managers prefer to talk instead of listen. Strong managers spend over 50 percent of their time listening to their employees' views, in an effort to support and respect their employees, and to receive excellent feedback and ideas that could advance the company. Strong managers avoid interruptions or jumping to conclusions when an employee is speaking; they stay attentive to and interested in what an employee is saying even if the delivery is overly wordy or boring, and avoid rushing the speaker or changing the topic unless the employee has finished. Strong managers ask questions to clarify points and to let the speaker know they are listening attentively. They treat every speaker with courtesy and respect.

Being Flexible

HSM managers are not satisfied being management generalists. In fact, in this day and age, any manager whose primary job is simply to manage people or integrate data is in a tenuous position. HSM managers strive to be strong general managers while also specializing in one or more areas of business most relevant to their company. For instance, HSM managers often try to specialize in such fields as law, research, sales, marketing, or finance. By being strong managers *and* talented specialists, HSM managers offer added value to their companies, especially companies that are trying to make do with fewer managers and staff. This flexibility is especially important at a time when certain management jobs are being permanently crossed off organizational charts, managers are being replaced by computers, and decision making gets pushed further down the line.

Surviving

HSM managers typically are characterized as high achievers whose careers have the potential to continually rise to new heights. Yet time-based managers never take their professional success for granted. In fact, HSM managers work very hard to avoid what Cynthia McCauley and her colleagues at the Center for Creative Leadership call the "ten fatal flaws" that lead to executive derailment (see McCauley & Ruderman, 1991). These flaws differentiate managers who succeed from those who fail. If the flaws are never eliminated from a manager's repertoire of behaviors, an early fall from grace can occur. The ten fatal flaws that HSM managers strive to avoid at all costs include (1) insensitivity, (2) aloofness, (3) betrayal of trust, (4) overmanaging, (5) being overly ambitious, (6) not thinking long term, (7) not adapting to a new boss, (8) being overly dependent on a mentor, (9) having poor hiring practices, and (10) being unable to handle problems of poor performance. These flaws, if not corrected, could derail a manager's career.

Psychological Predictors of Managerial Success

After more than twenty years of scientific research, Melany Baehr has identified the most important psychological factors related to successful job performance in managers. (She summarized her research in her 1992 book *Predicting Success in Higher-Level Positions*.) Baehr assessed these factors with a professionally developed psychological test battery known as the STEP (System for Testing and Evaluating Potential). A short description of each of these important factors is presented here. HSM managers should strive to develop and maintain these psychological orientations at all times.

Drive

Most successful managers possess a high level of drive, manifested in their ambition and initiative, and in what they have actually accomplished in both personal and work-related areas of their lives. They have a record of significant achievements, and are fueled by a relentlessness that allows them to continuously attain their ambitious goals even in the face of opposition or temporary setbacks.

Self-Reliance

Successful managers possess the ability to get the job done no matter what, and are characterized by a decisive, self-confident, and goal-oriented approach to work. Self-reliance enables quick and accurate managerial decision making and the confidence to stand behind those decisions. An extremely high level of self-reliance has its downside, however. If a manager is too goal-oriented, self-directed, and focused solely on the task at hand, that individual may be perceived as rude, abrasive, arrogant, even ruthless. Many management experts believe that this extreme could lead to a manager's ultimate demise, rather than to continuing success. Thus, self-reliance in moderate amounts is most highly related to success.

Responsibility

Another factor that enhances higher-level managerial performance is whether or not a manager is willing to take ultimate responsibility for the performance of his work unit. Managers who assume full responsibility believe their actions can have an impact on the productivity and profits of a work group, division, and ultimately the entire organization. For example, managers who readily accept financial responsibility for their units are generally very successful in their handling of budgets, financial planning, and forecasting. They are typically very good at planning, goal setting, motivating, and rewarding, and they do not blame their employees, peers, superiors, or the external environment for their problems.

Verbal Fluency

Consisting of both one's breadth of vocabulary and the ability to use it skillfully, verbal fluency is an important factor for almost everyone at any level of management. The importance of verbal fluency increases as one moves up in management, as does the actual linguistic ability of managers and executives. In fact, recent research on chief executive officers (CEOs) of organizations found that these corporate leaders showed superior facility for both written and spoken communication, including the ability to speak extemporaneously. Verbal fluency is the cornerstone of many of the interpersonal skills necessary in managerial and executive roles, such as delegation, team building, persuasiveness, public relations, and platform or high-level sales presentation skills.

Analytical Reasoning

Decision making is one of the most critical responsibilities of managers. The implications of decisions made at middle and top management levels are often far-reaching and, particularly at the top level, can have an immediate impact on the success, prosperity, and long-term viability of the entire organization. An important component in effective decision making is one's analytical and deductive reasoning—the ability to systematically analyze given facts and information to reach some decisive conclusion. Involved in this is the capacity to make important decisions with only partial or incomplete information.

Creativity

An approach to decision making and problem solving that differs substantially from the systematic, methodical, and analytical approach is a more creative or intuitive style. Many successful managers display high levels of creativity. Some research findings (see Moretti, Morken, & Borkowski, 1989) indicate that, on the average, high-level executives demonstrate even more creativity than middle managers. Innovation and creativity can play an important role in helping managers solve the vast array of business dilemmas for which no existing precedent has been set.

Parenthetically, research on CEOs found that while all scored relatively high in this area, CEOs in entrepreneurial companies had higher levels of creativity than their CEO counterparts in more established organizations. But one of the problems with high creativity, when it is not balanced with the proper amount of analytical and deductive skills, is that a highly intuitive style can be very frustrating to more systematic and analytical subordinates, peers, or superiors. The highly creative manager must strive to avoid exasperating and possibly alienating others.

Risk Taking

Research shows that highly creative managers, especially those with extroverted, outgoing personalities, have a tendency to engage in risk-taking behavior. This can be a highly valued attribute in many companies if the risk taking leads to more business opportunities, faster revenue growth, and greater profitability. In fact, many experts believe that the avoidance of at least moderate, high-percentage risks can lead to the downfall of a manager, ascribing such career-stopping terms as "ultraconservative" and "afraid to take a chance" to the manager. However, as is the case with creativity, it is important to consider on a macro level the organizational culture in which a person operates, and, more specifically, one's supervisor's style, before concluding that a proclivity for risk taking is automatically an asset.

Pressure Tolerance

A very valuable trait to possess as a manager is the ability to work under pressure or in distracting conditions. Certainly, stressful and distracting conditions are not uncommon to most managers. Most successful managers have a high ability to maintain or even increase productivity under pressure and are able to focus clearly on the pertinent, most critical aspects of a task while disregarding the irrelevancies. Such a quality is especially important when one is inundated with the wealth of information received and processed daily in our fast-paced, rapidly changing business environment.

Some managers' job stress manifests itself in neurotic behavior. The following summary (adapted from Kets de Vries & Miller, 1984, 1987) describes five neurotic managerial styles that should be avoided at all times. Managers who exhibit these

dysfunctional management orientations would probably benefit from career development counseling.

The depressed manager exhibits low self-esteem and self-
confidence and has little initiative. He is very negative and
tolerates mediocrity and, at times, failure. He prefers very bureaucratic and hierarchical companies. He creates a culture that
tends to be impersonal, resistant to change, and lacking in
motivation. A leadership vacuum and a lack of vigilance over
market conditions begin to surface. Under depressed management, the company begins to drift with no sense of direction,
and is often confined to mature and/or dying markets.

The overly compulsive manager requires allegiance to tightly
prescribed rules and regulations. She is a perfectionist who is
obsessed with routine, detail, and efficiency. She demands exact-
ness and perfection, and prefers subordinates who are sub-
missive, insecure, and uncreative. The corporate culture tends
to center around exhaustive and ritualized evaluation procedures. The compulsive manager tends to overrely on a single
aspect of management strategy (such as quality control, cost-
cutting, and so on).

The paranoid manager is suspicious and distrustful of others and demands loyalty. He manipulates others and implements rules to secure complete control over others. He is sometimes vindictive, and is prepared to counter any attacks and
personal threats. His management style leads to a centralization
of power, and a culture characterized by secrecy, fear of reprisal,
intimidation, and lack of trust. The company runs the risk of
becoming overly analytical, too conservative, and unable to
work in strategic alliances with other companies and vendors.

The dramatic manager seeks and creates excitement and
stimulation. She has a strong need for attention, yet is at risk to
engage in dangerously uninhibited and grandiose behavior.
The dramatic leader is usually surrounded by highly dependent
followers. This type of manager is rarely focused, and has a
tendency to prefer the sizzle instead of the steak. Oftentimes the
bold ventures, the distracting diversifications, and the un-
bridled growth are not part of an integrated set of strategic and

tactical plans, but are merely attempts to gain excitement while being in the limelight.

The detached manager is withdrawn and is indifferent to positive or negative feedback. She lacks genuine interest in the past, present, or future of her company. The detached manager provides insufficient monitoring of the external environment, which leads to an indecisive and inconsistent decision-making style. The corporate culture is characterized by conflicts, insecurity, and power seeking since strong leadership is lacking.

Ethical Approach to Business

One managerial trait that has long been considered desirable, if not critical, in developing lasting business relationships and a profitable company is a concern for ethics. There has been a strong resurgence of interest in business ethics over the past five years. Managerial psychologists (see Kouzes & Posner, 1990) have surveyed thousands of managers to uncover what attributes they look for and admire most in a successful manager. Out of hundreds of characteristics these managers listed as critical, managerial integrity, or ethics, was the most frequently cited. These results were replicated in other surveys of top-level managers, underscoring the importance of an ethical approach to management. The psychological predispositions of unethical managers that seem to differentiate them from their highly ethical counterparts include the following:

- A preference for autonomy and authority in the reporting structure; avoidance of cooperative and consultative relationships that include input from peers
- A slightly greater limitation in cognitive skills (for instance, lack of breadth of vocabulary) and creativity than ethical managers display, and a tendency to resort to doubtful or unacceptable business practices rather than deal competently with a variety of business situations
- Assumption of substantially less responsibility for their actions than ethical managers assume, and a tendency to feel

somewhat powerless, victimized, and blameful in relation to
the business environment
- Feelings of insufficiency, an inability to cope efficiently with
all the pressures of the workplace, and a generally low level
of overall emotional health (Based on Baehr, Jones, & Nerad,
1991)

Interpersonal Skills

Managers get their work done by leading and motivating other
people. Therefore, it is important to assess whether or not an
individual possesses the interpersonal skills needed to get maximum use out of his employees' skills and abilities. The following
list includes some of the fundamental techniques that HSM
managers should use when interacting with others:

- Avoid criticizing or complaining
- Show genuine interest in others
- Smile and show sincere appreciation
- Listen well
- Focus on the other person's interests
- Avoid arguments at all costs
- Respect the other person's opinions
- Begin most conversations in a friendly manner
- Empathize with the other person's issues
- Praise all improvements and key contributions
- Talk about their own mistakes before pointing out the other
person's mistakes
- Ask questions instead of giving directives
- Confront problems and mistakes in such a way that the other
person saves face
- Create a stress-free meeting atmosphere

Contemporary Models of Management

There are many different models of management that prospective HSM managers can learn from. These include management
by objectives, scientific management, situational leadership,

entrepreneurial management, group-centered leadership, and the controlled management of chaos. Three emerging management theories that are fairly consistent with the philosophy and goals of time-based management are briefly summarized on the following pages. They are (1) one minute management, (2) third-wave management, and (3) world-class management. These theories clearly illustrate both the challenges and the beauty of well-conceptualized approaches to management.

One Minute Management

In 1982, Kenneth Blanchard and Spencer Johnson wrote the now famous book *The One Minute Manager: The Quickest Way to Increase Your Own Prosperity.* This book quickly became a runaway best-seller. *The One Minute Manager* attempts to help novice and experienced managers focus on simplifying their game plan, while engaging in activities that can be completed in one minute or less. This pioneering book definitely reduces the manager's job to the basics. It is a good review course for all managers.

There are three basic techniques at the core of this time-based management philosophy: (1) one minute goal setting, (2) one minute praising, and (3) one minute reprimands. The diligent application of these three basic techniques saves a manager time while increasing the satisfaction and improving the performance of the employees. While successful managers need to learn more than these three techniques, mastering the principles of one minute management is a good place to begin.

In one minute goal setting, managers and employees must agree on their goals and write them in 250 words or less. Employees are required to review their goals and performance on a daily basis, to ensure that their behavior matches their goals. Hence, one minute goal setting keeps one's staff tightly focused on the most important management goals, yet it requires that the goal-setting and achievement process remains streamlined and nonbureaucratic at all times.

One minute praising allows managers to reinforce their employees' desirable work performance. Employees are told up front what they will be evaluated on, and how they will be evaluated. There are no surprises, and the employees' expectations of their work performance is consistent with management's expectations. The praising is very specific, with managers telling the employees what they did right, how they felt about what the employees did right, and how the organization and other employees will gain by the employee's high-level performance. Employees are encouraged to do more of the same, and they receive management's pledge to continue to support their success in the organization. It is clear why one minute praising serves to motivate employees toward continuous and higher-level achievements.

One minute reprimands are part of this bare-boned management philosophy. Employees must know beforehand that their managers expect them to achieve their goals, and that they will be reprimanded as soon as it becomes clear they are engaging in unproductive work activities. Managers must tell their employees what they are doing wrong and how it makes them, as managers, feel. Reprimanded employees need to experience the uncomfortable nature of the situation, but then managers need to let these employees know they are still valued. That is, reprimanded employees need to know that management thinks highly of them as workers, but *not* of their unacceptable performance. Finally, once the reprimand is over, it is over!

Third-Wave Management

HSM managers need to become familiar with the principles of third-wave management. John Sculley, chief executive officer of Apple Computer, and James Cook, former technology vice president of Computervision Corporation, collaborated on this model of new-age management. Their model is discussed in depth in Sculley's book (coauthored with John A. Byrne) *Odyssey: Pepsi to Apple. . . A Journey of Adventure, Ideas, and the Future.*

Sculley and Cook contrasted the management paradigms used by third-wave companies with those used by second-wave companies. Some of their contrasts include the following:

Organizational Characteristic	Second-Wave Companies	Third-Wave Companies
Structure	Hierarchical	Networking
Style	Bureaucratic	Highly flexible
Strength	Preserves stability	Promotes change
Culture	Traditional	Creative
Focus	Market share	Market creation
Leadership	Doctrinal	Inspirational
Quality	Affordable best	Perfection
Status goals	Title and rank	Making a difference
Greatest resource	Cash and assets	Information
Motivation	To complete projects	To build the future

Apple Computer was positioned as a leading third-wave company, while Pepsi was categorized as one of the best second-wave companies. The source of competitive strength in third-wave companies lies in their ability to quickly capitalize on change — the ability to rapidly transform the company and its products in response to new consumer preferences, unforeseen economic changes, and other societal demands. However, the source of competitive strength in second-wave or industrial-age companies is their stability. For example, second-wave companies emphasize a rigid corporate structure over a flexible structure. Second-wave companies also strive to preserve the status quo by promoting a more-of-the-same attitude, rather than continuously offering highly differentiated products and services.

Third-wave companies are flat, lean, and flexible. Their leaders work from a network model instead of a hierarchical model. The network is composed of unique groups and configurations of people that come together to work on very specific tasks and projects. It is possible for leaders to lead certain networks, be peers in others, and even be followers in some. In other words, networks allow leaders the opportunity to be very flexible in their team roles. Leaders basically try to empower networks. Ideas flow more naturally and quickly through networks than through hierarchies because the network was uniquely formed for the project at hand. Networks also require fewer employees, as Sculley describes:

> [At Apple Computer] we're able to keep so lean because we rely on an independent network of

> third-party business partners—independent soft-
> ware developers, makers of peripheral equipment,
> dealers, and retailers. We provide a conduit for
> creativity and innovation. The true entrepreneurs,
> then, are those who take advantage of the network.
> (Sculley & Byrne, 1987, p. 97)

Second-wave companies, on the other hand, are hampered and slowed down because each level of their steep hierarchy is a filter that can stifle flexibility, creativity, and innovation. Every level of the hierarchy is capable of voting down a new idea. If good ideas do percolate to the top of the corporate hierarchy, they usually do so very slowly, meaning that new products, services, and other competitive opportunities are not quickly recognized.

Third-wave companies are interested in inventing their own future while second-wave companies do everything in their power to defend the status quo. Third-wave companies invent the future by constantly finding a better way to offer their customers new products and services, even if it means making their own products obsolete. Third-wave companies study past and present business trends in an attempt to better anticipate the future. And third-wave companies are as interested in creating new markets as they are in retaining and expanding their share of old markets. Third-wave companies always look for ways to upgrade their customers to the next generation of products, and they constantly renew themselves so that they are prepared to supply their customers with those products that make a meaningful difference.

World-Class Management

More managers are being required to compete in the global marketplace. In a 1991 paper, Earl Young, a professor of management at DePaul University in Chicago, identified many of the essential characteristics exhibited by these world-class managers. Young admits that his concept of world-class manage-ment is still evolving, yet he points out that managers need to successfully master the following characteristics if they are to succeed in the highly competitive and rapidly changing global marketplace:

1. *A life-long commitment to management.* Young indicates that to be ranked among the top managers in the world requires the same life-long dedication, intensity, and focus that is associated with a successful career in medicine, law, or any other demanding profession.

2. *An internalization of the corporate mission.* This is a deep commitment to the company's overall mission statement. It involves the alignment of one's personal goals with the larger goals of the company, without compromising one's personal values. It does not mean blind loyalty! It means striving to achieve the socially approved and economically beneficial company mission and, in so doing, achieving personal and professional fulfillment.

3. *An uncompromising competitive attitude.* Anything less than a fearless competitive attitude can be seen as time serving — waiting for the eventual decline of the company into a marginal status or worse. A highly competitive spirit is needed as more managers than ever before strive to succeed in an increasingly crowded marketplace. Only those managers prepared for the inevitable and fiercely competitive battles can hope to survive, let alone dominate, in this business climate.

4. *A long-term profit orientation.* World-class managers do not endorse the short-term profit perspectives as reflected in an excessive preoccupation with quarterly performance. Instead, the top managers exhibit a willingness to wait for the benefits of a strategy to take hold, to invest rather than engage in premature profit taking, and to stay on the company's strategic course instead of reacting to temporary adversity.

5. *The pursuit of excellence.* Young points out that the search for excellence has become the rallying point for world-class managers. It is not enough to just make quality products or offer comprehensive service. These initiatives must be

done with the goal of achieving a number-one or best-in-
its-class rating.

6. *A customer service orientation.* World-class managers know
    that extraordinary customer service is fast becoming one
    of the key dimensions of a highly successful firm. A super-
    ficial commitment to service is not enough. Customer
    service must mean a total realignment of all company
    activities to immediately and consistently serve the cus-
    tomer within the scope of the company mission.

7. *An emphasis on continuous improvement.* Young points out
    that this is one of the primary contributions of Japanese
    management theory, and one of Japan's most successful
    management strategies. No attribute of a company's struc-
    ture, processes, products, services, or personnel should
    ever be exempt from close, never-ending scrutiny. The
    underlying philosophy of this organizationwide initiative
    should be that *everything* can eventually be incrementally
    improved.

8. *Mastery of a functional area.* A world-class manager must be
    both a generalist and a high-level specialist. Operational
    mastery of a key functional area is essential so that the
    principles of a given field — such as finance, research, sales,
    or marketing — can be translated into a more effective
    organization. In addition, in an age of cutbacks and reduc-
    tion of middle managers, the manager who is simul-
    taneously a generalist and a specialist brings more value to
    the company.

9. *Exceptional team leadership skills.* The ability to build and
    lead a high-performance team focuses on harnessing and
    directing a group/cooperative effort instead of an indi-
    vidual/competitive effort. Today's business tasks are in-
    creasingly complex and require the input of many skills
    and disciplines. Therefore, coordinating this group pro-
    cess requires a high level of management expertise in team
    dynamics and group leadership.

10. *Managing the future.* Young reveals that continued lead-
    ership by a world-class organization requires the early
    identification and interpretation of emerging trends and

events in the marketplace. World-class managers cannot wait for the security that comes with knowing that several other firms have profitably adopted a given course of action in response to some external trend or event. World-class managers must continually monitor and evaluate these trends and events for potential relevance to their company, and then develop and implement an appropriate response immediately. (Adapted from Young, 1991)

Conclusion

Prospective HSM managers must master the essentials of management before they try to conquer high speed management. This includes learning important management skills such as leadership, planning, motivating, rewarding, and communicating. Prospective HSM managers must also develop the thinking style and the level of emotional stability required of all top-level managers. Finally, prospective HSM managers should be familiar with different theories of management, including many of the contemporary theories. Once prospective HSM managers have mastered the basics, they are fully prepared to learn the principles of high-speed management.

Chapter Two

Manage Time Wisely

HSM managers do not waste time, but neither are they work-aholics. They strive to have a balanced lifestyle, with enough time for work, family, friends, and self. The extra time they earn through effective time management is not automatically used for more work. Instead, the HSM manager recognizes the importance of taking time for self-development and personal rejuvenation.

Unfortunately, many managers are unaware of their opportunities to control time and to put it to work *for* them rather than against them. These managers frequently live unbalanced lives, putting in long hours at work and spending little time with family and friends. There is no time for reflection, nor is there much free time for anything besides work. Time-management skills such as delegating effectively, planning one's work day, avoiding interruptions, and keeping organized allow HSM managers to put their available time to the best use.

With time management, HSM managers learn to do more than one important task at a time—for example, conducting conference calls on the car phone while driving to and from work, or listening to business education audiotapes while exercising. The HSM manager is skilled at overlapping and doubling up activities in an effort to get more done in the time available. In addition, HSM managers do many activities more quickly with the help of such time-management skills as speed reading, speed learning, and the adept use of computers. These and the time management strategies and technologies in the following list are commonly used by HSM managers:

Strategies	*Technologies*
Maintain a "to do" list	Portable and car phones
Organize paperwork	Speed reading and learning
Delegate	Air phones
Set priorities	Voice mail
Plan and schedule work	Electronic mail
Don't procrastinate	Laptop and notebook
Refuse low-priority work	computers
Control office socializing	Beepers and pagers
Keep a time log	Answering machines
Clarify objectives	Instructional audio and video
Block interruptions:	tapes
Drop-in visitors	Microcassette recorders
Unplanned meetings	Dictaphones
Telephone calls	Computers and business
Learn to say no	software:
Don't attempt too much	Spreadsheets
Complete tasks on time	Data-base manager
Maintain adequate staff	Word processing
Maintain efficient files	Desktop publishing
	Information management
	Communication links

It is not the intention of this chapter to provide comprehensive coverage of all time-management strategies. Rather the following sections give a brief overview of ten important time-control techniques. Major attention is given to delegation, probably the most important time-control strategy for the HSM manager. Readers are encouraged to thoroughly study the classic time-management texts listed in the reference section.

Delegate

High speed managers are excellent delegators. During the typical work week, most traditional managers perform important nonmanagerial activities that impede their own productivity as managers. HSM managers, on the other hand, delegate much of that work, thus relieving themselves of many time-draining projects. The delegated projects still get done, as they are supposed to, but the delegation process saves time and energy for more important managerial duties. By delegating, HSM managers bring more talent and resources to bear on the work at hand.

No-nonsense Delegation

The HSM manager uses delegation as a management tool to achieve certain work objectives — so that he can better focus on his specific management responsibilities and his employees can develop new work skills. That is, the HSM manager delegates in order to reduce his need to work overtime *and* so that he can train and cross-train his staff.

Conversely, traditional managers with poor delegation skills typically work long hours and work at a slower pace than HSM managers. They are often struggling to keep up. Poor delegators feel responsible for everything. They insist that everything must cross their desks for review and approval. Orders pile up, production becomes backlogged, and they keep everybody waiting for feedback. Moreover, they constantly run the risk of losing good workers because the workers do not have challenging tasks assigned to them.

Why Managers Fail to Delegate

Managers who fail to delegate generally experience one or more of the following eight psychological barriers to delegation:

1. *Egotism.* "I can do it better myself."
2. *Insecurity.* "What if the person I delegate to does a better job than I can do?"
3. *Fear.* "I am scared that anybody I delegate to will blow the entire assignment."
4. *Need for comfort.* "I am more comfortable working on non-managerial projects than I am managing."
5. *Overcontrol.* "I can best control the outcome of this project by doing it myself."
6. *Perfectionism.* "This project needs to be perfect, and no one can do it better than I can."
7. *Poor planning.* "It will take me longer to help someone plan this project than it will for me just to do it myself."
8. *Inefficiency.* " It will take me one hour to do this project, while it would take anyone else four."

Managers also fail to delegate because their employees block the delegation process through their anxiety, evasion of responsibility, or intimidation. Strategies that manipulative employees use to interrupt the delegation process include refusing to do any work outside of their job description; sabotaging any project that has been delegated to them; resenting the manager, as though he were merely attempting to pass off his own work; rejecting any new task out of fear and insecurity; taking on a delegated project in order to avoid regular job duties; and avoiding the opportunity to learn new job skills (see Weiss, 1988).

In these situations, the manager must clearly inform employees that delegation is a part of the managerial process, and that both managers and employees gain from it. Also, the steps involved in successfully completing a delegated project must be clearly spelled out to the resisting employees.

How to Delegate Effectively

Six steps need to be followed for successful delegation. These steps are (1) planning the delegation process, (2) choosing the best person, (3) establishing measurable action steps, (4) assigning responsibility and authority, (5) providing support and feedback, and (6) evaluating and rewarding the outcome.

Planning the delegation process. The HSM manager forecasts workloads, determines necessary resources, considers organizational obstacles, prioritizes the project in relation to other ongoing projects, and involves others in the planning process.

A working plan is prepared before formal delegation ever occurs. This plan covers the objectives of the project, available resources, action steps with due dates, contingency plans in case of problems, the supervisor's responsibilities, the employee's responsibilities, how progress will be measured, and when status reports are due. The HSM manager pays very close attention to the due dates since he or she is more inclined to set aggressive dates in keeping with the HSM philosophy.

Choosing the best person. The HSM manager, realizing he has the responsibility of not overloading anyone with work, delegates the project to the most qualified person—assuming that a qualified pool of people exists. The most qualified person has both the talent and the skills for the job. She tends to be one of the quickest people to complete projects successfully and usually requires little training. The most qualified person has time for the project, and will not let the delegated project interfere with her regular work duties. Of course, a person with minimal experience can be assigned the job instead, and can become trained in the process; but this person will often take much longer to complete the project.

Establishing measurable action steps. The HSM manager delineates measurable action steps and establishes a tight yet achievable time schedule for completion. The HSM manager defines the standards of acceptable work. The HSM manager makes sure the employee understands all critical checkpoints in the process. Finally, the HSM manager realizes that the employee needs to understand the plan, the action steps, the due dates, the consequences if the project is not successfully completed on time, and the rewards if the plan is completed far ahead of schedule.

Assigning responsibility and authority. The HSM manager assigns an employee all the responsibility for timely and successful completion of a project. Hence, the employee is responsible for providing regular progress reports and quickly informing the manager of any difficulties. The HSM manager also gives the employee the proper authority to complete the project. This means, for example, that the employee has the authority to obtain any resources she needs (such as clerical assistance, interdepartmental information, and funding) to successfully complete the project within the allocated time. Responsibility without authority will hinder the employee's efforts.

Providing support and feedback. The HSM manager continues to supervise the employee. That is, the manager listens to the employee's concerns, answers questions, resolves disagreements, provides advice, and helps to teach and develop the employee through the process of delegation. The HSM manager does not overcontrol the employee, and he encourages the employee to make key decisions about the project. Moreover, the HSM manager resists any upward delegation attempts by the employee — some employees might actually try to give the project back to the manager.

Evaluating and rewarding the outcome. Before a project begins, the manager spells out to the employee both the positive and the negative consequences of the outcome. And, as always, the HSM manager stresses the importance of meeting deadlines. If any deadline is ever declared impossible to meet, then it needs to be revised as soon as possible. Finally, the HSM manager rewards an employee for doing a job well, and reprimands poor performance — in doing so the manager is evaluating the effectiveness of the delegation process as a whole.

Using Delegation to Manage One's Time

The HSM manager is constantly confronted with the pressure to take on nonmanagerial responsibilities in order to meet the department's objectives. Yet a manager's time is best spent in hiring, training, coaching, directing, planning, problem solving, monitoring, rewarding, reprimanding, and delegating. Therefore, the manager must see to it that employees accomplish the bulk of the department's objectives.

Table 2.1 breaks down a typical poor delegator's sixty-hour work week. Forty-five hours are spent on direct managerial responsibilities and fifteen hours are spent on the nonmanagerial responsibilities that he has inadvertently taken on. This manager rationalizes his long work week by saying he is a working manager who must help out his employees in order to achieve positive departmental results.

Table 2.2 shows how an HSM manager uses delegation to gain firmer control of his work week. Not only does he delegate nearly 70 percent of the nonmanagerial responsibilities that he could have taken on, but he also delegates ten hours of his direct management duties in order to allow his employees to gain more diverse experience and to allot himself extra hours to engage in strategic planning and business development. In other words, the HSM manager is able to develop and practice

Table 2.1. An Ineffective Delegator's Workload: Sixty Hours/Week.*

Managerial Responsibilities	Nonmanagerial Activities
Maintain proper staffing (1)	Prepare public relations articles for business magazines (3)
Assign projects (4)	
Monitor production (6)	Input business letters and memos (2)
Assess quality (2)	
Maintain discipline (3)	Proofread all correspondence to customers to ensure quality (8)
Establish production standards (3)	
Prepare business reports (8)	Review products for possible acquisition (2)
Evaluate employees (2)	
Attend meetings outside department (6)	
Conduct departmental meetings (6)	
Control budget and expenditures (4)	
Managerial workload, 45 hours	Nonmanagerial workload, 15 hours

* Hours per week in parentheses.
Source: Adapted from Weiss, 1988.

Table 2.2. High-Speed Manager's Workload: Fifty Hours/Week.*

Managerial Responsibilities	Nonmanagerial Responsibilities	Delegated Responsibilities
Maintain proper staffing (1)	Proofread all correspondence to important clients (5)	Two supervisors monitor production rates (4)
Assign projects (4)		Special task force establishes production standards (2)
Monitor production rates (2)		
Assess quality (2)		Key supervisors represent department at some interdepartmental meetings (4)
Maintain discipline (3)		
Assist in development of production standards (1)		Senior scientist prepares public relations articles for business magazines (3)
Prepare business reports (8)		
Evaluate employees (2)		Executive secretary inputs letters and memos (2)
Attend meetings outside department (2)		Assists in proofreading correspondence to customers (3)
Conduct departmental meetings (6)		
Control budget and expenditures (4)		Product acquisition task force reviews products for possible acquisition (2)
Engage in strategic planning (10)		
Managerial workload, 45 hours	Nonmanagerial workload, 5 hours	Effective delegation, 20 hours

* Hours per week in parentheses.
Source: Adapted from Weiss, 1988.

his higher-level management skills, rather than doing his employees' work for them.

Assign Priorities

Most managers have more projects on their "to do" lists than they know what to do with. HSM managers realize that not all projects are equally important. By assigning priorities, HSM managers increase the odds of getting the most important projects done either on or ahead of schedule. A four-step strategy can be used to assign and accomplish high-priority projects:

1. Use the A–B–C coding system to categorize projects as being "top priority" (A–level projects), "must be done" (B–level projects), and "not important" (C–level projects).
2. Assign due dates to each project so that you can determine whether or not a project needs to be completed immediately. Completion dates also help you determine whether you are ahead of, on, or behind schedule when the project is completed.
3. Make a daily "to do" list of tasks that need to be accomplished that day or that week. Always complete tasks according to their priority and due date.
4. Decide what not to do. Many projects can be delegated immediately or dropped, especially if they will bring little value to the company. Low-payoff activities should be avoided at all times.

Organize Paperwork

HSM managers refuse to get trapped under piles of paperwork. Disorganized paperwork symbolizes indecision, procrastination, and confusion of priorities. It also reflects a failure to delegate.

HSM managers know the importance of an organized work area, an efficient filing system, and a strategy for handling correspondence and paperwork. The following six-step strategy can help managers to become more organized with their correspondence and paperwork:

1. Do not pile papers (phone messages, memos, notes, proposals) on your desk. Devise and utilize an efficient filing system instead. Also, do not let your staff pile papers on your desk.
2. Handle each piece of paper only once. Respond immediately and either file the paper, route it, or discard it.
3. Write brief replies to nonroutine correspondence. Use

form letters or standard memos for routine correspondence.

4. Do not overuse memos if issues can more easily be dealt with over the phone or in a brief face-to-face meeting. Memos can clog information channels. Memos should only be used to remind, clarify, confirm, or announce. Also, staff should be discouraged from sending memos that describe a problem without also offering a solution. This is a veiled form of reverse delegation. Finally, encourage colleagues not to send you memos unless they are absolutely relevant to your area of authority.

5. Have your mail and memos screened and prioritized so that the most important issues can be dealt with first. Correspondence can be put into one of four folders marked as follows: "sign," "immediate action," "deferred action," or "information only."

6. Periodically weed out unimportant, outdated, and unused information from the files. There is no good reason to hoard unnecessary paperwork.

An effective filing system can be developed as follows:

- File as you go. Don't let papers accumulate to be filed later.
- Put the most current information in the front of the file folders.
- Attach copies of replies to the front of the original correspondence.
- Don't overstuff file drawers. Allow yourself four to five inches of space in the drawers for easy handling and reviewing.
- File correspondence by subject, not by the date it was received or processed. File correspondence to individuals with last name first.
- Avoid creating too big a miscellaneous file. When you accumulate five to ten pieces of paper in this file, make another file category for the information.
- Lightly pencil in throw-away dates on all filed material.
- If papers are removed from the file for any reason, put an

OUT card in the file showing who has the material and the date it was taken.
- Have a place for everything. Don't leave paper lying around randomly; file it.
- Finally, weed out your files on a regular basis.

Block Interruptions

HSM managers believe that each minute in a work day is sacred. Hence, everything within one's power needs to be done to minimize interruptions. Four strategies commonly used by HSM managers are as follows:

1. Let employees know that you cannot be interrupted at certain times of the day. Employees will learn to respect this time. Also, set up times during the day when drop-in visits are encouraged.
2. Assertively tell interrupters that you are very busy and will get back to them as soon as possible.
3. Allow interruptions only if they are very important or can be dealt with in a few minutes. If they are unimportant or take longer, put them off.
4. Delegate most interruptions to someone else (such as your secretary or other qualified staff).

Never Attempt Too Much

HSM managers stay focused and try not to attempt too much. They know the difference between being cooperative and doing someone else's work. They stay uninvolved if others can handle the project. Finally, HSM managers know that everything can take longer than someone might think, so they strive to set realistic, achievable completion dates.

Be Assertive

Many traditional managers get involved in low-priority work and too many projects because they are unable to say "No." HSM managers must be assertive. They must realize that if they take on an extra project and fail to deliver, they may lose the respect of their superiors, colleagues, and subordinates. The unassertive manager is unable to say "No" for the following reasons:

- Desires approval and acceptance
- Fears offending
- Cannot turn down a project
- Cannot think of an excuse
- Cannot negotiate
- Cannot say "No" to boss

HSM managers, on the other hand, simply refuse to spread themselves too thin. They are able to say "No" if the project is inappropriate, low priority, or can best be done by someone else. If they have trouble saying "No," they delay their response and buy time. Most importantly, they tell others that a new project would interfere with their other priorities.

Avoid Procrastination

HSM managers do not put high-priority projects off, nor do they procrastinate. They put their important goals in writing, they are highly motivated to complete these projects on or ahead of schedule, and they always complete the assignments they are expected to do. HSM managers know how to break a larger project into smaller, more manageable parts. They are disciplined enough to work on the high-priority project even when they are not fully motivated. In brief, HSM managers know that if they do not *start* the project and continually work on it, then it will never get done.

Exhibit Self-Discipline

Good time managers are very disciplined. They set priorities to focus their efforts on high-return projects. They impose realistic but firm deadlines on all major steps of their projects. They use daily "to do" lists, progress reports, and project control charts complete with due dates in order to reach their objectives in a timely manner. Good time managers continually strive to replace poor work habits that waste time with habits that better manage, extend, and compress time. Most importantly, they realize that poor work attitudes and dissatisfaction with one's job make self-discipline more difficult. Hence, they always try to maintain a high level of enthusiasm and interest in their job.

Shorten Meetings

Most managers spend too much time in meetings. HSM managers do not attend a meeting unless it is absolutely necessary. Before attending a meeting, they ask themselves the following questions:

- Can I send a representative to the meeting?
- Can I get the main points from a summary report?
- Can I attend only part of the meeting?
- Can I participate in writing without attending?
- Can the meeting be shortened?

If an HSM manager is holding the meeting, he will always have an agenda, set short time limits, start and end on time, and quickly speak up if the meeting gets off target. Moreover, he will skillfully change the style of presentation to keep the meeting interesting, use eye-catching visual aids, and get attendees involved so that the meeting remains fast-paced and productive. Only the people who absolutely need to attend the meeting are invited. Most importantly, the HSM manager summarizes the conclusions of the meeting and always follows up with the attendees to ensure that all agreements are kept.

Utilize Commuting Time

HSM managers organize commuting time so they can implement time-extending strategies. For example, if one shares a ride or takes public transportation, then commuting time can be used to read and write. If one drives a car, then commuting time can be used to rehearse speeches, listen to business tapes, make phone calls, and dictate letters. Commuting time should never be wasted.

Conclusion

In summary, HSM managers are masters at managing their time. They consistently try to replace time-wasting behaviors with time-control behaviors, they use time-saving technologies, and they strive to achieve a more balanced and stress-free lifestyle.

Chapter Three

Anticipate the Future

HSM managers realize that, for their companies to survive and grow in the 1990s, they must show more foresight than ever before. This is why *futuristic thinking*, rather than mere *strategic planning*, is starting to find its way into management literature — and why future-based planning sessions are kept separate from strategic planning sessions.

HSM managers never rest on their company's past accomplishments. They are as concerned about predicting what will happen to their company three, five, or even ten years from now as they are about forecasting the next quarter's earnings (although in most companies it is a departure from tradition to think beyond the one- to two-year plan). By learning how to anticipate the future, HSM managers are realizing that the course of the future can be influenced.

HSM managers believe that it is possible to predict the future accurately, although they realize that the degree of prediction will never be perfect. By carefully documenting past and present trends, the HSM manager can project trendlines forward in time. These trendlines can map out the *probable* routes that companies will need to take if they want to succeed in the twenty-first century.

A variety of strategies are required to prepare one's company for the future. First, HSM managers must learn how to anticipate and plan for the future using the techniques described in this chapter. Second, HSM managers must routinely study the predictions of the leading business futurists, with the hope of determining which products and services will be best received by consumers in the near and distant future. Then, managers can combine their predictions with the predictions of other future-oriented thinkers to gain a better consensus on what the future will bring. Before discussing these issues, however, a word of caution is in order.

Limitations in Predicting the Future

Spyros Makridekis, in his 1990 book *Forecasting, Planning, and Strategy for the Twenty-First Century,* points out that the major purpose of predicting the future is to provide companies with a *general direction* in which to guide their resources now to ensure success in the future. Companies should also try to forecast the future to improve their strategic planning. But Makridekis warns managers to be aware of the limitations in predicting the future.

For example, the longer the time horizon of the forecasts, the greater the chance that established trends and relationships between variables will change, thus invalidating the forecasts. Key people and unforeseen events can also disrupt the course of the future, making the task of forecasting more difficult. Finally, improper research methods can lead to faulty forecasts.

Therefore, Makridekis encourages managers to study only those forecasts made by legitimate futurists with a solid track record of successful predictions. In addition, research has shown that a pattern of similar predictions made by different forecasters is usually more accurate than a single prediction made by a single forecaster. If three highly reputable futurists use independent methodologies to come up with the same prediction (for instance, that we will be in the Age of Leisure by the year 2020), then the odds of this event actually occurring in the future are much greater than if only one futurist made the prediction. Finally, a forecast is more likely to be accurate if it is based on scientific research and statistical models of prediction than if it is based on someone's biased and unscientific hunch.

Business forecasting typically includes (1) collecting and categorizing all relevant information and data, (2) choosing an appropriate statistical model, (3) accurately estimating the relationship between events past and present and events in the future, and (4) determining the degree of confidence one has in one's own predictions. While HSM managers still view the prediction of the future as being as much an art as a science, they all agree that a less than perfect snapshot of the future will always give them more competitive advantage than no snapshot at all. The following sections highlight both the methods and the predictions of some of the more successful futurists of our time.

The Leading Futurists

There are two major types of business futurists: content futurists and process futurists. *Content futurists* specialize in different areas of information about the future (such as societal change, customer preferences, technological advances, and so on). They try to forecast what the future will look like by monitoring both the frequency and the content of emerging trends. Most of these trends, which take years to fully materialize, can be tracked because they have a history and they leave a path from which managers can forecast their future shape and direction. *Process futurists*, on the other hand, deal with the way people think about the future. While there are many popular books that describe what to expect in the future, there are very few that explain why and how the future is unfolding in a particular manner.

Joel Barker: Anticipating Paradigm Shifts

Joel Barker is a process futurist. In his 1992 book *Future Edge: Discovering the New Paradigms for Success*, he provides key insights that will help HSM managers better anticipate the future in turbulent times.

Anticipate the Future. Barker lists thirty-nine dramatic changes in technology (such as satellite communications, fiber optics, and biotechnology) and society (for instance, civil rights legislation and environmentalism) that have emerged over the past thirty years. If a manager had been able to anticipate even one of these trends during its initial, formative years, he would have identified an extremely profitable investment opportunity. A wide variety of innovative products and services were triggered by these changes. For example, entire industries are starting to emerge around environmentalism. Barker estimates that environmentally based industries will form a trillion-dollar industry worldwide by the year 2000, even though the environmental movement did not even exist in 1960.

Barker contends that managers need to spend more time trying to anticipate these types of changes. Barker cites Peter Drucker, author of *Managing in Turbulent Times*, as stating that one of the most important management skills during times of change and high turbulence is anticipation. Traditional managers spend too much time defensively reacting to a variety of unexpected business problems. HSM managers, on the other hand, try to use an offensive and proactive style of management, in which they anticipate and avoid potential business problems while actually identifying new business opportunities in the process.

Understand Paradigm Shifts. Most of the thirty-nine changes Barker lists in his book were driven by paradigm shifts. Barker defines a paradigm as "a set of rules and regulations (written or unwritten) that does two things: (1) it establishes or defines boundaries; and (2) it tells you how to behave inside the bound-aries in order to be successful" (1992, p. 32).

A paradigm is a scheme for perceiving, understanding, and explaining certain aspects of reality. A paradigm is an agreed-upon way of thinking and doing associated with one's perception of reality. A highly accepted paradigm often exists as an unquestioned understanding that is passed on to succeeding generations through experience rather than through education. Knowing that the paradigm concept is difficult for some manag-ers to fully grasp, Barker lists a collection of traditional words that capture its essence. Some of these include model, stan-dards, protocol, routines, assumptions, habits, mind-set, con-ventional wisdom, traditions, and frames of reference.

Barker feels that outstanding leaders are able to antici-pate, facilitate, and then capitalize on future paradigm shifts. He points out that while a paradigm "tells you that there is a game, what the game is, and how to play it successfully," a paradigm shift "is a change to a new game, a new set of rules." Finally, Barker states that "when the rules change, the whole world can change."

For example, for years Switzerland was the leader in watch making. They built high-quality, accurate watches that were continuously improved. The Swiss invented the minute hand, the second hand, and waterproofing. They sold the best self-winding watches while constantly inventing better ways to man-ufacture the mainspring and gears. By 1968 the Swiss had 65 percent of the world watch market. Yet by 1980 their market share dropped to less than 10 percent. What happened?

Barker points out that the Swiss had ignored or mini-mized the importance of a paradigm shift. The fundamentals of watch making had shifted from mechanical to microelectronic mechanisms. Everything the Swiss were good at was irrelevant in the new paradigm. Japan benefitted from the paradigm shift because Japanese companies like Seiko were in the midst of refining electronic quartz technology that could be used in watches. Their share of the world watch market grew dramatically, from 1 percent in 1968 to about 33 percent in 1990. It was the Swiss who invented electronic quartz movement. Yet Swiss watch manufacturers firmly rejected this revolutionary idea in 1967. The Swiss inaccurately assumed that the electronic quartz watch could not possibly be the watch of the future. The Swiss failed to anticipate the future role of the new technology.

HSM managers are aware that new paradigms put everyone practicing the old paradigm at great risk. The more a company has invested in the old paradigm, the more it has to lose by changing paradigms. Therefore, in order to help managers better understand and anticipate paradigm shifts, Barker provides the following information:

1. Because companies usually benefit from their current paradigms, they almost always resist using the new paradigms.
2. Usually an outsider to the industry creates a new paradigm, because the outsider is not emotionally attached to or biased by the old paradigm.
3. Companies that change to a new paradigm gain a new way of perceiving their industry, along with new approaches for meeting customers' needs.
4. A paradigm shift puts all companies back to point zero. Companies that benefitted from the old paradigm eventually lose much if not all of their leverage and advantage.
5. Significant competitive advantage lies with those companies that accurately anticipate, and possibly even create, a paradigm shift. (Adapted from Barker, 1992)

Finally, Barker points out that companies usually have three choices when confronted with a paradigm shift within their industry. They can (1) keep their current paradigm, yet seek out new customers and markets; (2) change to the new paradigm to keep their current customers; or (3) change their paradigm *and* change their customers. HSM managers typically prefer model one or two, or some combination of both, since model three is very risky and time-consuming. The following case study illustrates how one quick-response company used models one and two to successfully cope with a paradigm shift.

Deluxe Corporation is an industry leader in check printing. Even though Deluxe accurately printed checks faster than their competitors, the emerging trends in electronic banking (the paradigm shift) were threatening Deluxe's core business. Deluxe chose model one as its competitive strategy (that is, keeping the original paradigm, but changing customers) because it realized there was still value in its original paradigm of putting ink on paper better than anyone else. Deluxe continued to print checks but also started printing bank forms, office forms, computer forms, and even direct-mail greeting cards. Deluxe's original paradigm was still capable of generating new and expanded customer bases. In addition, Deluxe also experimented with model two (changing to the new paradigm to retain current customers) by getting into the electronic funds transfer business. Deluxe Corporation is an excellent example of an HSM company.

Gerald Celente: Trend Tracking for Profit

Gerald Celente, a process futurist, is co-author of *Trend Tracking: Find Out How to Transform Trends into Opportunity and Profit*. He defines a trend as "a definite, predictable direction or sequence of events, like the warming of the earth's climate" (1991, p. 13). His staff identifies significant trends by following social, political, and economic events through the past into the present and the future. Celente's goal is to teach clients how to profit by translating a trend into specific competitive strategies, products, and services. In brief, trend tracking can show HSM managers how they got where they are and where they need to be headed in the future.

Celente uses a very sound methodology for identifying future trends. It yields fairly accurate results and is recommended for all prospective HSM managers. The following are six key aspects of his model.

Look everywhere. Some futurists maintain that trends originate in a few states (such as California) and then move eastward. In actuality, trends have many sources, including world leaders, the middle class, inventors and innovators, and social, economic, and political events. A broad view of where trends can come from is needed, not an overly restrictive view.

Identify trends. Trends are based on a progressive sequence of events that assumes a predictable direction. Two common or interrelated events are typically needed. A trend must have social, political, and economic significance. Finally, a trend should have an identifiable cause and a meaningful effect on something of importance. Fads are not to be confused with trends since they are unpredictable and have no real significance.

Acquire factual information. HSM managers must exhibit discipline and objectivity when trying to predict future business trends. They must focus on specific facts about the past and present, and avoid inaccurate, biased, misleading, and exaggerated information. HSM managers must ignore junk news, headline-only news, and media hype. Hyped-up trends seem true at first glance because they appear to be based on facts. Unfortunately, actual facts might be overemphasized and exaggerated, or removed from their original context. Apparent facts might actually be inclinations or intentions, and not yet reality. The following is a list of some of the best sources of objective and accurate information (adapted from Berkman, 1980, and Celente & Milton, 1991).

On-line Information Services

- CompuServe, 5000 Arlington Centre Boulevard, P.O. Box 28212, Columbus, Ohio 43220 (800-848-8199)
- Dow Jones News/Retrieval Service, P.O. Box 300, Princeton, New Jersey (800-522-3567)
- Gannett/USA Today Online Library, Data Times, Parkway Plaza, Suite 450, 14000 Quail Springs Parkway, Oklahoma City, Oklahoma 73134 (800-642-2525)
- Prodigy Interactive Personal Service, P.O. Box 791, White Plains, New York (800-284-5933)

Newspapers

- *Investors Business Daily* (Los Angeles). A solid financial daily that provides strong coverage of economic and business trends.

- *The Times* (London). An influential foreign newspaper with an excellent business section.
- *The New York Times.* Solid, comprehensive news reporting on a wide variety of topics.
- *USA Today* (Washington, D.C.). Filled with essential information covering a wide range of trends.
- *The Wall Street Journal* (New York). A premier financial daily information source that also covers controversial topics.

Magazines

- *Advertising Age.* Focuses on consumer spending trends.
- *American Demographics.* Covers trends in demography and marketing research.
- *Asia Week.* Covers local, regional, and world news from the Asian viewpoint.
- *Business Week.* Provides timely coverage of leading corporations, international business, the economy, marketing trends, the government, science and technology, and other issues.
- *Common Cause.* Covers current political views and programs aimed at making government more responsive.
- *The Economist.* Covers global politics, finance, and science along with major economic trends.
- *Forbes.* A very readable business magazine that covers investment news, government policies, and major business issues.
- *Fortune.* Covers topical business news, corporate performance, management strategies, society, technological advances, and politics and public policy.
- *The Futurist.* Official publication of the World Future Society. Summarizes the latest professional research.
- *The Nation.* Focuses on politics.
- *National Review.* Covers international events and politics.
- *Science News.* Covers a wide range of news in science and technology.
- *The Washington Monthly.* Focuses on political areas including presidential policies, federal agencies, congressional activities, and the courts.

- *World Press Review.* Contains excerpts from major news-papers and magazines covering current world affairs.

Books

- Berkman, R. I. (1990). *Find it Fast: How to Uncover Expert Information on Any Subject.* New York: Harper & Row Pub-lishers. An innovative handbook that shows managers how to quickly locate the best information sources, how to find and utilize the experts behind those sources, and how to combine a wide variety of techniques to conduct a complete information search. This book also provides a listing of books, magazines, and associations that are useful for a wide variety of information findings.
- Glossbrenner, A. (1987). *How to Look It Up Online.* New York: St. Martin's Press. Focuses on computerized data-base searches. Provides a comprehensive resource guide to avail-able data bases.

Adopt proper discipline. HSM managers must incorporate trend-tracking into their daily routines—from fifteen minutes to one hour a day. Most managers already watch TV news and read newspapers, magazines, and newsletters for more than an hour a day without formally tracking trends. As trend trackers, managers will now be reading and watching with a purpose. HSM managers must also be willing to accept change and take advantage of it. Anticipated changes should not be denied or ignored. HSM managers must always strive to be objective in their review of past, present, and future trends. They must stay open-minded, because some trends actually contradict popular thinking.

Identify targets. HSM managers cannot track everything. This would be a waste of time. They need to select the most relevant fields of inquiry that can prove most profitable to their companies. They must try to track true trends instead of fads. HSM managers should try to track a variety of trends that might become interrelated in the future. For example, if one were tracking trends in travel and in communications, one would look for future connections between these two fields. In the future, auto and airline travel will probably become more difficult as the roads and skies become more congested. Environmentalism might also block the expansion of highways and access to overcrowded air routes. So it seems feasible that more of the travel load, especially business-related travel, will shift to the communications arena (teleconferences, videoconferences, and so forth).

Profit from trend tracking. To profit from trend tracking in a reliable and consistent manner, Celente recommends using this four-phase standardized procedure:

1. *Trend tracking.* Identify and track meaningful and ongoing trends that have social, economical, and political significance.
2. *Forecasting.* Project the trend into the future. Use information from the past and present as the foundation for the forecast.
3. *Planning.* Develop specific strategies to take advantage of the projected changes. Brainstorm as many strategies as possible, and select the ones that have the highest probability of success.
4. *Implementation.* Pick a time and date to actually implement the strategy or strategies. Continually monitor the effectiveness of the strategy to ensure that you are actually benefitting from the trend tracking, forecasting, and planning.

Celente offers many excellent examples of how people profit from these trend-tracking methodologies. One example dealt with the 1979 Iran crisis. During the *trend-tracking* phase, Celente followed the political trends in Iran. He also tracked the declining ability of the United States to transform the world into its own image. Finally, he tracked worldwide economic trends, such as inflation.

During the *forecasting* phase, Celente projected the political trends in Iran into the future. He predicted the Shah would be overthrown, primarily because the Shah was seen as "America's boy." Celente also predicted that Europeans and Middle

Easterners would view the overthrow of the Shah as an international crisis, would feel their security threatened, and would become even more disillusioned with America. To protect themselves financially, they might convert their assets into dollars as they had done in similar crises, except that due to increasing inflation the dollar was quickly losing value. If there were another oil crisis in addition to the Iran crisis, having their assets in dollars would only make their financial situation worse. So Celente predicted that the safe haven for investors would be the purchasing of gold.

The *planning* phase was straightforward. In order to profit from his projected trends, Celente decided to buy as much gold as he could afford, and to hold it until its price was driven up by people reacting to the fall of the Shah and related crises. In the *implementation* phase Celente selected a reputable broker, opened a trading account, and started buying gold. Needless to say, events unfolded exactly as predicted and Celente and his clients profited from his four-step program.

John Naisbitt: Identifying Megatrends

John Naisbitt is a content futurist. His best-seller *Megatrends: Ten New Directions Transforming Our Lives*, published in 1982, identified the ten trends summarized in the following list:

John Naisbitt's Original Ten Megatrends

From	*To*
1. Industrial society	Information society
2. Forced technology	High tech/high touch systems
3. National economy	World economy
4. Short-term considerations	Longer-term time frames
5. Centralization	Decentralization
6. Institutional help	Self-help
7. Representative democracy	Participatory democracy
8. Hierarchical structures	Informal networks
9. North	South/west
10. Either/or society	Multiple option society

Naisbitt's book convinced many companies to change some of their long-term goals, and these trends continue to prove valuable to business leaders seeking to understand and take advantage of the ways in which our society is changing.

HSM managers always strive to stay out in front of change to ensure maximum competitive advantage. For example, accepting the trend toward self-help and self-care probably facilitated the offering and improvement of such home-based products as tests for pregnancy, cholesterol, and diabetes. Certain pharmaceutical companies will surely benefit from this megatrend. Health care costs can also be reduced if companies can discover ways to effectively promote to their employees such free self-help groups as Alcoholics Anonymous, Narcotics Anonymous, Overeaters Anonymous, and Emotions Anonymous.

Naisbitt points out that his book focuses on the megatrends, or "broad outlines," that will shape and define the new society. His findings are based on a thorough content analysis of more than 2 million articles about local events in cities and towns across this country during a twelve-year period. Naisbitt categorizes trend information from approximately two hundred daily newspapers, then isolates trends in relation to the amount of space they were allotted in the newspapers.

Naisbitt (with Aburdene) published his most recent book, *Megatrends 2000: Ten New Directions for the 1990's*, in 1990. In this book, he confirmed that the ten original megatrends are pretty much on schedule, but he also presented ten new "millennial megatrends" that should continue to influence society in the 1990s and will serve as gateways to the twenty-first century. Again using content analysis, Naisbitt was able to delineate the following overarching megatrends:

Naisbitt's Millennial Megatrends

1. The booming global economy of the 1990s is ushering in a period of worldwide economic prosperity.
2. A renaissance in the arts will occur; the arts will replace sports as society's primary leisure activity.
3. The emergence of free-market socialism will mark the demise of classical socialism.

4.   Global lifestyles and cultural nationalism will be made possible thanks to a thriving world economy, global telecommunications, and expanding travel.

5.   The privatization of the welfare state will occur, whereby governments will reduce the number of state-owned enterprises.

6.   The Pacific Rim (including such cities as Los Angeles, Sydney, and Tokyo), which will have two-thirds of the world's population by the year 2000, will continue to emerge as an economic powerhouse.

7.   The decade of women in leadership will evolve, as women are starting new businesses twice as fast as men and continuing to take the majority of the new jobs created in the information era.

8.   The age of biology is unfolding, as evidenced by advances in biotechnology and genetic engineering.

9.   The religious revival of the new millennium is expected; baby boomers who rejected organized religion in the 1970s will return to the church with their children.

10.   The triumph of the individual will come to serve as the foundation of society and the basic unit of change.

Robert Tucker: Profit from the Future

Robert Tucker is a content futurist who points out that more and more companies are being devastated by events they failed to anticipate, even though the majority of these events were predictable. Any company that does not know how to gain competitive advantage from future events is at risk of being devastated by change. In his book *Managing the Future*, Tucker proposed the following four-point strategy to meet this challenge successfully.

Manage the future. HSM managers must go with the dominant forces of change in the business world instead of resisting them. Tucker conducted both extensive library research and in-depth interviews with CEOs of companies that were "just slightly ahead of their time" in order to document the following ten major forces of change for the 1990s:

1. *Speed.* Whole businesses will be built around speed.
2. *Convenience.* Customers will prefer the ultimate in convenience before, during, and after the sale.
3. *Age waves.* American companies must deal effectively with three age-related markets: mature, baby-boom, and baby-bust.
4. *Choice.* Customers want choice — to have it their way — even if companies must continuously customize.
5. *Lifestyle.* Businesses must learn to benefit from changes in the way people live, such as an increase in fitness and health consciousness.
6. *Discounting.* Discounting will probably spread to all industries in the 1990s, the era of price competition.
7. *Value-adding.* Companies must continually add value to their products and services in order to create alternatives to price competition.
8. *Customer service.* Companies must continuously work to build lasting customer satisfaction and loyalty.
9. *Technology.* Businesses must strategically use computers and related technology to gain a competitive edge and to become industry leaders.
10. *Quality.* Quality products must conform to and even surpass customer requirements to ensure a satisfied and profitable customer base. (Adapted from Tucker, 1991)

Innovate and improve. HSM managers must be able to respond to future changes by creatively improving their products and services and differentiating them from the competition. Companies must be able to develop new products, services, delivery channels, and marketing strategies that best fit with the expectations of the future. For example, both pharmaceutical companies and allergists should be developing new medications and more effective treatments as they anticipate an increase in pollution-related allergies.

Keep your eyes on the customer. HSM managers must always be poised to meet new and emerging customer needs, a rapidly moving target in the 1990s. HSM managers must stay slightly ahead of their customers at all times. Tucker points out that

when companies take their eyes off the customer, then the customer finds a way to avoid or bypass the company.

According to Tucker, Robert Hazard, president of Quality
Inns International, stayed very close to customers and rein-
vented his hotel chain based on consumer feedback. After talking to his barber, Hazard realized that the typical customer
preferred to stay at budget motels on the road, yet splurge on
more upscale hotels in major downtown areas. Hazard realized
that his motels were probably too expensive, while his big city
hotels were definitely too cheap. He knew his company was
poised for disaster unless he quickly corrected the situation.
Hazard pioneered market segmentation with his hotel chain.
He introduced economical Comfort Inns and Sleep Inns for
budget-minded travelers on the road and the more upscale
Clarion Hotels to satisfy travelers in big cities. By staying close to
his customers, Hazard quickly identified and responded to a
consumer trend and thus saved his company.

Be aggressive. Tucker believes that HSM managers need the
mind-set of an attacker instead of a defender. The 1990s will
surely bring constant competitive attacks from companies that
offer superior technology, faster and better ways of doing business, increased service and convenience, better quality, and so
on. Tucker believes that attackers are more apt to anticipate,
identify, and exploit lucrative markets, while defenders, often
blind to competitive threats against them, have trouble anticipating what to expect from the future.

Frank Feather: Tracking Global Forces

Frank Feather's *G-Forces: The 35 Global Forces Restructuring Our
Future*, published in 1989, is based on a comprehensive analysis
of information on global trends affecting business, government,
education, and society. Feather identifies thirty-five global forces
(G-Forces) currently effecting change that will be restructuring
the world through the twenty-first century. Feather believes that
these G-Forces provide a more global, long-term structure for
understanding the future than Naisbitt's megatrends.

Feather provides two useful schemes for understanding

Table 3.1. North America's Six-Wave Economy.

Social Wave	Peak Year*	Focus
1st	1880	Agriculture and natural resources
2nd	1915	Industry and manufacturing
3rd	1950	Services (such as educational, health, and personal)
4th	1988	Information (such as knowledge and high technology)
5th	2020	Leisure and tourism
6th	2050+	Outer space

* Based on percent of people employed in that sector. The peak years are estimates.

Source: Adapted from Feather, 1989.

the future. His six-wave economy—an expansion of Alvin Toffler's work on first-wave, second-wave, and third-wave economies (see Toffler, 1980)—highlights the industrial sectors that employ the majority of a country's work force at certain points in time. For example, Table 3.1 gives a brief sketch of the evolution of North America's six-wave economy. By the year 2000, the leading companies in America will probably be those that are firmly committed to fourth- and fifth-wave categories.

Feather also identified thirty-five G-Forces that should radically shape the future of the world over the next sixty years. He grouped these forces into four categories: (1) social motivation, (2) technological innovation, (3) economic modernization, and (4) political reform. While it is beyond the scope of this chapter to summarize all thirty-five G-Forces, a few of the most important ones are summarized in the list that follows. HSM managers around the world are probably already exploring ways to gain competitive advantage by developing products and services that are consistent with these G-Forces.

Feather's Major G-Forces Shaping the World's Future

1. *Social motivation.*
   - Stabilize the global population
   - Economically feed the world

- Provide clean water for all
- Create global wellness and health

2. *Technological innovation.*
   - Eliminate hard work to create a leisure society
   - Create a real-time globalized network of information utilities
   - Establish geo-strategic corporations
   - Push back high-tech frontiers with scientific advances

3. *Economic modernization.*
   - Industrialize the Third World
   - Improve the global financial system
   - Eliminate worldwide energy shortages
   - Redirect the military to worldwide ecological development projects

4. *Political reform.*
   - Disarm the planet
   - Modernize China
   - Solidify and unify the Third World
   - Revitalize America by forming alliances with Canada and Mexico

Peter Lorie and Sidd Murray-Clark: Approaching the Year 3000

Planning far into the future has different levels of importance to different companies. For most, planning one or two years into the future is the norm. Some strategically oriented companies also think in terms of three to five years. Donald Kennedy, former Stanford University president, projected nearly thirty years into the future in an effort to envision what higher learning at Stanford should look like in the year 2020. Japanese industrial leader Konosuke Matsushita was reported to have prepared a 150-year business plan for his company. These two executives are very committed to having their organizations be leaders in their fields far into the future. However, the farther into the future one projects, the greater the chances are that the future will become harder to predict, more unbelievable, and therefore even more anxiety provoking.

Peter Lorie and Sidd Murray-Clark wrote *History of the*

Future: A Chronology in 1989. They make predictions about the state of the world through the year 3000. They base their predictions on a variety of scientific writings including the work of leading physicists and metaphysicists. Some of their major predictions are summarized below. One caveat: Many people would argue that these predictions read more like science fiction than future realities. Yet HSM managers try to approach all predictions about the future with an open mind, and they always try to use their future visions to strengthen their company's competitive posture.

Lorie and Murray-Clark's Predictions
Through the End of the Third Millennium

Date Range	Major Predictions
2000–2100	World government experiments; genetic catastrophes; a global financial structure; preventive medicine overtakes curative medicine.
2100–2200	New family structures; the space age takes hold; genetically engineered people; independent countries begin to give way to a world state; computer systems interface with the human brain; biochips permanently store a person's mind; hypersonic travel (mach 15 to mach 25).
2200–2300	Contacting other species in the universe; joining the galactic community; computer-controlled emotions; higher levels of consciousness; machines that feel; instant travel on a molecular transfer level.
2300–2400	Global security forces; time travel; interplanetary communications; underwater cities; significant longevity gains through medicine and chemicals; bionic body parts; super-minds through genetic engineering.
2400–2500	Time manipulation; fabricated planets away from earth; androids; a new math; cryogenic advances; robopathic labor; tunnelling the planet; population control advances.

2500–2600   Mental sports competitions; galactic war poten-
             tial; strange events in space; extensive leisure
             time creates problems; increase in human phys-
             ical power.
2600–2700   New types of test-tube bodies; regrowing, re-
             building, and transplanting body parts; a new
             era of pleasure seeking; entertainment through
             self-created dream states.
2700–2800   Spread of multiplanet communication; better
             understanding of the root cause of all diseases;
             development of super-consciousness; visits from
             alien super-beings.
2800–2900   New planets discovered; mankind begins to leave
             earth for new worlds; infinity found to have
             boundaries; computers write whole books and
             print out on their own; para-sciences (for exam-
             ple, parapsychology) become more mainstream.
2900–3000   Peace on earth as more of the human race
             departs; a broader understanding of life and
             death evolves.

John Sculley: "Back to the Future" Planning

John Sculley, chief executive officer of Apple Computer and a
process futurist, reflects on a hypothetical trip to the 1939
World's Fair to highlight the importance of planning for the
future:

> The sponsors of the [1939 world's] fair attempted to
> predict the technologies and advances that would
> shape the world through 1989. They envisioned
> space travel, then only a fantasy in scientific movies
> and books, becoming a reality. They thought televi-
> sion, then a mere curiosity, would be in every home.
> And they believed that air travel would make the
> world seem much smaller. Yet they never even men-
> tioned the computer, the laser, the transistor, or the
> microprocessor. (Sculley & Byrne, 1987, p. 292)

Sculley illustrates how planning for the future was incredibly complex and difficult in 1939, and is even more complex in the 1990s. Many companies have lost millions of dollars placing bets on the wrong products and services. When planning for the future at Apple Computer, Sculley prefers to talk about ideas and beliefs about the future instead of basing his predictions solely on numerical figures and taking a totally analytical approach.

Sculley uses a "back to the future" planning strategy to ensure that his company will be ready to compete in the lucrative markets of the 1990s and beyond. He points out that most traditional managers look forward when they plan for the future. They make extrapolations about the future based on their company's past accomplishments. At Apple, the planning process is different. Apple's managers project themselves into the future and then work their way back in small increments of time.

For example, planners at Apple might ask themselves what the year 2000 will be like and then create in their minds an image of what the economy, their industry, their company, and their products will look like that far into the future. These planners then slowly work their way back to the present in order to envision what they need to do in the 1990s to achieve their vision of the year 2000.

Apple's planners then compare their readiness for the future with their major competitors' readiness. In the late 1980s, to prepare Apple for the 1990s, Apple's planners confidently envisioned a computer industry of the future that was focused on high-quality graphics and a good user interface. These already were Apple's strong points, yet Apple recommitted itself to making major investments in these technologies to ensure domination of these markets in the future.

Planners at Apple use two additional strategies to enrich their efforts at planning for the future *different viewpoints* and *insightful questions*. Uncensored brainstorming sessions allow for a strong generation of ideas. Planners are also encouraged to use "unconstrained dreaming." Idea creation is never limited! In addition, Apple's planners always try to articulate questions that

yield the most diverse and insightful answers, rather than getting hung up on any one particular answer.

Once planners lock into some highly probable scenarios
of the future, they ask themselves what they should be prioritizing and doing differently in the present, based on how they
envision the future. They then discuss their vision of the future
with other managers to get additional input, perspective, and
eventual buy-in. The planners also want the managers to think
about the implications of the future vision for their own units.
Sculley wants future-oriented thinking to become part of the
entire company's mind-set and culture, where managers will
think constructively about the future all the time. He wants both
the anticipation and the invention of the future to become a
permanent part of Apple's identity, values, and culture.

Conclusion

HSM managers must become very skilled at anticipating and
predicting the future if their companies are going to gain and
retain their competitive advantage. HSM managers must learn
to use methodologies such as trend tracking (Gerald Celente)
and "back to the future" planning (John Sculley) in order to
anticipate the future of their industry, company, products, and
competitors. HSM managers need to seriously study the writing
of both content futurists (John Naisbitt) and process futurists
(Joel Barker). By focusing on the prediction of the future, HSM
managers and their companies have a better chance of inventing
it. In addition, a future-oriented philosophy increases HSM
managers' odds of conceptualizing, producing, and marketing
products and services that will be most relevant to the markets of
the future.

Chapter Four

Make Decisions Faster

In *The Effective Executive,* published in 1967, Peter Drucker concludes that making effective business decisions is one of the most important managerial activities. But Drucker sends a mixed message on the importance of speed in executive decision making.

Drucker reports that executives are "not overly impressed by speed in decision making" (p. 114). Yet he points out that some of the most effective executives in history (such as Alfred P. Sloan, Jr., of General Motors and Theodore Vail of Bell Telephone) avoided working on too many major decisions at one time. Instead, they concentrated on the decisions that required the highest level of conceptual understanding. Focusing only on the most important decisions is definitely a time management strategy. This strategy typically leads to quicker and more accurate decision making because the executive does not become distracted with an abundance of less important problems.

Drucker also discovered that effective executives use a five-step model, summarized in the following list, to guide their decision making. Managers who use a well-formulated decision-making model usually make quicker and more accurate decisions than less-disciplined decision makers who do not use a proven method to reach effective decisions.

1. *Determine the nature of the problem.* Determine if the problem being addressed is *generic* (that is, it generalizes across different situations) or *unique.* Generic problems should be solved with a decision that establishes a rule, policy, or principle. Unique problems must be handled individually; they usually require no rule.

2. *Determine the purpose of the decision.* Establish clear specifications as to what the decision has to accomplish. Determine what goals and objectives the decision has to attain. The decision always needs to satisfy its purpose.

3. *Determine the correct solution.* Seek the opinions of others. Discussion and disagreement lead to more alternatives. Intelligently determine the best solution to fully satisfy all specifications before considering any concessions or adaptations needed to make the decision acceptable. By determining the right solution first one can avoid making wrong concessions later on.

4. *Convert the decision into action.* Decisions must be carried out. Converting a decision into effective action requires commitments from the parties responsible for executing and monitoring the decision.

5. *Test the decision's effectiveness.* Decisions can often be wrong and they can eventually become obsolete. Therefore, they must continuously be tested against actual events to determine their effectiveness, and revised if necessary.

In fast-paced work settings like the computer and financial industries, the tumult of technical change places a premium on rapid strategic decision making. Fast decision making allows executives to keep one step ahead of their competitors. Research conducted by Kathleen Eisenhardt shows that fast decision making is linked to high levels of sales growth and profitability in high-velocity industries. Fast decisions apparently helped the executives learn faster and capitalize on market opportunities sooner. Compared to slow strategic decision makers, fast decision makers typically:

- Make decisions up to four times quicker than traditional managers
- Collect and use more information to form a decision
- Develop more alternative solutions to their business dilemmas
- Encourage input from a wide variety of sources, including experts and senior managers
- Are able to more rapidly and effectively resolve conflicts
- Quickly integrate the strategic decisions with their operational plans (Adapted from Eisenhardt, 1989)

How Fast Strategic Decisions Are Made

Management specialists disagree about the importance of speed in decision making. Some experts feel that fast decision makers tend to base their decisions on quick-and-dirty analyses with input from too few sources. These experts also believe that rapid decision makers tend to limit others' involvement in the decision-making process. However, some current research suggests these views are inaccurate. Scientific research conducted by Eisenhardt has identified the following five effective strategies used by fast decision makers (see Eisenhardt, 1989).

Use Real-Time Information

Eisenhardt found that managers who make fast decisions typically use more information than slower decision makers. However, the information is not "forecasted" information. Instead, it tends to be "real time" information. Real-time information is information about a company's business operations or competitive environment that is reported shortly after or as it occurs. The greater the use of real-time information, the greater the speed of the strategic decision-making process.

Managers making fast strategic decisions about their company's business operations or competitive environment pay close attention to a wide variety of quantitative indicators, such as daily, weekly, and monthly records of sales, inventory, cash flow, product development milestones, and competitors' moves. These highly effective executives prefer immediate face-to-face conversation, electronic mail, or voice mail rather than time-delayed media like lengthy formal reports.

Fast decision makers are constantly communicating with other executives, their employees, customers, prospects, and vendors. Conversations typically focus on the current status of a wide variety of important company projects, rather than on speculations about where the projects will stand in the future.

The use of real-time information allows executives to spot both problems and opportunities sooner. Fast decision makers use strong business controls and tracking systems so that they are always updated on the status of major projects. However, they do not get bogged down with overly complicated, lengthy, or time-consuming tracking systems. They tend to use very brief status reports that focus on the major milestones, due dates, completion dates, and the reasons a project is behind schedule at any stage.

Slow decision makers do not seek out and base their decisions on real-time information. They hold few meetings to check on the status of important corporate projects. Slow decision makers are more detached from day-to-day operations. Many are also unfocused in their priorities.

Simultaneously Consider Multiple Alternatives

Eisenhardt found that fast decision makers generate and consider more alternative solutions to their problems than slow decision makers. Moreover, fast decision makers tend to simultaneously consider multiple alternatives, while slower decision makers tend to sequentially consider fewer alternatives. Fast decision makers often compare and contrast their options with the help of a support team whose sole purpose is generating multiple alternatives to a business problem. The process of comparing alternatives helps fast decision makers quickly determine the alternatives' strengths and weaknesses, and builds their confidence that the most viable alternatives have been thoroughly reviewed and considered.

The consideration of simultaneous alternatives provides a fallback position for fast decision makers. They are able to tolerate a great deal of ambiguity since they must think about a wide range of options simultaneously. They tend to have a lower psychological stake in any one alternative and can quickly shift between alternatives if they receive any negative information about one of them. In contrast, slow decision makers usually consider fewer solutions to their problems and tend to seek out a new alternative only when an old one is no longer feasible. This sequential procedure of slow decision makers is in stark contrast to the simultaneous considerations of fast decision makers.

The notion that the consideration of multiple alternatives is time-consuming is not justified. Slow decision makers spend a great deal of time on only one alternative. Fast decision makers pursue several alternatives that are analyzed very quickly. The breadth-not-depth decision-making strategy is highly efficient in situations in which time pressure is high.

Use Experienced Advisors

Eisenhardt discovered that it is a myth that centralized power leads to quicker decision making, since fewer managers need to be involved. The truth is, some autocrats are fast decision makers and some are slow. Even autocratic decision makers can be delayed because of anxiety, inadequate information, confusion, procrastination, or even fear.

Fast decision makers typically use a two-tier advice process — not only do they seek input and feedback from from other members of the management team, but they also focus on obtaining advice from one or two of the company's most experienced counselors, who can provide information that only a true expert in the field would know. The experienced counselor serves as a sounding board for all of the executive's ideas. An executive can be very open with a trustworthy counselor, and can share his or her concerns about the various alternatives without hesitation. The experienced counselor provides perspective and can relate possible alternatives to past decisions.

Actively Resolve Conflicts

Conflict resolution is a critical skill for high-speed decision makers. Eisenhardt found that fast decision makers establish a decision-making support team that is skilled at dealing with conflict. Yet if an impasse is reached among team members, then the key decision maker quickly resolves the conflict.

Fast decision-making teams take an approach to conflict resolution that has been called *consensus with qualification*. This consensus-making strategy is a two-stage process. First, a team attempts to reach consensus by involving every team member. However, if consensus is not reached, the relevant member of the senior management team, often the president or chief executive officer, makes the final decision. Of course, the decision is always shaped and guided by the input of the entire team.

In contrast, conflict resolution is problematic for slow decision-making teams. Slow decision-making teams tend to delay their decisions until external events force a choice. Sometimes such teams wait too long for group consensus. In addition, slow teams often wait for deadlines rather than make a critical decision before the deadline.

Integrate Strategic Decisions with Tactical Plans

Finally, Eisenhardt found that fast decision makers quickly integrate their strategic decisions with one another *and* with the complete set of tactical plans. New strategic decisions are usually examined in relation to their integration with past and current strategic decisions, and in relation to current tactical plans such as the budget, product release schedules, sales goals and objectives, and so on. Fast decision makers also know their way out of each decision—they develop plans to manage the worst-case outcome of the new strategic decision.

Slow decision makers typically do not analyze their new strategic decisions relative to other strategic decisions or to tactical plans. Lack of decision integration keeps decision making at an abstract, rather than a functional, level. For example, a slow decision maker and his team struggled for over a year to conceptualize and develop a new product. Only after the decision was made to develop a new product did the executive consider how to integrate the new product idea into the existing product line. This led to very lengthy delays. Not only did it take a long time to decide to develop the product, but it took even longer to determine where the product fit into the overall company strategy.

A Strategy for Making More Accurate Decisions

Richard Cosier and Charles Schwenk have conducted research that shows that fostering conflict and disagreement in a structured decision-making setting may actually lead to better overall decisions. This is because the most thoughtful decisions surface only after intense debate and careful consideration of several points of view. In fact, Cosier and Schwenk went so far as to suggest that "[w]idespread agreement on a key issue is a red flag, not a condition of good [corporate] health" (1990, p. 69). Their views are consistent with a story Peter Drucker shares about the late Alfred P. Sloan of General Motors:

> Alfred P. Sloan is reported to have said at a meeting of one his top committees: "Gentlemen, I take it we are all in complete agreement on the decision here." Everyone around the table nodded assent. "Then," continued Mr. Sloan, "I propose we postpone further discussion of this matter until our next meeting to give ourselves time to develop disagreement and perhaps gain some understanding

of what the decision is all about." (Drucker, 1967, p. 148)

Some of the top business leaders in the country believe that successful business decisions are reached only in companies that advocate open and intense discussions before adopting a solution. For example, Cosier and Schwenk report that Scott McNealy, Sun Microsystems' CEO, actually encourages noisy, intense debate among his senior executives. Similarly, Jack Welch, General Electric's CEO, prefers a tough and aggressive decision-making climate that benefits from constructive arguments and confrontations. In brief, many successful leaders actually prefer conflict and dissent as part of the decision-making process.

Conflict and dissent can occur naturally in decision-making settings, yet it is safer and less time-consuming to plan for the conflict and program it into the process. There are two ways to do this. The first is the *devil's advocate technique,* whereby everyone in a decision-making group questions the major assumptions underlying the most popular decision. Another alternative is to assign an individual the role of devil's advocate. This person presents an in-depth critique of the decision under consideration. The conflict created by the devil's advocate technique generates more alternative solutions. Potential problems and false assumptions can also be more easily avoided.

The second technique for programming conflict into the decision-making process is called the *dialectic method.* Cosier and Schwenk describe this method as a structured debate between conflicting views, "a struggle between opposing forces," or "the conflicting views of a thesis and an antithesis" (1990, p. 73).

Key decision makers typically request a structured debate between the people who support the original decision and those who have been asked to develop a counterproposal based on totally different assumptions. Proponents for each point of view must present and defend the key assumptions that support their arguments. False and misleading assumptions are usually avoided by using this method. Some form of compromise decision is almost always made—one that is usually more promising than the original decision.

In brief, programmed conflict is needed to foster more effective and innovative decision making in organizations. Programmed conflicts lead to a healthy debate of all critical issues and more alternative solutions are generated.

Avoid Decision-Making Mistakes

Management consultants J. Edward Russo and Paul J. Schoemaker, authors of *Decision Traps: The Ten Barriers to Brilliant Decision-Making and How to Overcome Them,* discovered that even though decision making is the most important activity of a manager's career, few managers have ever had any systematic training in how to make decisions. They identified the four key elements of decision making as (1) *framing*—accurately conceptualizing the problem to be solved; (2) *gathering intelligence*—collecting all relevant factual information along with reasonable estimates of all unknowable information that is needed to make a decision; (3) *drawing conclusions*—using a systematic approach to examine all aspects of the problem and then basing one's judgment on relevant information alone; and (4) *learning from feedback*—keeping track of and learning from the lessons of past decisions.

These researchers also learned that untrained decision makers typically make the same errors over and over again, frequently defining the problems they are contemplating in ways that cause them to overlook the best choices. Poor decision makers often fail to collect the most critical factual information because they are overconfident about their initial opinion. The list that follows summarizes this and other barriers to effective decision making that are thoroughly discussed by Russo and Schoemaker. Comprehensive strategies for conquering these decision-making flaws are also presented in their book. HSM managers realize that if these errors in decision making can be reduced or eliminated, then quicker and more accurate decisions will ensue.

Russo and Schoemaker's Ten Most Dangerous Decision Traps

1. *Plunging in.* Trying to immediately solve the problem without first clearly delineating its scope and nature, and without thinking through how the decisions should optimally be handled.

2. *Frame blindness.* Setting out to solve the wrong problem because the mental framework for conceptualizing the problem did not take into account all of its aspects.

3. *Poor frame control.* Not conceptualizing the problem in more ways than one. Accepting without question other people's limited or erroneous definition of a problem.

4. *Overconfidence.* Being too sure of one's assumptions, opinions, and judgments. Failing to diligently collect and analyze necessary information.

5. *Taking shortcuts.* Failing to thoroughly research the topic. Overrelying on convenient information regardless of quality or accuracy.

6. *Being unsystematic.* Trying to keep all relevant information straight in one's head instead of following a systematic procedure when making the final decision. This flaw is often characterized as shooting from the hip or winging it.

7. *Poor group process.* Failing to manage the group decision-making process. Inaccurately believing that smart members of a group will generate the best group decision regardless of the group structure and decision-making process.

8. *Ignoring negative feedback.* Overlooking or underestimating evidence that suggests that the decision led to a bad outcome. Failing to acknowledge and learn from past mistakes.

9. *Not keeping records.* Failing to keep systematic records to track the success and failure of one's decisions. Not being able to study the lessons learned from past decisions.

10. *Not auditing.* Failing to audit the decision-making process to ensure that all flaws in thinking are avoided.

Decision-Making Styles of Top CEOs

Warren Pelton, Sonja Sackman, and Robert Boguslaw wrote *Tough Choices: The Decision-Making Styles of America's Top Fifty CEOs* because they felt that corporate leaders must begin to make bolder and more innovative decisions to optimally compete in a rapidly changing business environment. In their study they analyzed and distilled the decision-making styles of leading executives, among them Frank T. Cary (retired chairman and CEO, IBM), Richard J. Flamson (chairman and CEO, Security Pacific Corporation), C. Joseph LaBonte (president and COO, Reebok International Ltd.), Robert S. McNamara (former U.S. secretary of defense and former president of Ford Motor Company), Carl E. Reichardt (chairman and CEO, Wells Fargo & Company), and Walter B. Wriston (retired chairman and CEO, Citicorp and Citibank). Fifty executives were thoroughly interviewed so that Pelton, Sackman, and Boguslaw could construct a model for making extremely tough executive decisions.

> Our interviewees' distilled experiences and insights. . . provided a framework for [understanding] tough situations — the uncharted, unexpected, unprogrammed areas of decision-making for which no executive can truly be prepared, because these situations offer no clue on which to base a computed solution and, indeed, there are no guidelines by which to prepare. (1990, p. 4)

Pelton, Sackman, and Boguslaw focused primarily on what they called the tough problems. Some examples of tough executive decisions that they cited are listed below. The primary decision makers' names are in parentheses.

- Deciding to divest a corporation of over sixty of its companies within the first year of one's leadership. (Martin Davis, CEO of Gulf & Western)
- Radically changing a bank's objectives and goals for allocating funds to developing Third World countries that were encountering serious problems related to poverty. (Robert McNamara, former president of the World Bank)
- Deciding on the best time for introducing a new product (such as the personal computer) that was designed to both

create a new market and become the industry standard. (Frank Cary, former chairman and CEO, IBM)

The following list (adapted from Pelton, Sackman, & Boguslaw, 1990) attempts to draw some clear distinctions between the routine and the more complex decisions that modern-day managers must make:

Routine Problems	*Tough Problems*
Expected	Unexpected
Simpler	More complex
Analyzable	Unanalyzable
Predictable	Unpredictable
Solutions exist	Solutions may or may not exist
Programmable	Not programmable
"A" causes "B"	"A" may or may not cause "B"
Similar problems existed	Unlike any other problem
Can be planned for	Cannot be planned for

Based on their interview data, the three researchers extracted the following six elements that are critical to making tough business decisions:

1. *Long-term focus.* The long-term implications of all tough decisions must be examined. A long-term focus can mean five-, ten-, or fifteen-year cycles. This perspective can then be translated into specific decisions and actions through strategic planning. A vision must be translated into a highly probable future reality.
2. *"Big picture" focus.* The decision maker must be fully cognizant of the full range of factors affecting major decisions (societal, political, economical, educational, and so on). The "little picture" addresses the definable here and now. The "big picture" includes all internal and external factors and their interrelationship. The unfolding levels of perspective regarding the "big picture" are as follows: task, indi-

vidual, department, corporation, industry, nation, world, and humanity.

3. *A talented team.* A team of outstanding people must be hired, trained, and properly deployed so they can contribute to successfully resolving the problem. Good people get the job done and make things happen. They also keep pace with change, are team players, and self-manage if necessary.

4. *Flexibility.* The team of talented employees must be flexible throughout the decision-making and implementation phases. They must accept the fact that everything may be subject to change at any time. New and innovative solutions are constantly needed to cope with the unpredictable. The team members should be able to thrive on all the unforeseen challenges, keep their options open at all times, and constantly anticipate and plan for new contingencies.

5. *Bottom line focus.* All proposed strategies need to be creatively related to the bottom line. The bottom line can have three different yet interrelated meanings: (a) the last line of an income statement, (b) the outcome of a business activity, and (c) the highest aspirations of a dedicated management team (for instance, Steve Jobs, former CEO of Apple Computer, expected his company to not only become a formidable challenger to IBM, but to also improve the quality of the entire world by improving information technology). The outcomes of tough decisions should not only enhance a company's financial and competitive positions, but should also enhance the image of the company to customers, employees, and policy makers.

6. *Personality.* The top fifty executives possessed four character traits that seemed to enhance their ability to make tough decisions about complex situations. These traits include (a) a lack of self-delusion, (b) the ability to make tough decisions with accuracy, despite limited information and the absence of predictive models, (c) the ability to simplify extremely complex situations to facilitate decision making, and (d) a tolerance for rapid change and ambiguity. (Adapted from Pelton, Sackman, & Boguslaw, 1990).

Conclusion

In brief, HSM managers need to be quick and effective decision makers. They should strive at all times to rely on real-time information, simultaneously consider multiple alternatives to business problems, use experienced advisors as a sounding board, actively encourage constructive conflicts but resolve conflicts that could delay a decision, and finally, quickly integrate different strategic decisions with one another and with the operational plans. HSM managers must always strive to avoid common errors in decision making. Finally, they must be able to make both routine *and* tough decisions. Mastery of high-speed decision making can quickly yield a competitive advantage for time-based managers and their companies.

Chapter Five

Conduct Winning
Negotiations

Effective negotiating is needed to work more productively and profitably with superiors, peers, subordinates, customers, competitors, and government regulators. HSM managers realize that failure to assert their interests through well-planned negotiations allows other parties to impede their progress. Negotiations are also needed to resolve business conflicts and to improve all relationships, in business and in life.

HSM managers choose to be *strategic negotiators* by using the strategies most effective for each situation, rather than limiting themselves to using only one style of negotiating. Certain conflicts might be more amenable to a win-win, or cooperative, style of negotiation, while other conflicts might be better dealt with using a competitive style. The HSM manager utilizes both of these styles of persuasion, depending on the situation, in order to guarantee the desired outcome in the shortest amount of time.

Effective Negotiating Strategies

A thirty-item survey called the *Negotiating Style Profile* was developed by Rollin and Christine Glaser. It identifies the following five negotiating styles (adapted from Glaser & Glaser, 1991):

1. Win-lose. A high degree of concern exists for the substance of the negotiation, and a low degree of concern is expressed for the relationship with the other party. The negotiation is usually adversarial. The goal is to defeat the other party at all costs.
2. Win-win. A high degree of concern exists for both the substance of the negotiation and the relationship with the other party. The process is described as collaborative. Both parties need to have their needs met for the negotiation to be successful.
3. Accommodation. The primary focus is to build a strong interpersonal relationship that alone will lead to a fair outcome. Substantive differences are avoided to promote harmony.
4. Indifference. There is a low degree of concern for both the substance of the negotiation and one's relationship to the other party. The negotiation process is characterized by feelings of indifference, withdrawal, and resignation. The goal is to take whatever is conceded.
5. Compromise. There is a moderate degree of concern for both the substance of the negotiation and the quality of the relationship with the other party. This style is characterized by compromise, trade-offs, and splitting the difference. Conflict reduction is valued.

For a successful negotiation to take place, strategic negotiators must have confidence in both their communication and deal-making skills. They must be effective problem solvers while trying at all times to understand and satisfy the needs of the other party. That is, strategic negotiators must repeatedly listen to, understand, and empathize with the other party's positions on key issues. They must be able to anticipate what the other party is willing to accept as a reasonable outcome.

Strategic negotiators must also clearly communicate their own needs to the other party. They typically strive to build trusting, long-term relationships with the other party so that future negotiations are resolved more quickly and successfully. Strategic negotiators must seek a workable, timely, and profitable solution as opposed to a perfect solution—which rarely takes place, especially in a timely manner.

Finally, strategic negotiators must avoid disruptive confrontations with their opponents. Instead, they need to remain objective and rational at all times over the issues being negotiated. This approach helps to avoid any delays or breakdowns in the negotiating process due to ill feelings between the two parties. In brief, the HSM manager must attempt at all times to exhibit strategic negotiating skills, while avoiding the predictable barriers to effective negotiations. Some of the major barriers to successful negotiations are:

- Being unprepared for negotiations
- Having a negative attitude toward negotiations
- Lacking confidence in one's negotiating skills
- Being unable to build trusting relationships
- Failing to understand negotiating styles and tactics
- Viewing negotiations as an aggressive act
- Believing there must be a winner and a loser
- Using faulty information to establish a negotiating position
- Becoming overly emotional when negotiating
- Not understanding the wants and needs of others
- Feeling awkward when communicating
- Being unassertive and passive
- Being confrontational and driving people apart
- Defining problems in terms of an injustice that has been done to you
- Making extreme demands, which push people apart

- Feeling obligated to defend extreme demands
- Being too self-righteous ("I am right and everybody else is wrong!")

Win-Win Negotiating

The HSM manager is open to using many different negotiating styles, yet he typically favors a win-win style, which attempts to meet the needs of all parties involved. Win-win negotiators do not regard their opponent as an adversary. With this cooperative style of negotiating, no one feels like the loser. The four major stages of the win-win negotiating process are:

1. *Adopt a win-win attitude.* Focus on how to identify and meet each party's needs. Identify mutually beneficial outcomes and work with the other party to achieve these objectives. Problem solve by entertaining many possible ways to meet the other party's needs, and be open to alternatives for meeting your own needs.
2. *Maintain positive relationships during the negotiation.* Establish trust by listening to and understanding the other party's concerns. Do not become impatient, and respect the pride and ego of all parties involved. Remain objective and rational. Avoid overly emotional outbursts, both positive (such as extreme joy and excitement) and negative (such as lingering anger and frustration), because they can be distracting and can ultimately disrupt the negotiating process. The major benefits of a trusting relationship include improved communications, less tension, and quicker resolution of problems.
3. *Implement a strategically planned negotiation.* Conceptualize and prepare a thorough negotiating game plan whenever possible. Understand the parties you are negotiating with, including their mind-sets, negotiating styles, and hidden agendas. Shorten the negotiating process by knowing when to communicate your key points, offering possible break-through solutions, and reaching agreements on key issues that quickly move the negotiating process forward.

4. *Keep the negotiation focused on fundamental issues.* Avoid adversarial interactions by which you might try to intimidate and overpower the other party. If the other party attacks you or strays from the main issues, simply say, "I feel we are off the main issues that we need to discuss and resolve in order to meet our mutual objectives." Keep the negotiations focused on the fundamental issues and avoid personal issues. Continually encourage a successful conclusion to the negotiation, and try to avoid any tactics that will lead to an inordinately long negotiation or a stalemate.

Competitive Negotiating

Another popular style of influence is the competitive style of negotiating. In its extreme form, it has also been referred to as win-lose, confrontational, and positional negotiating. The HSM manager is keenly aware that an extreme form of competitive negotiation can create permanent enemies. If mutual satisfaction is not sought and achieved through the win-win process of negotiation, there is a risk of lingering anger, vindictiveness, and ongoing animosity between the two negotiating parties. An enemy created during a win-lose negotiation is capable of repeatedly blocking the HSM manager's future negotiating efforts. In fact, stalemates and other delays frequently occur with confrontational negotiations.

Competitive negotiators typically think in terms of fixed resources and outcomes. The fixed-pie mentality is based on the notion that if one party wins the other party must lose. Competitive negotiators tend to make extreme demands, which drive people apart, and feel obligated to defend their extreme positions at all costs. The HSM manager usually tries to avoid this style of negotiating because too much time and effort go into establishing and defending these extreme positions. Extreme demands can escalate and all parties can be driven even further apart. Win-lose negotiations are always at risk of stalling or breaking down.

The HSM manager knows that many negotiators use the competitive style in an attempt to reach their objectives at the other party's expense. Competitive negotiators feel that unless they control the negotiation process through manipulation and intimidation they will lose their advantage and the other party will take control of the negotiations. Despite the limitations of the competitive style, many win-lose negotiators are successful. Therefore, the HSM manager must be able to identify and counter the different manipulation strategies and tactics used by the competitive negotiator. In addition, the HSM manager might need to use some of these tactics himself from time to time, especially if he chooses to employ confrontational negotiation tactics. A few of the most common negotiating tactics used by both cooperative and competitive negotiators are discussed in the next section.

Common Negotiating Strategies

The following negotiating strategies can be used to speed up or facilitate a negotiation, or to slow down and delay a negotiation. HSM managers must be able to use both types of strategies depending on the situation. That is, the HSM manager will want to facilitate negotiations that are in his company's best interest, while delaying or even blocking negotiations that are not.

Facilitative Strategies

The following strategies are routinely used to speed up negotiations. These strategies are essential if HSM managers are to achieve quick yet successful resolutions to negotiations.

Remain cooperative. Avoid "getting into the ring" with a win-lose negotiator unless you are prepared for a confrontation. Instead, keep your strategies focused on your goal—a "win-win" solution. Stick to objective and rational issues, and do not succumb to personal attacks or pressure tactics which could delay or possibly destroy the negotiations.

Strike while the iron is hot. Act decisively when it is advantageous to do so. The success of many negotiations depends more on fortunate timing than anything else. The negotiator must see the opportunity and then quickly seize it.

Beat the other party to the punch. Be the first to thoroughly research a problem, submit a proposal to a prospect, offer a workable solution to a business problem, and so on. Many negotiations are won by the first one on the scene.

Surprise moves. Make unexpected moves while maintaining your original objective. The surprise move can quickly change the direction of the negotiation since it usually catches the other party off guard and unable to effectively counter it. A negotiator's goal can be quickly reached if the opposing party is unable to anticipate and block a surprise move.

Fait accompli. Impose a solution on the other party as though it were an accomplished fact. Minor issues are sometimes quickly resolved with this strategy. The negotiator hopes that the other party will cooperate and go along with the situation, rather than trying to return the situation to the status quo.

Set limits. Use a wide variety of limits (such as time, space, cost) to speed up the negotiation. Limits quickly bring a problem into focus, test the strength of the other side, create urgency, and often bring about change sooner.

Find an ally. Try to find someone who is also interested in your problem and who is willing to negotiate on your behalf. This achieves a stronger front since two heads are better than one. Two people can also work twice as fast as one person.

Association. Link your goals and objectives with those of an influential person or campaign. This can inspire respect and lead to quicker approval of your plan since you will not have to work as hard and long to establish your credentials or to defend your motives and actions.

Salami. "Slice" your demands into smaller pieces to make your proposals easier to focus on. This strategy is very effective since presenting all of one's demands at once is often seen as asking for too much and can seriously delay a negotiation.

Refer to your partner. Indicate that you must meet with your partner or colleague to discuss where you are in the negotiation and what your partner wants to do next. Often this strategy of referring to a partner is not questioned and you immediately have more leverage at your disposal.

Delay Strategies

The following strategies are often used to slow down, seriously delay, or even kill a negotiation. HSM managers need to immediately identify and counter these strategies if they want to quickly achieve successfully negotiated settlements. In addition, there might be times when HSM managers will need to use these strategies to block an undesirable negotiation.

Refuse to negotiate. Do not negotiate with another party if there is no reason for you to enter into the negotiation, or if it is clear that you have nothing to gain in the process. Wait until the other party is willing to negotiate in a fair and cooperative manner, in which the needs of both parties are met. Negotiations can be stalled indefinitely with this tactic.

Stall. Use this tactic when the time pressure on the opposing party is greater than the time pressure on you. Stall in order to place even greater pressure on the adversary, who will eventually capitulate.

Intimidate. Use a real or implied threat aimed at winning a negotiation. For example, you might ask the other party to make an immediate decision due to deadline pressure, or you might try to discredit or make fun of the other party if they do not accept your terms. This strategy often leads to anger and delays in reaching an agreement.

Withdraw. Leave the room or make a phone call to buy time and think about new strategies and opportunities. This gives the impression that the negotiator is in a strong position and is not overly concerned with the outcome of the negotiation. The negotiator appears both nonchalant and indispensable to reaching an agreement. The other party must wait until the negotiator returns to the negotiating table.

Shotgun approach. Attempt to cover a very broad area with this negotiating attack in hopes of hitting the target in the process. The opponent is never quite sure of the true target with this approach. This strategy often prevents both parties from immediately focusing on and quickly resolving the key issues of concern.

Make demands high. Start by making the highest possible demands. Then attempt to slowly work downward from the high-demand position. This is risky since it can seriously delay and even stall the negotiations.

Agent with limited authority. Delegate members of your organization who have limited authority or decision-making power to attend negotiation sessions. This can slow or even halt the negotiation process, since too many meetings are required. Your opponent may use this strategy to get a preview of your position or to undermine your strategies — you never quite know whom you are negotiating with.

Present non-negotiable demands. Present your demands as unalterable, to demonstrate the strength of your conviction. This lowers opponents' expectations, and forces them to reevaluate their positions. Making non-negotiable demands can often wear an opponent down.

Good guy/bad guy. Set up a situation in which you (the good guy) appear to be agreeing with your opponent, while someone else from your side (the bad guy) appears hopelessly negative. This strategy is used to get your opponent to trust and confide in the good guy but, unfortunately, the bad guy often creates a negative negotiating climate that is hard to change. Trust breaks down when this ganging up strategy is used.

Let the problem worsen. Sit back and wait until the problem gets worse before you begin negotiating. This way everyone knows about the problem and will be seeking a solution. Once the problem is solved, however, many people will wonder why a solution was not formulated much earlier.

Only a handful of negotiation strategies were reviewed in this section to illustrate the difference between those that facilitate and those that delay. Other authors (for instance, Richard Buskirk, 1989, and George Fuller, 1991) have written about hundreds of other effective strategies that could also be classified as facilitative or delay tactics. When dealing with very difficult people, consult William Ury's *Getting Past No: Negotiating with Difficult People*, which thoroughly reviews a wide variety of effective strategies for finding common ground and eventual agreement with extremely resistant negotiators.

Finally, negotiating styles differ by country. That is why Trenholme Griffin and Russell Daggatt wrote *The Global Negotiator: Building Strong Business Relationships*. HSM managers must be aware of all these nuances of the negotiation process if they are to become effective strategic negotiators.

Controlling the High-Stakes Negotiation

The HSM manager realizes that the most successful negotiations are focused, measurable, and achievable. The HSM manager knows what she wants to achieve, discerns what the other party wants, and seeks a win-win solution that is good for all. This sometimes means settling for an alternative yet acceptable solution rather than holding out for an ideal solution, which would seriously delay the resolution of the problem.

The HSM manager is also aware that certain negotiations are for very high stakes (see Kuhn, 1988). These are the big deals that can make or break a person's career. When negotiating a high-stakes deal, the nature of the issue being negotiated is quite important to both parties, and the value of the matter under consideration often is relatively high. The HSM manager observes the following cues to determine if he is in a high-stakes deal.

The higher the level of the person you are negotiating with, the higher the stakes. High-level negotiators are usually more powerful in their organizations, and they are better able to establish and control strong opening positions that can immediately skew the results of the negotiation in their favor. In addition, the more attention that your opponent and his company place on the deal, the higher the stakes.

The more active party in the negotiation typically views the deal as being more important than the less active party. For example, the party that frequently schedules meetings and is constantly discussing deadlines usually has more at stake. In addition, the party that becomes more stressed during the negotiation, as evidenced by signs of anxiety, displays of temper, and other nervous habits, usually has more at stake in the negotiation.

The HSM manager realizes the importance of monitoring his own emotional reactions, while remaining rational during a high-stakes negotiation. He controls unplanned anger that could seriously delay the timely outcome of the negotiation. He refuses to intimidate, threaten, or insult the other party, knowing that these tactics will only build resentment and could stall or even stop the negotiations. He avoids talking too much and showing other signs of excessive emotion. Finally, he never enters a high-stakes negotiation without being fully informed and prepared. His information must be both accurate and appropriate and it must give him the competitive edge.

Computer-Based Negotiating

The HSM manager occasionally uses interactive software programs to help him quickly and effectively prepare for extremely important negotiations. Negotiating software can be used to quickly lay the groundwork for a successful outcome. A number of negotiating software programs are available.

The Art of Negotiating Program

This popular package is based on the expertise of Gerard Nierenberg, one of the top instructors of negotiations in the world. Nierenberg has taught more than 200,000 executives how to succeed in all types of business negotiations.

Nierenberg's computer-based program (1990) leads you through crucial (and often neglected) areas of preparation. In each section, the program asks an integrated series of questions and offers suggestions and perspectives about people on both sides of the negotiating table. This expert negotiator-on-a-disk stimulates your thinking about the upcoming negotiation and records important data for you to use in the actual negotiating session. The program can help you develop a sound plan of action, a sharp awareness of your opposition, and an overall feeling of confidence. The following are some of the highlights of Nierenberg's negotiating software program.

1. *Subject matter.* The program clearly profiles the negotiating parties and delineates the general purpose of the negotiation. It helps you determine what you and your opponents want from the negotiation. It also develops alternative objectives based on your needs and those of your opponent. Hence, it builds in flexibility to avoid stalled negotiations.

2. *Key issues and obstacles.* The program documents the key issues most likely to divide and/or unite the two parties. The program identifies emotional issues and rewords them in neutral ways, thereby helping to control the emotional environment of your negotiation. It helps you plan a series of questions to guide the negotiation process, and it points out how to transform a negative negotiating situation into a positive one.

3. *Strategies and counter-strategies.* The program helps you determine how, when, and where to approach your opponent and how your opponent will probably approach you. It allows you to be fully prepared in advance with the most effective negotiation strategies and counter-strategies. Nothing is left to chance with this software program.

4. *Agenda and report.* Finally, the program prints out a comprehensive agenda and game plan to guide your negotiations. It is capable of preparing a secret agenda as well, so you will have a solid fallback position. The customized report can be shared with colleagues and conegotiators.

The Negotiation Edge Program

All negotiations involve dealing with people. Therefore, gaining insight into the key person you are negotiating with is the first step in planning any successful negotiation. *The Negotiation Edge* (Malin, Montgomery, & Gallagher, 1984) was specifically designed to help you understand the personality, motivation, and thinking style of the other party. Moreover, *The Negotiation Edge* produces a comprehensive report that offers strategies and tactics on how to optimally interact with and positively influence the other party.

The Negotiation Edge helps you answer a wide variety of questions that need to be answered before you can finalize your negotiation strategy, including:

- What are my needs and goals?
- What are my options and how much can I compromise on my goals?
- Who will I be negotiating with and what are this person's strengths and limitations when negotiating?
- How much time can I spend negotiating and how will the negotiations change over time?

The Negotiation Edge can be used to develop a psychological profile of your opponent so that your personality and attitudes toward the negotiation will not clash with his. Strategic negotiators know that it is always best to avoid an atmosphere of tension, suspicion, and outright aggression. The Negotiation Edge assists you in understanding the specific issues and situations that can lead to a confrontation with your opponent, and helps you identify the specific situations that facilitate a mutual attitude of partnership and cooperation in negotiations. Since The Negotiation Edge provides you with the insight into the needs and expectations of your counterpart, it will help you to quickly move the negotiation to a successful close.

Conclusion

In summary, the HSM manager is aware that successful negotiators know how to use knowledge, power, and time to influence the behavior of other people. HSM managers usually attempt to use a win-win style of negotiating—they cooperate with their opponent in an attempt to reach a timely and equitable settlement. Confrontational negotiators, on the other hand, want to reach their objectives at the expense of the other party. Confrontational negotiators do not trust their opponents. This type of suspicion can lead to interpersonal aggression, and a deadlock often ensues. The HSM manager strives to develop a trusting relationship with the other party instead of a confrontational encounter, and he is receptive to using negotiating software programs in order to quickly develop a comprehensive and effective game plan to guide his actions. The HSM manager has the skills and confidence to quickly advance his objectives in business and life through timely negotiations.

Chapter Six

Excel in the
Information Age

Michael McCarthy, an information management expert, reports in *Mastering the Information Age* that by 1995, 80 percent of all managers will be knowledge workers, involved primarily in collecting, analyzing, synthesizing, structuring, storing, retrieving, and sharing information. Therefore, HSM managers will need to know how to derive value from the following sources (adapted from McCarthy, 1991, and Weitzen, 1988):

Forms of Information

- Data
- Text
- Images
- Pictures

- Time
- Sound
- Voice

Acts Performed on Information

- Generating
- Capturing
- Checking
- Isolating
- Processing
- Consolidating
- Sorting
- Upgrading
- Integrating
- Storing

- Protecting
- Retrieving
- Transmitting
- Communicating
- Copying
- Customizing
- Generalizing
- Leveraging
- Updating
- Potentiating

Technologies

- Computers
- Software
- Printers
- Modems
- Telephones
- Facsimile machines
- Pagers
- Radios

- Televisions
- Audio players
- Video players
- Compact disc players
- Transmission networks
- Satellite carriers
- Multimedia systems

Services

- Data base providers
- Information brokers
- News services
- Time sharing
- Service bureaus
- Business research
- Educational services
- Product enhancements
- Systems design and improvement
- Libraries and indexes
- Consulting and managing
- Information transferring

- Broadcasting and delivering
- Packaging
  Computer disks
  Compact disks
  Audiotapes
  Video cassettes
  Books
  Films
  Directories
  Newspapers
  Advertisement
  "Informationalized" products

McCarthy believes that the major challenge of the Information Age is for managers to create knowledge out of information —

focusing on the essence of the information, making quick sense of it, then making the information meaningful and useful to their company and customers.

Many traditional business managers are panicking because they feel there is too much information coming at them and too little time to assimilate it. HSM managers, on the other hand, realize that for them to succeed in today's rapidly changing business climate, they must skillfully control this information, rather than let the information overload control them. The HSM manager likely to excel in the Information Age is able to:

- Quickly find all relevant business information in an accurate and up-to-date form
- Know the difference between essential and superfluous information
- Research information using the latest technology (such as on-line databases and CD-ROM)
- Quickly read, study, and learn vast amounts of information while attaining high comprehension rates
- Give full attention to speakers to enhance understanding and retention of important facts and information
- Review a wide range of information sources (such as cable news, on-line databases, best-selling books, premier business magazines, informative audiotapes, and financial newspapers) that bring them into touch with new ideas and diverse points of view
- Think critically about information that is not consistent with other facts and figures
- Deliver information clearly and succinctly to other people in either written or spoken formats
- Disseminate information using the latest information technology (such as presentation graphics, video conferencing, and voice mail)

While traditional managers are becoming more susceptible to "information anxiety" (anxiety related to the gap between what they need to know and what they actually understand), HSM managers have minimized the gap between available information and their knowledge of it. Moreover, HSM managers realize that in the near future an ever-widening gap will differentiate those managers who have the requisite skills to meet the increased demands of an information-intensive economy from those who do not. The following sections highlight a few of the most important skill areas that prospective HSM managers need to master quickly in order to excel in the Information Age. They include (1) quickly finding and accessing relevant information, (2) becoming familiar with portable computers and business software, (3) acquiring speed reading and accelerated learning skills, (4) mastering telephone and related communication technology, and (5) improving mental functioning.

Finding Information Fast

HSM managers must be able to quickly and conveniently find information that addresses their unique business needs. This task is especially formidable since book publishers, government agencies, trade associations, research centers, and the news media are adding daily to our store of knowledge. H. Skip Weitzen, author of *Infopreneurs: Turning Data into Dollars*, describes this dilemma:

> Today massive quantities of data, random facts, and isolated communications have constituted a desperate search for meaningful information. This information explosion is highlighted by the proliferation of scientific articles. In 1986, between 8,000 and 10,000 articles were written each day. By 1990 the number of articles will double. . . . Yet the discipline of information access is a relatively new phenomenon. (1988, p. 54)

HSM managers need to find the right information in a timely manner. Hence, they need to utilize a quick yet accurate information-access model that will guide their search activities. Robert Berkman, author of *Find It Fast: How to Uncover Informa-*

tion on Any Subject, has developed the following six-step model for this purpose.

Define goals. The information-finding project needs to be clearly defined. HSM managers must know exactly why they need a particular type of information, how much information they need, and precisely what they plan to do with it to bring more value to their company and customers.

Locate nontechnical sources. The HSM manager should first understand the basic concepts and operational definitions of the subject matter. She might want to consult nontechnical and more general information sources at this stage, since she probably knows very little about the topic.

Locate technical sources. More specialized information is obtained with this step. HSM managers should only examine technical information when they understand the basic concepts of their subject. Reference materials to check include technical books, scientific journals, trade publications, government reports, and copies of conference presentations. The focus should be on the classic research studies, the very latest research, and the reports that summarize the best-designed studies.

Interview experts. Most traditional managers skip this step. Once they have gotten all the relevant material from both the nontechnical and the technical sources, they should interview the experts — people who have published a comprehensive review of all the research on a topic, written a key scientific article, or conducted a seminar that thoroughly covers the topic. The experts can usually clarify any questions that may still exist, and describe their as-yet-unpublished research activities.

Redirect focus. At this point the HSM manager must step back and review her progress to date. She must make sure that the information she is obtaining actually meets her information-seeking goals and objectives. If necessary, she should quickly make an adjustment by redirecting the focus of her search. She will also fill any identified gaps in her information base by quickly going back through the previous steps.

Get expert review. Exemplary HSM managers get one or more experts to review their near-final synthesis of the information for accuracy and soundness. The synthesis can be in the form of an unwritten opinion, an internal report, a written speech, a popular article, a technical study, a pamphlet, a book, and so on. If experts are not available, then well-respected colleagues should review the material.

Berkman also warns his readers that occasionally they will need to make very quick searches and therefore his six-step plan will simply not be feasible. At this point they need to quickly identify the one best source of information (perhaps a key expert, a specialized reference library, or a trade association report) that will provide the most credible information on the topic in the shortest amount of time. One of the best resources for a quick search is an on-line data-base search, as the next section illustrates.

On-Line Data-Base Searches

An on-line data base is a collection of information that is related in some way and that can be easily accessed by subscribers to an on-line data-base vendor. The vendor sells access to various data bases and provides users with the ability to quickly search them for relevant information. To access an on-line data base, the user needs a personal computer, communications software, a modem, a telephone, and a password. Charges for the on-line data base can range from a standard monthly fee to an hourly connect-time rate.

There are many benefits to HSM managers who utilize on-line data bases. The service can be used to (1) quickly screen data, (2) download information into the computer for instant analysis, (3) print out studies and reports, (4) interact with others via on-line bulletin boards, and (5) order materials and supplies on-line. Robert Berkman isolated the following four biggest benefits of on-line information services.

Enormous scope. On-line vendors provide managers access to vast amounts of useful information, including dozens of business data bases, scores of technical reports and trade pub-lications, thousands of company profiles, and hundreds of direc-tories. It would be literally impossible to quickly and accurately search for relevant information in these data bases without using an on-line vendor service.

Timeliness. Late-breaking news can be easily accessed through an on-line data base. That is, managers can scan what was recently published in the *Wall Street Journal*, the *New York Times*, *Business Week*, and so on. This is especially important if managers want up-to-the-minute information about an investment opportunity or a competitor's recent activity. Finally, news wire information that will not be published until the next day can usually be accessed.

Speed. HSM managers can spend a few minutes at a computer instead of an entire day at the library. They can obtain printouts immediately instead of having to request time-consuming photocopying. Finally, most computer data bases are accessible twenty-four hours a day, seven days a week, 365 days a year!

Specificity. Computer searches typically make use of "keywords" to allow HSM managers to immediately zero in on the exact information they need from the most relevant data bases. For example, lawyers can access a legal research data base to quickly identify the latest research and debates on a new tax law. Investors can access a data base of leading companies in America to scrutinize their earnings potential for the next three to five years.

Many on-line data base services are available, yet there are only a handful of major vendors. Before selecting a vendor, a manager should always examine the total cost of the service, its ease of use, the timeliness of data base updates, and any special features (for instance, toll-free hotlines, electronic mail, electronic shopping). Two of the most popular on-line data bases are CompuServe and the Dow Jones News/Retrieval Service.

CompuServe (Columbus, Ohio). The CompuServe Information Service offers user-friendly access to more than thirteen hundred data bases, as well as comprehensive member assistance, and excellent subscriber resource materials. Three very popular reference materials are *How to Get the Most Out of CompuServe*, a book by Charles Bowen and David Peyton, the *CompuServe*

Almanac: An Off-line Reference of On-line Services, and the *Compu-Serve Navigational Chart.* This on-line data-base vendor also provides the monthly periodical *CompuServe Magazine* to subscribers.

Some of the general CompuServe data bases available to subscribers are travel planning and reservations, hotel and car rental information, and a wide variety of educational forums, telephone directories, electronic shopping, educational resources, and entertainment and games. CompuServe also offers the Executive Option, a special package of all business-related data bases and services available to the busy manager, for which the manager pays an additional one-time upgrade fee. Some of the key services offered in this executive package are:

Financial	*Managerial*
SEC Information	Daily News Monitoring
Company Screening	AP Online (Business News)
Return Analysis	Executive News Service
Current Quotes	Over-the-Counter Stock News
Earnings and Estimates	Target Marketing Reports
Market Highlights	Demographic Reports
Economic Outlooks	Government Information
Investment Data	U.S./State/County Reports
Financial Forum	Public Relations and
	Marketing Forum
	Legal Research Center

Dow Jones News/Retrieval Service (Princeton, New Jersey). This data base specializes almost exclusively in economic and business information. The available information services fall into six major categories: (1) business and world news wires, that is, national and international business and investor news; (2) text-search services including reviews of the *Wall Street Journal,* the *Washington Post,* and *Business Week;* (3) company and industry information, including Dun & Bradstreet Reports, Standard & Poor's Online, and Worldscope; (4) stock quotes, statistics, and commentary, such as the Dow Jones Real-Time and Historical

Quotes, Mutual Funds Performance Report, technical analysis reports of more than forty-five hundred stocks; (5) general services, such as book reviews, on-line brokerage services, and electronic stores; and (6) customized information, such as clipping services, stock tracking, and the like.

While on-line data bases provide volumes of useful information, HSM managers realize that they must be able to effectively use a personal computer to benefit from these services. The following section provides a brief introduction to the use of personal computers in business settings.

Establishing the Managerial Workstation

Traditional managers often take the position that they do not need to learn to use a computer because they can delegate the task to someone else. This might be the attitude of managers who find themselves out of a job within a few years for a couple of reasons. First, it is appropriate that other employees do computer tasks for the manager, but the manager should be accomplishing something entirely different on the computer. While a manager can easily delegate computerized planning, accounting, and desktop publishing activities to his subordinates, he can still benefit by using the computer to, for example, track and forecast the key financial indicators of his company on a real-time basis; use software to generate, outline, and organize creative ideas for an important meeting; or use negotiation software to strategically plan for a high-stakes deal-making session.

Also, a manager who does not utilize the latest computer hardware and software advances might shy away from viewing technology as a major source of competitive advantage. That is, managers who shun computers never learn the full capabilities of this technology at a personal level; therefore, they will be more limited when it comes to conceptualizing new hardware and software applications for their company and customers. Finally, the computer-illiterate manager will obviously not become a role model for his people.

Robin Nelson, writing in *Personal Computing* magazine,

reported that many executives view computing as a good idea for everyone but themselves. Yet Nelson feels that a lack of computer expertise will be a serious detriment to these managers in the near future:

> [T]here is growing sentiment [that] top executives who do not use computers in their work, and those who never will, are slowly losing ground to a lot of other people who do—like their employees. Because of this, many people are strenuously urging [executives] to question their decision to shun the technology. (Nelson, 1989, p. 70)

Nelson summarized a 1989 poll that revealed that only 21.4 percent of five hundred executives regularly use a computer at home or work. The main reason computers were shunned is because managers thought they were too difficult to learn. Other reasons included a belief that only subordinates should use them, or that there was actually no critical application for them among executives.

The Managerial Workstation

HSM managers believe that executives should fully enter the world of computing as soon as possible. Use of the computer as a business tool gives a manager an electronic edge. One way to begin using a computer is by developing a streamlined managerial workstation. Ideally, the HSM manager would start with a very fast desk-top computer (for example, an Intel 386, 386 SX, or 486 microprocessor-based system with 20 megahertz running speed or higher). He would also utilize a VGA color monitor to present hundreds of different colors at a time. These monitors are usually more readable and more aesthetically pleasing to work with. Seriously committed managers should consider using portable computers (laptops, notebook size, palmtops) so they can have access to computing power while working at home or on the road.

The HSM manager should equip himself with a high-quality laser printer (for instance, the Hewlett-Packard Laserjet series) for exceptional printouts. (He can use a portable printer when using a portable computer.) The HSM manager will also need a two- or three-line phone jack, a high-speed modem (that is, Hayes-compatible), and a top-notch communications software package so he can handle modem, voice, and fax calls. This equipment provides the hardware and software linkups to collect, create, analyze, and edit information, print out the information, and send the information to others. This equipment establishes the core managerial workstation.

Key Software Applications

Managers interested in becoming familiar with computers should probably begin with a highly rated and very useful yet easy to learn desk-top-organizer software program. A core package usually features an appointment calendar, a "to do" list, a phone directory, a dialer, a calculator, and a memopad. Some computerized organizers even include a built-in alarm to alert managers to upcoming meetings.

Then, interested managers should probably learn a powerful yet user-friendly spreadsheet program. This would allow them to quickly analyze financial figures and other corporate and employee performance data. This software can be used to plan, analyze, and forecast a company's financial performance. Top-tier managers can also use spreadsheet software to review their staff's spreadsheet work and even to develop their own what-if scenarios. The major applications for Lotus 1-2-3, a leading spreadsheet software package, are:

- Budgeting
- Forecasting sales
- Preparing financial statements
- Financial analysis (ratio analysis)
- Financial forecasting (cash flow projections)
- Cost-volume-profit analysis
- Invoicing
- Accounts receivable management

- Inventory management
- Managing capital assets (depreciation)
- Determining time value of money
- Statistical analysis
- Graphic presentations
- Data base management
- Outlining ideas
- Customizing formulas

Next, interested managers should learn how to use their computer to facilitate communication. Managers could use their communications software to access on-line data bases and services. These on-line resources can be useful for keeping track of industry trends and the competition. The communications software can be used in conjunction with a fax board to send and receive faxes. A manager can also benefit from electronic mail by acquiring the appropriate communications software and a high-speed modem. Electronic mail would allow the manager to send or receive messages at any time of the day. A description of how electronic mail has helped Finn Caspersen, chairman and CEO of Beneficial Management Corporation, is described by Dean Meyer and Mary Boone in *The Information Edge*:

> Finn M. W. Caspersen, the chairman of the board and chief executive officer of Beneficial, says, "For me, the computer is a communication device, and the primary function of the chairman is to communicate." Caspersen routinely sends and receives electronic mail; he finds it to be a much faster means of running the company than paper memos and the telephone. "I use it both to send and receive all of my internal mail. . . . It allows me to operate in a whole different time frame. Instead of having a memo wind its way through the system for five to seven days, I can get a response in half an hour." (Meyer & Boone, 1989, p. 228)

The next step might be to have the company's in-house computer expert develop an Executive Information System (EIS). The EIS is a customized software program that includes a menu of the most commonly used executive application programs. This menu facilitates the executive's use of the computer. The EIS also allows the executive to access the company's mainframe computer or local area network. Real-time data that summarizes the year-to-date status of key financial and corporate performance figures can be pulled out of the mainframe computer. Ideally, these figures will be run through a program that consolidates the information into easy-to-read graphics.

There are many ways for a manager to begin utilizing a computer and related equipment. The bottom line is that Information Age managers will gain a competitive edge by being able to access, process, summarize, and send information in a quick, accurate, reliable, and useful manner.

Mastering Speed Reading and Learning

Despite personal computers and on-line data bases, it is imperative that HSM managers become speed readers and learners. For example, managers constantly face high-volume reading and learning demands simply to keep pace with their day-to-day business operations and to stay ahead of the competition. They must read memos, reports, business newspapers, news magazines, sophisticated journals, financial printouts, computer screens, and so on. HSM managers must be able to review, read, and comprehend this material faster than more traditional managers. Hence, all HSM managers must study speed-reading and accelerated-learning techniques to enhance their mastery of information.

Speed Reading

Increasing reading speed does not necessarily correlate with having higher intelligence or more education. Instead, it involves breaking slow reading habits and acquiring faster ones. HSM managers have usually learned to read six hundred words or more per minute, with some time-based managers exceeding eight hundred and even one thousand words per minute! The average manager reads between 180 and 300 words per minute. The three major slow reading habits that prospective HSM managers must overcome include:

1. *Speaking each word to oneself.* Reading by speaking the words silently to oneself (subvocalization) is a habit a person picks up when learning to read. A person can read only as fast as he can speak, about two hundred and fifty words per minute. By retaining this slow reading habit, one's reading speed will never exceed the average.
2. *Reading only one word at a time.* This is another bad habit a person typically picks up in the first grade. Most people are taught by their teachers how to read from left to right, word by word, one word at a time. These slow readers usually linger over each word and feel they must recognize and understand a word before going on to the next.
3. *Backtracking.* This bad reading habit causes the reader to go back and constantly reread words, phrases, and/or sentences because he was being inattentive the first time while his eyes followed the lines automatically. He loses the meaning of the reading or fails to understand something because of this lack of concentration.

Prospective HSM managers must be willing to attend training seminars or participate in self-study programs to break their slow reading habits. For instance, the *Evelyn Wood Reading Dynamic Program* is one of the most effective speed reading systems available. It is offered in seminars and is also available in a software training program. The following are a few of the key elements of this program.

Eliminate subvocalizations. A master speed reader uses the index finger of his dominant hand to pace his reading. He guides his eyes so swiftly over a sentence that he reads without speaking words to himself. His rate of speech no longer limits his reading speed.

Read groups of words. A person's eyes awkwardly start and

stop when they attempt to read sentences from left to right, one word at a time. A master speed reader knows his eyes do not stop naturally at each and every word. Instead, the eyes are capable of seeing groups of words. The speed reader uses swift underlining hand motions to group and quickly read chunks of words.

Stop backtracking. Master speed readers use their pacing hand as a guide to avoid backtracking. They are forced to concentrate since they are reading so fast. Diligently following one's pacing hand naturally eliminates backtracking.

Improve reading comprehension. Speed reading improves comprehension by increasing concentration. Master speed readers read with a purpose; they know exactly what they want to get out of a particular reading. They preview the reading ahead of time to locate sections of interest. They avoid the trap of trying to learn everything from the reading. Finally, skilled speed readers stay relaxed when reading, and they avoid frequent use of dictionaries, highlighters, and underlining.

Accelerated Learning

HSM managers must be especially skilled at only learning the relevant facts and figures, and just staying familiar with the less relevant information. They can accomplish this by using the following accelerated learning program:

Step One: Establish clear and concise learning goals. Define and write out exactly what you need to learn using as few words and sentences as possible. Establish realistic learning goals that can quickly be achieved—in days, not years. For instance, in some cases it is better to quickly learn and act on most of the available information in a few days or weeks than to wait to act on 100 percent of the information in a few months or even years.

Step Two: Collect all of the information in one place. Eliminate redundant and irrelevant material. Then, rapidly skim all of the remaining material. Put the material in a logical sequence and then re-read it using speed reading techniques so that you understand most of the important details.

Step Three: Group the material into the smallest possible study units. Eventually condense the contents of each study unit into a single short paragraph that contains only the most important facts about the topic of concern.

Step Four: Reformat your own self-created learning course. That is, put the reassembled material on flash cards, on audiocassettes, or in outlines. Format the material in a style that you will want to study over and over again.

Step Five: Review the material at least twice a day. Use the review format of your choice. This procedure will help you quickly comprehend the material and memorize it accurately. By mastering speed-reading and accelerated-learning techniques, HSM managers can learn a high volume of extremely important business information without experiencing information overload or anxiety.

Mastering Telephone Technology

HSM managers try to acquire more advanced telephone skills and utilize more modern telephone technology than traditional managers. Moreover, they know how to keep phone costs under control.

Advanced Telephone Skills

HSM managers know how to courteously put a caller on hold or transfer a caller. They are able to speed dial important clients, colleagues, and employees. They can forward their calls to another location if needed. They know when to activate the "mute" button on the speaker-phone in case they need a quick and private consultation. Finally, they know how to use the phone for a teleconference. While a teleconference lets the HSM manager interact with people from around the city, country, or world without traveling from his desk, he must mandate the following rules to deal with a few of the limitations of the teleconference:

- The teleconference should be scheduled ahead of time.
- The agenda should be set and made available before the call.
- Only one person should speak at a time.

- Individuals should identify themselves before they speak.
- Questions should be addressed to specific individuals.
- The teleconference leader should make sure that no one dominates the discussion.
- A note-taker should summarize and distribute the minutes of the meeting and all agreements reached.

Advanced Telephone Technology

HSM managers try to keep pace with and utilize all of the telephone-related technological advances that have occurred in recent years, such as the following:

Automated attendants. A recorded message system welcomes callers and asks them to press an extension number, or to press zero for the operator, or to briefly hold the line. The automated attendant gives instant access to the appropriate party and eliminates caller waiting time. Some of the procedures for ensuring the proper use of an automated attendant include informing prospects and customers of this service in advance and giving them your extension number, keeping all recorded messages brief, presenting the system as a benefit that reduces waiting time, making sure callers can always reach an employee if they wish, and limiting all menus to no more than three options.

Facsimiles. Faxes are messages transmitted over the telephone lines from one facsimile machine to another. The types of materials faxed include brief messages, quick confirmations, sales orders, and last-minute information for a meeting. Fax cover sheets are used to ensure the privacy of the message. Messages can literally be faxed around the world with extraordinary speed. Personal computers can now be equipped with a fax board so that text, data, and graphics files can be transmitted over the telephone lines from one computer to another.

Beepers and cellular telephones. HSM managers use beepers and cellular telephones to stay in touch with their office and customers during busy times. Pagers are less expensive and are typically used on routine incoming calls. Cellular phones are more often used when communication is urgent. Callers should announce that they are using a cellular phone, for two reasons. First, it lets the person called know you believe the issue to be discussed is important. Second, the person called understands that the call will probably be kept brief in order to keep costs down.

Voice mail. HSM managers realize that, if used correctly, voice mail is a powerful tool that enhances the manager's personal effectiveness. Managers can program their phones to play back a series of short greetings that can be used with specific caller groups (for instance, external customers or internal co-workers). The callers know they can immediately record brief or detailed messages in the manager's voice mail–box, which the manager can access at any time from any place. Most importantly, the message is delivered immediately—not when the manager eventually returns the call. Finally, the HSM manager knows how to quickly scan his voice mail messages so that important messages and return calls are promptly handled.

There are a lot of advanced voice mail features. For example, HSM managers can program a message to be delivered to an employee at a future date. A group messaging feature allows a single voice mail message to be quickly delivered to the mailboxes of targeted recipients. Voice mail allows people doing business with you nationwide or globally to leave a message in your system regardless of time zone differences. Finally, voice mail bulletin boards allow callers to quickly and conveniently help themselves to frequently requested information.

Psychological Preparedness for the Information Age

HSM managers must always try to improve their mental readiness and functioning in order to optimally locate, study, analyze, learn, and utilize vast amounts of information. They accomplish this in three ways: (1) staying relaxed and watching their health, (2) learning to think more critically about information, and (3) developing their memory skills.

Staying Relaxed and Healthy

A relaxed mental state facilitates quick learning, concentration, and memory. One's physical condition is also critical to optimal mental performance. For example, long-term alcohol abuse kills brain cells and dulls thinking. Long-term heavy smoking can adversely affect the lungs so that eventually lower levels of vital oxygen reach the brain, reducing mental functioning. Increased aerobic exercise, on the other hand, improves oxygen intake by the brain and improves mental functioning. The blood supply to the brain can become restricted if cholesterol from fatty foods clogs the arteries. This process also adversely affects mental functioning. Finally, as the following list suggests, certain vitamins and minerals might be related to proper mental functioning; for reasons of health alone, nutritional deficiencies should be avoided at all costs.

Vitamins Linked to Improved Mental Functioning

- *Vitamin B_1 (thiamine).* This vitamin protects nerve tissue from the adverse effects of oxidizing agents, such as alcohol, and breaks down carbohydrates into sugars, such as glucose, which fuel the brain.
- *Vitamin B_3 (niacin).* This vitamin can enhance memory. One double-blind, placebo-controlled study with young and middle-aged normal adults showed that memory was improved by 10–40 percent following a 141-milligram dose of niacin per day.
- *Vitamin B_5 (pantothenic acid).* This vitamin is known as a powerful antioxidant and stamina enhancer and is especially important for people under stress. It contributes to mental alertness.
- *Vitamin B_6 (pyridoxine).* This vitamin is necessary for the manufacturing of neurotransmitters (norepinephrine, serotonin, dopamine). These neurotransmitters are very important to optimal mental functioning and clarity. For example, deficiencies in serotonin can cause depression, which impairs mental performance.
- *Vitamin B_{12} (cyanocobalamin).* This vitamin aids in the development of the myelin sheath that carries the electrical impulse from one nerve cell to another. It also helps form blood cells that carry oxygen to the brain. A deficiency can lead to depression, confusion, and memory limitation.

- *Vitamin C (ascorbic acid).* A key antioxidant that assists in the manufacturing of neurotransmitters and the nerve cell structures.
- *Vitamin D.* This vitamin improves mental alertness by aiding in the assimilation of calcium and magnesium.
- *Vitamin E.* This vitamin facilitates the nerve cells' utilization of oxygen. It preserves our cells by preventing the oxidation of important molecules.
- *Choline.* A food substance that prevents memory loss. Choline possibly increases the amount of acetylcholine in the brain. It also appears to regulate cholesterol and nourishes the sheaths of nerve cells.

(See the books listed in the reference section by McCarthy, 1991, and Dean and Morgenthaler, 1991, for a list of any precautions related to the use of these nutrients. Research on some of these vitamins is in its infancy.)

Developing Thinking Skills

HSM managers must be critical thinkers if they are to excel in the Information Age. Joan Baron and Robert Sternberg, authors of *Teaching Thinking Skills: Theory and Practice,* define critical thinking as follows:

> Critical thinking is reasonable reflective thinking that is focused on *deciding what to believe or do.* . . . [This] definition does not exclude creative thinking. Formulating hypotheses, alternative ways of viewing a problem, questions, possible solutions, and plans for investigating something are creative acts that come under this definition. (1987, p. 10)

To be a critical thinker, an HSM manager must have the proper disposition, along with a host of critical thinking abilities. The following is a list of general and situation-specific dispositions of both effective and ineffective critical thinkers.

General Disposition

Effective Thinkers	*Ineffective Thinkers*
• Use critical thinking skills	• Use unsophisticated thinking skills
• Keep well-informed	• Are out of touch
• Seek maximum precision	• Are sloppy and careless
• Are confident thinkers	• Are insecure problem solvers
• Are rational thinkers	• Are overly emotional
• Work in organized manner	• Stray in their thinking
• Stay open-minded	• Are closed-minded
• Seek facts first, position second	• Seek position first, facts second
• Use multiple thinking styles	• Use one style of thinking
• Act decisively	• Are extremely indecisive
• Are active, responsive thinkers	• Are passive, lazy thinkers
• Use objective rules	• Use subjective and biased strategies
• Study top thinkers	• Do not practice thinking
• Seek truth	• Are easily fooled
• Appreciate ideas	• Resist ideas
• Enjoy thinking	• Find thinking frustrating

Situation-Specific Disposition

• Clearly define thinking task	• Are unclear about goals and objectives
• Precisely state problem	• Give weak conceptualization of problem
• Seek reasons	• Do not make cause-and-effect inquiries
• Focus on total situation	• Have difficulty concentrating
• Use credible sources	• Use inaccurate sources
• Focus attention	• Drift from idea to idea
• Seek alternatives	• Have a one-solution bias

- Accurately state facts
- Focus on key points
- Weigh the truth of all statements
- Continuously ask questions

- Exaggerate and mislead
- Treat all points the same
- Accept statements on faith
- Avoid in-depth questioning

Baron and Sternberg (1987) identified the following six major critical thinking abilities:

1. *Focus on the right questions.* Formulate the best possible questions for getting the answers you seek. All key terms should be accurately defined and all critical issues should be listed.
2. *Analyze arguments.* Identify and examine conclusions, stated and unstated reasons, positions, overlooked and needed assumptions, and summaries. Determine the structure of the argument and locate any irrelevance.
3. *Question, challenge, and clarify.* Ask the who, what, when, where, and why questions. Seek factual examples to support stated positions. Separate fact from fiction. Ask for additional information and explanations whenever needed.
4. *Judge the credibility of sources.* Assess the expertise, reputation, and possible conflicts of interest of all sources. Assess if their observations were objective and corroborated, or biased and inaccurate. Determine if their observations were accurately coded, analyzed, and presented.
5. *Use proper logic.* Appropriately apply inductive and deductive reasoning. Ask such questions as (a) Were adequate hypotheses formulated and tested? (b) Were proper studies conducted to infer significant relationships between variables? and (c) Were the proposed conclusions plausible?
6. *Employ high-level strategies.* Use other thinking strategies, such as (a) analyzing—identifying the elements of the event; (b) comparing the properties of different objects and events; (c) inferring—predicting, hypothesizing, testing, and concluding; (d) evaluating the significance of findings; (e) clarifying—formulating questions and defining important terms; and (f) problem solving—identifying reasonable alternatives.

HSM managers realize that critical thinking must be the basis of action. High-level thinking allows managers to better establish goals, develop plans to achieve these goals, and then take action in order to successfully complete the plan.

Baron and Sternberg (1987) offer ten reasons that many intelligent managers fail.

- Poor motivation and lack of perseverance
- Inability to translate thoughts into action
- Unfamiliarity with a company's products and strategies
- Fear of failure, self-pity, and excessive dependency
- Personal problems and stresses
- Overextending themselves and poor time management
- Poor concentration and distractibility
- Procrastination and problems initiating projects
- Lack of follow-through on projects
- Much academic but little practical intelligence

Intelligence per se is not important; successful managers need the ability to translate high-level critical thinking into effective plans and actions.

Finally, McCarthy (1991) points out that to be effective, managers must avoid the following ten sources of faulty thinking:

1. *Overgeneralization.* General statements like "All customers will prefer this product" sound appealing, but only one exception exposes the generalization.
2. *Emotion-laden words.* Trying to influence an argument by using words that elicit strong emotions, that may not be based on sufficient facts and logic. Removal of the words with strong emotional connotations might reveal the argument's weaknesses.
3. *Selected cases.* Trying to prove a point by using a few specific cases that support it while ignoring the rest. A wide-based foundation of facts should actually be used.
4. *Quoting experts.* Claiming that an expert or celebrity supports a particular position is not necessarily evidence of

truth. Determine if the argument stands when the endorser's opinion is removed.

5. *Distractions.* Letting one's mind wander away from the key points of the argument when distracting, unrelated, and irrelevant points are made. One must always be sure to keep one's eyes on the ball.

6. *Inadequate sources.* All sources must be defined if the information is to be trusted. Information should not be seriously considered if it is unverifiable. Always ask for facts that can be confirmed.

7. *Repetition.* If a position is repeated enough times in a wide variety of places by different people, it becomes more believable, regardless of its truthfulness. Repetition shifts people's attitudes in a desired direction. One should constantly be on guard against this powerful tactic.

8. *Acceptable statements, unacceptable conclusions.* A person might present a series of believable statements that win favor with an audience. This makes it easier to introduce a few doubtful or blatantly false statements, which go unquestioned. One must therefore constantly evaluate the logic and flow of each component of an argument as it leads to a conclusion.

9. *High ambiguity.* Highly ambiguous language and poorly defined terms hinder effective thinking and can lead to multiple interpretations. One must offset this vagueness by constantly asking for clarification until the terms become crystal clear.

10. *Denigration of opponents.* The other party is put down ("He is an amateur." "He probably has a hidden agenda.") to discredit his arguments, even though the arguments might be quite sound. An issue should therefore always be considered separately from the person presenting the issue.

Develop Powerful Memory Skills

One of the realities of the Information Age is that so much information is disseminated that a manager cannot remember it all. Therefore HSM managers must develop their memory skills.

A good memory saves time, since they can quickly recall specific facts and figures without having to look them up. But because they usually need to recall only certain key points, instead of all of the information they reviewed about a topic, they need a powerful *selective memory*.

Michael McCarthy, author of *Mastering the Information Age,* identified four keys to a powerful memory. The first key is *trusting one's memory*. One must overcome any negative beliefs and feelings about the ability to remember ("I feel terrible about my lack of memory skills"). One must focus only on the positive aspects of memory development ("If I work hard enough and improve my memory skills a little bit at a time, I will soon become a more effective manager").

The second key is *intending to remember.* Quite simply, one must make a conscious effort to remember more of the important things related to one's work. McCarthy presents several skills that are needed for this step, such as being fully attentive, putting oneself in a relaxed learning state, defining the "information target-zone," and effectively transferring information from short-term to long-term memory by frequently summarizing, reviewing, and recalling the material.

The third key is *exercising one's memory.* Memory skills and abilities can be lost if they are not regularly used. In fact, McCarthy cites research suggesting that the more information a person takes in and tries to remember, the more extensive a person's neuronal networks will become. A number of techniques can be used to exercise one's memory, including using multichannel input (such as reading, writing, and drawing the material to be remembered), mnemonics, memorization, associational learning, organizing the material to be memorized ("chunking" and classifying), creative visualization, and mind maps.

Finally, the fourth key in McCarthy's model is to *decide what does not need to be remembered.* HSM managers are skilled at determining what is worth remembering and what is not. If a person wants to have information available, but does not want to remember it, then he needs to develop an effective yet streamlined personal filing system. Computer filing systems and electronic organizers are quite useful in this capacity.

Conclusion

HSM managers continually strive to excel in the Information Age. They have exemplary information search skills and they try to focus their prime attention on the most critical problems at all times. They know how to access comprehensive on-line data bases for fast and accurate searches. They establish electronic offices, which include a powerful desktop computer, a laser printer, a modem, a quality fax machine, and an advanced telephone, at a minimum. They familiarize themselves with useful yet user-friendly software. They use portable computers to give them computational power at home and on the road. They strive to master speed reading and accelerated learning skills. Finally, they try to maintain a high level of psychological preparedness at all times so they can mentally and emotionally cope with the demands of the Information Age. It is very hard for traditional managers to compete against this type of information expert.

Chapter Seven

Avoid Job Burnout

HSM managers know that they must avoid chronic job stress or they will become burned out. Burned out managers are slow and ineffective. Although most managers encounter many stressful events in their jobs, only some of them become burned out and unproductive. HSM managers strive to be hardy, stress-resilient managers who are able to remain healthy and productive despite the pressures of work.

Case Studies

Two case studies are presented below that illustrate the hardiness phenomenon. Case one depicts a stress-prone manager. He is unable to cope with the current restructuring of his com-

126

pany and experiences adverse stress reactions. Case two presents a hardy manager employed at the same company. This executive manages to cope with organizational change without becoming ill or counterproductive.

Case One: The Stress-Prone Manager

Mark is a stress-prone manager who works for a large computer services company. He is in his late thirties. He sees himself as a link in the chain of command, doing work that he thinks is routine rather than creative. His company recently reorganized. This has him very worried. He feels heightened job stress due to increased responsibilities, heavier workloads yet fewer people, new supervisors and subordinates, and continual job insecurity. He regrets that the company is far different from what it was when he first joined. At times, he even finds himself wishing that the reorganization would fail. He tends to focus on the negative, wishing that the company's plans and objectives were clearer. Some days things seem out of control at work, and he is confused about what to do first.

Mark rationalizes that work is not important to him anymore. He does not feel part of a strong management team attempting to accomplish important and worthwhile goals. He becomes more withdrawn and apathetic. The company now seems too complex and stressful to be positively influenced by him or anyone.

Mark is under a great deal of mental and physical strain. He is irritable, has trouble sleeping, worries, and has lost his appetite. He has high blood pressure and gets frequent heart palpitations. Mark takes medication for an ulcer. He is drinking more and more alcohol to calm his nerves. His stress symptoms appear to be increasing as the pressure at work mounts.

Case Two: The Stress-Resilient Manager

Anita is the manager of the Customer Relations Division at the same company where Mark works. She is in her mid-forties and describes herself as someone who enjoys solving problems. She maintains a relaxed manner. She noted a slight increase in stress following the company reorganization, but added that her job is becoming all the more interesting and challenging as well. She has a clear sense of both the type and the magnitude of coming changes, but she welcomes them. She shows no signs of panic!

Early in her tenure Anita formulated divisional plans for a more comprehensive approach to customer relations in support of the reorganization efforts. She jogs and remains in fine physical health. She eats a healthy diet. She has never suffered a serious illness. When asked about her general attitude toward life, she points out that she wants a full, active, and demanding life. It is clear that Anita, the hardy manager, coped better with the company reorganization than Mark did. HSM managers strive to cope with stress as Anita did.

Managerial Stress Syndrome

The direct cost of managerial stress has been estimated at $10 billion to $20 billion in the United States alone. This cost figure includes such clearly measurable items as work days lost, hospitalization, outpatient care, and death benefits. Indirect costs that result from lowered productivity, poor decisions, and ineffective leadership were not included.

Managerial stress is the adverse emotional and physical response executives and managers have to any source of pressure in their environment. Some examples of stress response commonly reported by distressed managers include:

- Increased feelings of dissatisfaction with work
- Frequent irritation with superiors, peers, subordinates, and customers
- A tendency to rationalize poor leadership performance by blaming employees or the company
- Actual withdrawal from job duties and contact with other employees
- Obsessions with and fantasies about leaving the company and looking for a new job

Managerial Stressors

Managers continually face "stressors"—forces that challenge a manager's ability to cope. Stressors have varying levels of impact and can be categorized as either *personal* or *work-related.* Major personal stressors are death of a spouse, marital problems, financial difficulties, legal conflicts, and family problems. Major managerial stressors include the following:

- Organizational rules and policies
- Excessive number of meetings
- Deadline pressure
- Gaining financial support for projects
- Personnel conflicts
- Evaluating employees' performance
- Work overload and time pressure
- Interruptions
- Organizational changes and restructuring
- Long hours and increased demands on time
- Being advanced too slowly
- Decrease in status
- Lack of recognition
- Reprimands
- Acquiring new subordinates
- Difference of opinion with superiors
- Fear of job loss
- Unsatisfactory work relationships
- Changing business climate
- Organizational politics
- Nonparticipation in decisions
- Competition
- Lack of authority
- Challenges for leadership
- "Up or Out" pressures
- Increased responsibility

Because stressors challenge a manager's ability to cope, they must be effectively dealt with.

Managerial Coping Styles

Managerial coping styles include both desirable coping skills and undesirable coping deficiencies that each manager uses when confronted with stressors. Managerial coping is best defined as efforts to master conditions of harm, threat, or challenge in the workplace. In 1984, Salvadore Maddi and Suzanne Kobasa (*The Hardy Executive*) identified two general types of coping styles used by managers: *transformational coping* and *regressive coping*.

Transformational Coping. Managers must take decisive action to constructively change stressful situations so that they become less stressful. Transformational coping skills are usually called into action *before* a stressful situation causes excessive strain. Examples of transformational coping skills include:

Behavioral and Interpersonal

Taking decisive action to change stressor
Managing time and delegating tasks
Remaining task-oriented
Negotiating solutions
Helping others cope
Seeking help and asking for advice
Using social support networks
Gathering information
Proactively managing resources
Motivating employees
Retaining control over staff
Using effective planning
Showing persistence
Exercising and relaxing
Maintaining a healthy lifestyle

Mental and Emotional

Staying optimistic and confident
Finding positive aspects in situations
Selectively ignoring sources of stress
Thinking rationally
Accurately appraising problems
Remaining problem-focused
Assuming responsibility for actions
Maintaining positive view of self
Employing problem-solving strategies
Tolerating and welcoming change
Acknowledging and expressing feelings
Exhibiting self-control
Remaining patient
Focusing on the present and the future
Keeping problems in perspective

Transformational coping skills provide an effective buffer against stress. Stressful events are kept in perspective and dealt with in an optimistic manner, which decreases strain by neutralizing the stressful events. Through decisive actions, the manager alters the situation surrounding the stressful event so that both the intensity and the duration of the strain are reduced. Thus, the manager avoids stress-induced burnout, illness, and lost productivity.

Regressive Coping. This deficient coping style is characterized by withdrawal, avoidance, and emotionalism. Managers who favor regressive coping strategies usually have a pessimistic outlook on life and work. Stressful events are seen as terrible disruptions and as unavoidable and unchangeable. Regressive coping does not effectively ward off the disease of stress. In fact, the chronic use of many regressive coping strategies (for example, internalizing problems) can actually cause illness.

Regressive coping strategies do little to cut down on the intensity of stress and even less to curtail the duration of stressful episodes. Hence, regressive coping approaches are very undesirable. Examples of regressive coping styles include:

Behavioral and Interpersonal	*Mental and Emotional*
Avoiding all sources of stress	Remaining pessimistic and
Withdrawing and isolating	fearful
self	Tolerating change poorly
Drinking or using drugs to	Thinking irrationally
relax	Inaccurately appraising
Blaming others	problems
Giving up	Devaluing self and others
Cutting off communication	Becoming overly fatigued
Keeping problems to self	Internalizing problems
Becoming overly dependent	Denying or minimizing
on others	problems
Exhibiting aggression and	Engaging in self-blame
hostility	Becoming excessively angry

Participating in gripe sessions	Becoming apathetic
Avoiding staff and superiors	Fantasizing about leaving
Failing to support staff	company
Acting out at work	Focusing on past
Reactively managing resources	Avoiding responsibility
Punishing staff	Becoming impatient
Complaining	"Catastrophizing" problems

Signs of Managerial Stress

If managers are unable to effectively cope with stressors, they may experience signs and symptoms of managerial stress, such as cardiovascular problems (for instance, increased blood pressure, elevated heart rate, and stroke), digestive disorders (burning sensations, nausea and vomiting, and increased or decreased appetite), muscular tension (headache, backache, and fatigue and lethargy), and mental health problems (alcoholism, drug abuse, depression, eating disorders, and suicide). Additional indicators of health problems include accidents, sleep disorders, sexual dysfunction, and diabetes. Current research even shows a link between stress and cancer.

Other signs of managerial stress include dysfunctional thought processes and substandard job performance. For example, distressed managers exhibit greater indecisiveness, make poorer decisions, and experience more anxiety-provoking thoughts than unstressed managers. Distressed managers also avoid stressful situations, become less productive, and provide ineffective leadership. It is obvious why HSM managers need to effectively manage stress.

The Hardiness Factor

Exposure to work pressures does not cause all managers to become ill or nonproductive. A personality characteristic that Maddi and Kobasa (1984) call *hardiness* — which helps managers cope with pressure and prevent stress-induced diseases — can be developed over time.

Hardy managers have three personality traits that offer a

buffering or protective effect against stress. Maddi and Kobasa's research shows that hardy managers tend to be more *committed* to family, friends, and their jobs than stress-prone managers; they have a greater sense of *control* over what occurs in their lives, and they experience life pressures as *challenges*. An examination of each of these dimensions of hardiness follows.

Challenge

Hardy managers perceive organizational changes as opportunities rather than threats. Change presents a challenge that can enhance personal and professional development. Hardy managers know that a satisfying career will always present problems, and once a problem is confronted and resolved, they move on to the next. They experience their jobs as demanding yet exciting.

In contrast, stress-prone managers feel threatened by change because it seems to disrupt their comfort and security. These managers are pessimistic and fearful. They are at high risk to become burned-out and unproductive.

Control

Hardy managers believe they can positively affect their work environment. Rather than avoiding pressure situations, they take charge and choose among various courses of action to diffuse threatening, stressful events. These managers always reflect on how to turn challenging yet stressful events to their advantage.

In contrast, stress-prone managers believe that stressful events are outside their span of influence. They feel powerless, and act as if they are the passive victims of forces beyond their control. These managers have little sense of resource and prepare themselves for the worst.

Commitment

Hardy managers have the ability to become committed to their jobs, family, and friends. They view stressful business challenges

as purposeful, interesting, and important. They involve themselves in their work wholeheartedly. They enjoy their work.

Stress-prone managers are less involved with their jobs.
They often find their jobs boring or meaningless and consequently feel alienated from them. They often fantasize about
quitting their jobs. Their lack of commitment causes them to
slow down on the job and become poor performers.

Lee Iacocca, chairman and chief executive officer for
Chrysler Corporation, exemplifies the hardy executive, as reflected in his comments made during an interview when his
company was in financial trouble:

> [Management consultants] came [to Chrysler], paid
> by the government, and recommended that I de-
> clare [bankruptcy]. They had all their people on
> hand to say there's no way to survive. . . . They were
> paid something like a million dollars to come up
> with a paper that said we can't make it in the car
> business. I saw in three years we could make it. It
> wasn't defiance. It was a leader and a good team of
> 25 top officers who got together and said, "We'll
> show them how to do it." (Foell, 1984, p. 5)

Iacocca exhibited commitment, control, and a sense of
challenge in the face of tremendous pressure. His quick turnaround efforts at Chrysler serve as a model for HSM managers
to emulate.

Coping Skills Used by Hardy Managers

The following sections describe some of the coping skills used
by hardy managers.

Positive Thinking. Hardy managers think positively and rationally. They maintain an optimistic outlook on work and
business—in contrast to stress-prone managers, who think negatively and irrationally and have a pessimistic frame of reference.

HSM managers can use the following four-step model to begin thinking more positively.

Step One: Identify negative thinking. Immediately examine your thoughts and internal self-talk when you are feeling distressed or emotionally upset. Learn to discriminate between your use of optimistic/rational thoughts and your use of pessimistic/irrational thoughts. Some examples of irrational beliefs that are commonly held by stress-prone managers are:

- "I must have approval from every significant person in my life, including my subordinates and superiors."
- "I must be thoroughly competent, adequate, and achieving in all aspects of my job to consider myself worthwhile."
- "It is catastrophic when things at work are not the way I would like them to be."
- "When things start going wrong at work, they will only get worse."
- "My stress is caused by external situations that I have little or no ability to control or change."
- "It is easier to avoid than to face potentially stressful situations."
- "I must find good solutions to all the problems that I encounter at work."
- "All jobs are boring, meaningless, and stressful."
- "Some of my employees, peers, or superiors are bad, wicked, and villainous, and they should be blamed and severely punished for their villainy."
- "I can avoid stress by taking a passive and uncommitted approach to work that is free of risks."
- "Major changes at work should be avoided since they will surely disrupt my comfort and security." (Adapted from Ellis, 1972)

Endorsement of these beliefs and similar ones contributes to higher levels of stress. Hence, they need to be vigorously scrutinized and disputed.

Step Two: Dispute negative thoughts. Challenge and dispute any negative thoughts and irrationalities that you identify. Deter-

mine if the negativity and pessimism are fully warranted. Attempt to understand why negative thoughts can increase your
feelings of stress.

Step Three: Substitute positive thoughts. Once you are convinced that you are thinking negatively and irrationally, then
substitute more rational and optimistic thoughts for negative
thoughts. Feelings of stress should decrease.

Step Four: Reinforce positive thinking. Positively reinforce
yourself whenever you substitute positive, optimistic thinking
for negative, pessimistic thinking. This increases the probability
that you will remain rational and optimistic in the face of future
challenges at work.

Rationality and optimism are key mental characteristics
of a hardy manager. HSM managers must learn to identify their
irrational thoughts and begin to think more rationally and
realistically.

Problem Solving. A problem can be defined as a failure to find an
effective response to a stressful situation. Managers can make
stressful problems worse by employing a response that seems
somewhat effective at the time but proves to be disastrous in the
long run. An example would be to continuously rely on alcohol
as a way of coping with a stressful day of work, but then coming
to overrely on this habit. The following five-step problem solving
process can be used to better assess the consequences of ineffective, short-term solutions to job pressure, and to come up with
alternative responses that pay off in the long run.

Step One: State your problem. Managers normally experience
problems in the areas of work, social relationships, finances, and
family life. Different types of solutions are needed for each
problem area.

Step Two: Outline your response. Thoroughly describe the
problem and your usual effective and ineffective responses to
the situation. Use this information to try to understand why you
get upset over the problem and how you can best cope with the
situation.

Step Three: List alternative solutions. Brainstorm new solutions for effectively solving your stressful problem. Generate as

many solutions as possible. For example, list at least five new solutions for each problem. Seek input from others if necessary (family, friends, work colleagues, professional counselors).

Step Four: Review the possible consequences. This step involves prioritizing and then selecting the two or three most promising solutions from your list. Take the time to thoroughly review both the positive and the negative consequences of your most promising strategies. Next, select the one strategy for which positive consequences most greatly outweigh the negative consequences. Then decide on the exact steps you will have to take to implement this strategy. List concrete steps for implementing your new problem-solving strategy. Again, seek input from others.

Step Five: Evaluate your results. This last step is the hardest. Once you implement the new response, observe the consequences. Did the new strategy reduce the problem that caused increased stress in your life? If you still have the stressful problem, then try another strategy from your final list of three. Keep trying new strategies until the original problem is solved. Again, if you cannot solve the problem yourself, seek assistance from a friend, your boss, or even a professional counselor.

Assertiveness. Behaving assertively means standing up for your rights in a way that shows you also respect the rights of others. Assertive behavior is an honest, direct, and appropriate expression of your current feelings and attitudes. It communicates respect rather than aggression. Types of assertive behavior include:

1. *Basic assertion.* A simple, direct expression of your feelings or rights without violating those of others.
2. *Empathic assertion.* A paraphrase of your understanding of another's feelings or rights along with the expression of your own.
3. *"I-Language" assertion.* Specific feedback. "When you do (or say) _____, it affects me this way: _____."
4. *Escalating assertion.* An increase in the intensity of your message when faced with persistence from others, by which you repeat your assertive statement using one or more of the

above forms; provide an honest statement of the probable consequences if they continue to persist; provide a statement that shifts focus from content to your perception of the process going on between you and others.

Aggressive behavior is standing up for your rights in a way that humiliates, browbeats, or degrades another person. It is frequently an over-reaction to other people whom you perceive as responsible for your anger. Humiliating and being sarcastic toward others are examples of aggressive behavior.

Personal rights need to be preserved and protected at all times. The HSM manager asserts himself in an effort to preserve his personal rights, which include the following:

- The right to say no and to disagree with others
- The right to refuse requests without having to feel guilty or selfish
- The right to feel and express feelings, including anger, as long as the rights of others are not violated
- The right to be competitive and to achieve
- The right to enjoy rest and leisure
- The right to have one's needs be as important as those of others
- The right to make mistakes
- The right to have one's opinions given the same respect and consideration as those of others
- The right to be treated as a capable and mature adult who should be taken seriously (based on conversations with Rose Ramirez, The St. Paul Companies, 1984)

Deep Breathing Exercise. A commonly used deep breathing exercise (DBE) combines physical and mental relaxation, using your breathing as a focusing device to give the body rest from prolonged stress. By systematically focusing on your breathing, you gradually turn off tension-causing thoughts, thus breaking the chain of mental strain. Like all skills, the DBE does require regular practice. It is recommended that you perform it twice a day for ten to fifteen minutes per session, following these steps:

1. Choose a quiet environment with as few distractions as possible.
2. Either sit or lie down.
3. Close your eyes and adopt a completely passive attitude.
4. Take a deep breath, then exhale to the sound "ah."
5. Inhale deeply through your nose to the count of five.
6. Hold your breath to the count of five.
7. Exhale slowly to the count of seven.
8. As you inhale, imagine you are calmly bringing energy into your body; as you exhale, feel your body releasing all worries and tension.
9. Initially, continue the deep inhalations and exhalations for about ten minutes, increasing gradually to fifteen minutes.
10. When distracting thoughts enter your mind, simply disregard them.

Physical Exercise and Stretching. Physical exercise improves the HSM manager's mental skills and flexibility, builds muscle strength and tone, relieves tension, reduces weight, and improves the body's general physiological condition. Excellent forms of exercise include jogging, walking, skiing, biking, and swimming. Other, non-aerobic exercises (such as golf, bowling, and archery) improve skills and strengthen and stretch some muscles, but they do little to condition the cardiovascular system.

In order for any exercise to be of benefit for stress management, it requires repetition (minimum of three times per week), exertion (elevate pulse rate to approximately 130 beats per minute), duration (minimum of twenty to thirty minutes per session), and a noncompetitive attitude. However, before starting any rigorous exercise or stress management program, it is important to check with your doctor to assess your age demands, health status, and present physical condition.

Overall Lifestyle Management

The hardiest managers adopt healthy lifestyles. Significantly reducing sedentary activities, alcohol misuse, overeating, and cigarette smoking would save more managers' lives in the forty- to sixty-year age bracket than the best current medical practices. Managers unable to improve their health behavior should seek professional counseling.

I developed an informal health-risk questionnaire (Exhibit 7.1 on p. 142) that allows managers to measure their risk of heart attack. In addition, the guidelines in Tables 7.1 and 7.2 can be used to determine if a manager is overweight. However, managers should consult with a professional (such as a physician, psychologist, nurse) if they have any questions or concerns about their health due to their answers on this questionnaire. By reducing all modifiable health-risk factors, managers can greatly reduce their risk of disease.

The questionnaire and tables do not attempt to identify people who are severely underweight. These people are advised to consult with their physician. These tables allow managers to

**Table 7.1. Desirable Weights for Adult MEN
(in indoor clothing).**

Height (with shoes, 1-inch heels)		Small Frame	Medium Frame	Large Frame
Feet	Inches			
5	2	112–120	118–129	126–141
5	3	115–123	121–133	129–144
5	4	118–126	124–136	132–148
5	5	121–129	127–139	135–152
5	6	124–133	130–143	138–156
5	7	128–137	134–147	142–161
5	8	132–141	138–152	147–166
5	9	136–145	142–156	151–170
5	10	140–150	146–160	155–174
5	11	144–154	150–165	159–179
6	0	148–158	154–170	164–184
6	1	152–162	158–175	168–189
6	2	156–167	162–180	173–194
6	3	160–171	167–185	178–199
6	4	164–175	172–190	182–204

Source: Adapted from Metropolitan Life Insurance, 1960.

Table 7.2. Desirable Weights for Adult WOMEN
(in indoor clothing).

Height (with shoes, 2-inch heels)				
Feet	Inches	Small Frame	Medium Frame	Large Frame
4	10	92–98	96–107	104–119
4	11	94–101	98–110	106–122
5	0	96–104	101–113	109–125
5	1	99–107	104–116	112–128
5	2	102–110	107–119	115–131
5	3	105–113	110–122	118–134
5	4	108–116	113–126	121–138
5	5	111–119	113–130	125–142
5	6	114–123	120–135	129–146
5	7	118–127	124–139	133–150
5	8	122–131	128–143	137–154
5	9	126–135	132–147	141–158
5	10	130–140	136–151	145–163
5	11	134–144	140–155	149–168
6	0	138–148	144–159	153–173

Source: Adapted from Metropolitan Life Insurance, 1960.

compare their *current* body weight with their *ideal* body weight. The tables should only be used to get an estimate of your ideal weight. A physician should be consulted for the most accurate assessment.

Conclusion

Due to their strong sense of commitment, control, and challenge, hardy managers view stressful situations much more optimistically than do stress-prone managers. Stressful events are seen in perspective, as stressful yet changeable. Such optimism increases the likelihood of decisive actions that will quickly lead to stress reduction. That is, hardy managers are more likely to use transformational coping skills than regressive coping strategies. Transformational coping strategies can allow HSM managers to be high-level achievers in the face of business pressures, challenges, and insecurities. By using these strategies, HSM managers will be able to maintain their health in the face of stress.

Exhibit 7.1. Manager's Heart Disease Risk Assessment Questionnaire.

Yes	No	Risk Factor
—	—	1. Are you more than 55 years of age? (Heart disease risk increases with age.)
—	—	2. Are you a male? (Males have greater risks than females.)
—	—	3. Do you have one or more blood relatives with a known history of heart disease or other cardiovascular diseases? (Heart disease runs in families.)
—	—	4. Have you had one or more cardiovascular health problems (such as a heart attack, heart surgery, or stroke)? (Cardiovascular problems are recurrent.)
—	—	5. Do you have diabetes and now are on insulin or other medication? (Diabetics have a high frequency of cardiovascular problems.)
—	—	6. Do you regularly smoke cigarettes, pipes, or cigars? (Smokers have a much greater health risk.)
—	—	7. Is your cholesterol level greater than 275? (High cholesterol contributes to cardiovascular problems.)
—	—	8. Do you eat (a) red meat at least five to seven times a week, (b) eggs six to seven times a week, and (c) use butter, whole milk, and cheese daily? (High-fat diets lead to atherosclerotic deposits in arteries.)
—	—	9. Do you have extremely high blood pressure? (Diastolic/systolic is greater than 160/100.)
—	—	10. Are you 25 pounds or more overweight? See the guidelines in Tables 7.1 and 7.2 to help make this determination. (Obesity aggravates health problems including heart disease.)
—	—	11. Do you refuse to engage in aerobic exercise (such as brisk walking, jogging, bicycling, swimming) three or more times per week? (Lack of physical exercise aggravates cardiovascular problems.)
—	—	12. Are you constantly frustrated when waiting in line, often in a hurry to complete work, easily angered, and often moody? (Stress-prone personality types are more likely to have cardiovascular health problems.)
———		Total "Yes" answers

Interpretation based on number of "yes" responses

0–1 = below average risk
2–3 = average risk
4–6 = above average risk
7 + = very high risk

Note: Remember, a high score does not mean a manager will definitely develop heart disease. Exhibit 7.1 is merely a guide I developed to make managers aware of a potential risk. Please consult your physician to obtain a better understanding of your heart disease risk factors. For a more thorough and scientifically based assessment of heart attack risk for individuals or corporate groups, contact National Health Enhancement, 3200 North Central Avenue, Suite 1750, Phoenix, Arizona 85012 (Phone: 602-230-7575). Also review the Arizona Heart Institute's Heart Test for a more sophisticated prediction (see Diethrich, 1981).

Part Two

ORGANIZATIONAL STRATEGIES

Chapter Eight

Hire the Best

HSM managers prefer to hire job applicants who have the greatest chance of quickly succeeding at work. The cost of replacing an unproductive employee has been estimated at approximately two and a half times his or her annual salary. These costs include recruiting dollars and interview time, as well as lost productivity while the position remains vacant. High-quality personnel assessment programs lead to improved personnel selection, promotion, and career development decisions, thereby reducing costly personnel selection errors.

Making Accurate Selection Decisions

HSM managers use a wide variety of assessment methods to help select individuals they think will quickly become good, productive workers. These methods include reference checks, interviews, work samples, and psychological tests. When considering a selection method, however, HSM managers must take into consideration the *validity* of the method—that is, how accurate is the method at predicting future job performance.

Imagine a hypothetical situation in which a manager assesses a thousand job applicants, using a highly valid screening method such as a paper-and-pencil employment test. Each individual has received a score on the assessment procedure. Let us assume that we also have in our possession future job performance scores for these thousand job candidates. We now have two scores for each individual, one score from the assessment instrument and one job performance score.

Let us then assume that five hundred, or 50 percent, of the applicants received acceptable scores on the test, while 50 percent received unacceptable scores. Finally, let us assume that fifty percent of the candidates received good job performance evaluations from their supervisors, while the other fifty percent received poor evaluations. Because a high-validity procedure was used, it is likely that, for the most part, the better test scores were obtained by the applicants who later received superior performance evaluations.

Figure 8.1 shows how a highly valid assessment procedure (the psychological test) was 90 percent accurate in predicting job performance in our hypothetical example, while an assessment procedure that had no validity (a poorly designed interview) was only 50 percent accurate. In other words, with the invalid procedure one was just as likely to make an inaccurate classification decision as an accurate classification of each individual. While no assessment procedure is 100 percent accurate, HSM managers always try to use highly valid methods to maximize accurate assessment decisions while minimizing inaccurate ones. The next section highlights different types of valid testing applications that HSM managers routinely consider.

Common Applications of Employment Testing

The predictive accuracy (validity) of professionally developed selection tests has been demonstrated in relation to a wide

Figure 8.1. Assessment Scores and Job Performance Ratings.

Valid Procedure

Assessment Score

		Acceptable	Unacceptable
	Good	450	50
Job Performance			
	Poor	50	450

Agreement Rate = 90% (900/1,000)

Invalid Procedure

Assessment Score

		Acceptable	Unacceptable
	Good	250	250
Job Performance			
	Poor	250	250

Agreement Rate = 50% (500/1,000)

range of important job-related criteria—including productivity, sales performance, manager effectiveness, job advancement, turnover, safety, and dependability (see Jones, Bray & Steffy, 1991). Moreover, high-quality personnel tests are more accurate predictors of job performance than traditional interviews, résumé ratings, and reference checks. It is no surprise then that HSM managers prefer personnel tests over most other procedures.

The most common use of employment tests is for *personnel selection.* Employment tests are used to quickly obtain a comprehensive assessment of job applicants' knowledge, skills, abilities, and attitudes in order to facilitate an accurate hire/no hire decision. Selection tests can be used to quickly hire competent managers, successful sales professionals, honest retail clerks, skilled computer programmers, and safe drivers.

Personnel tests are also used for *placement.* Placement tests differ from selection tests in that no one is rejected. Instead, all individuals are assigned to relevant training programs or jobs; the goal is to find the best fit between each person's skills and the organization's needs. In selection, the test score leads to a hiring decision—the person accepted will generally be more satisfactory than the person rejected. In placement, however, a test score predicts that a person will probably be more satisfactory in one job than in another. Placement testing is a good strategy when there are only a few applicants for the number of available jobs.

Employment tests are also used for *career counseling*. Career counseling tests provide both employers and employees with useful information about how employees' thinking styles, personalities, and life experiences either facilitate or inhibit their career development. The HSM manager uses these tests to help employees capitalize on the facilitative aspects of their personalities while better controlling the hindering aspects. Career counseling test scores can be shared with employees to document whether they have the knowledge, skills, and abilities for other employment opportunities within the company. These tests can also be used to assess whether employees are approaching their careers in a mature and responsible manner—employees can learn how to modify their attitudes and behaviors in order to better achieve their career goals.

Employment tests are also used for *training and development*. Tests can be used to identify limitations in an employee's job knowledge and work skills. For example, a company can use a test designed for management trainees to assess whether a candidate has the proper math skills, energy level, and commitment to become a first-rate manager. If a person scores poorly in any of these areas, the company may recommend a training program so the employee can develop the necessary business skills, motivational levels, and attitudes needed for the demanding position.

Groups Commonly Assessed

HSM managers can use employment tests with a wide variety of employee and job applicant groups. Employment tests are often used to assess entry-level workers. They are used for clerical staff and office-worker positions, typically to assess whether an applicant has the aptitude and skills for such work (for instance, organizational, typing, and word processing skills).

Employment tests are also used to select service-oriented employees such as retail clerks, hotel workers, and bank tellers. These tests can help determine whether job candidates are hardworking, courteous to customers, dependable, cooperative with management, and likely to exhibit a commitment to the company.

Employment tests are used to select skilled workers, such as mechanics, drivers, assemblers, and production workers. An employment test can be used to determine whether a motor vehicle operator has the requisite driving skills and knowledge of motor vehicle operation laws, and is both emotionally stable and safety-conscious. These skills and personality characteristics are needed to ensure safe and efficient motor vehicle operation.

Employment tests can be used with unskilled and semiskilled workers. Some of these tests assess basic reading and writing skills, so that the person can receive remedial training if needed. Some tests assess the different types of jobs the lessskilled worker groups might be interested in as part of an employee development or retraining program. Still other tests assess manual dexterity and psychomotor skills for placement in jobs such as janitorial, labor, or material handling.

Employment tests are used to assess professional-level employees, for selection, placement, and development purposes. Those tested include sales professionals, technicians, accountants, statisticians, writers, instructors, scientists, engineers, and computer programmers and analysts. Typically, a battery of tests is used to assess these professionals' overall intelligence and/or specific mental abilities, background and past work experience, personality, and specific job skills.

More comprehensive test batteries are used for managers and executives. Like those used for professionals, these test batteries tend to assess intelligence (both general and specific); personality traits appropriate to management, such as ambition, drive, maturity, and discipline; and job-relevant life and work experiences. One test battery even includes a test that assesses the probability that a manager will consistently engage in ethical workplace behavior. Again, HSM managers use employment tests so that they can more quickly, accurately, and successfully match a person to a job.

Estimating Bottom-Line Savings

HSM managers use employment tests that have a proven track record of containing costs and enhancing profits. They are familiar with three approaches that have been used to determine the return on investment of improved selection decisions. The three methods include (1) time series analysis, (2) control group comparisons, and (3) mixed designs. Studies conducted in a number of different companies are reviewed to illustrate each procedure.

Time Series Analysis

The first procedure, time series analysis, allows HSM managers to document empirically the impact of a personnel selection program both before and after test implementation. With this longitudinal strategy, companies must first determine which bottom-line variables need to be tracked over time. These could include, for example, production output, sales, turnover, and accidents. Companies should expect a bottom-line improvement after the implementation of a testing program.

Figure 8.2 shows how a major transportation company evaluated the impact of a personnel safety test on the cost of paid insurance losses. The selection inventory was designed to screen in the most safety conscious and reliable truck drivers and support personnel (such as dispatchers and maintenance workers). The study was conducted over a forty-one month period.

Results showed that the average monthly paid insurance losses due to companywide injuries (for instance, over-exertion or lacerations) equaled $25,600 per month before the safety testing program was implemented and $5,400 per month after the program was implemented. Annual paid insurance losses

Figure 8.2. Impact of Personnel Selection on Accident Criteria.

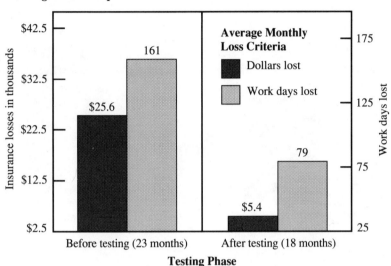

were reduced from approximately $307,200 per year before testing to $64,800 per year after testing. This yielded an annual company savings of about $242,400.

The company also tracked work days lost due to injuries. When using the time series method, it is preferable to track multiple outcome variables. The average number of work days lost per month was reduced from 161 before safety testing to 79 after testing. This company recovered approximately 984 days of lost productivity per year due to their safety assessment program, an outcome that is consistent with the HSM manager's goals.

A number of time series studies have shown that pre-employment tests that screen in reliable employees have effectively reduced inventory shrinkage (that is, loss) rates by millions of dollars per year. Yet a recent study, summarized in Figure 8.3, shows that discontinuation of a preemployment integrity testing program caused an increase in shrinkage. During the pretest phase, companywide shrinkage was 2.8 percent of sales. After implementing the integrity testing program, shrinkage was reduced to 1.9 percent of sales. After the testing

Figure 8.3. Shrinkage Analysis: Impact of Testing Program.

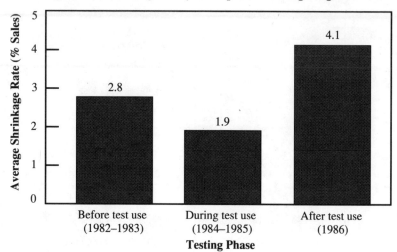

program was discontinued, shrinkage increased to 4.1 percent of sales. The director of loss control at this company, which eventually went out of business, attributes most of the increase in shrinkage to the fact that the testing ended. HSM managers never allow themselves to go out of business due to poor personnel selection decisions.

Control Group Comparisons

This procedure typically compares organizations that use personnel selection systems with organizations that do not. The companies must be relatively similar on all other variables, including type of industry, number of employees, and geographic location. For example, companies can randomly assign stores to testing or nontesting groups, or they can match pairs of testing and nontesting stores on critical variables to ensure similarity between these stores.

Employee theft is a major source of inventory shrinkage in supermarkets: approximately 40 percent of all supermarket employees admit to the theft of company cash or merchandise. A control group analysis was recently conducted in the super-

market industry. Two large supermarket chains used preemployment integrity tests to hire job applicants with the least potential
to steal company cash, merchandise, and property. The two
chains were composed of 125 separate supermarkets. Four supermarket chains did not use any type of integrity test to screen
applicants. These four nontesting chains were composed of 367
individual stores. The two supermarket chains that used integrity tests were expected to have significantly less insider theft.

A unique strategy was used to estimate the dollar amount
of all employee theft at all the supermarkets, both those that
used and those that did not use preemployment integrity tests.
Anonymous questionnaires were sent to randomly selected employees of the six supermarket chains. A total of 233 usable
surveys were analyzed; 64 of the usable surveys were from the two
test-using companies and 169 were from the other companies.
Each employee surveyed was randomly selected from a different
store, so 233 individual supermarkets were represented in this
study. The survey material was designed to be part of a major
university research project. This situation should have led to less
bias in responses.

Employees were asked to estimate the total amount of
money, merchandise, and property the average employee at
their store took weekly without permission (that is, stole). Results showed that for respondents from the 64 test-using stores,
the average employee was estimated to be taking $13.76 per
week. Respondents from the 169 nontesting stores, however,
estimated that the average employee was taking $26.98 per week.
This difference was statistically significant. The findings suggest
that the average employee in the nontesting stores steals almost
twice as much as the average employee in the testing stores.
Although both strengths and limitations exist in this study design, it allows companies to estimate the potential impact of a
personnel testing program on company losses. The results
would be even more compelling if average shrinkage rates were
compared between the testing and nontesting stores.

The weekly estimates just mentioned were converted to
annual estimates using a fifty-week work year. Table 8.1 reveals
that the average annual theft rates based on perceptions of the

Table 8.1. Estimated Annual Theft at Supermarkets.

Unit of Analysis	Selection Tests Used	No Tests Used	Difference in Dollars
Average employee	$688	$1,349	$661
150-employee store	$103,200	$202,350	$99,150
25-store chain	$2,580,000	$5,058,750	$2,478,750
50-store chain	$5,160,000	$10,117,500	$4,957,500
100-store chain	$10,320,000	$20,235,000	$9,915,000

average employee were $688 and $1,349 for the test-using and nontesting supermarkets, respectively.

It is speculated that the average annual theft rate is as high as it is for the test-using supermarkets because their work forces still contained some unscreened employees. Also, not all stores in the test-using chains consistently used the testing program. Table 8.1 shows how a large supermarket chain can forecast how much money it could potentially save per year through diligent personnel selection. HSM managers are committed to using tests to reduce theft-related losses and contain costs.

A Mixed Design

Some program evaluators combine two or more research designs when evaluating the effectiveness of a selection system. These are called mixed designs. For instance, a company might use both a time series analysis and a comparison-group design to assess the impact of a testing program on the bottom line.

The fundamental equation for business is "revenues minus expenses equals profit." This equation can be used to demonstrate how preemployment screening can help maximize a company's profitability through both increased revenues and reduced expenses. Multipurpose test batteries that assess job applicants on a wide variety of job-relevant skills and abilities allow companies to select the highest-quality applicants with the greatest potential for increasing revenues and containing costs. The following list describes how multipurpose selection tests can actually contribute to bottom-line earnings.

Enhanced Performance (Revenues)

- *Enhanced sales ability.* Preemployment screening helps to guarantee that new sales representatives are conscientious, courteous, and service-oriented. These are the people most likely to bring in the tough sales.
- *Enhanced productivity.* Quality employees increase the efficiency of the production line and the quality of the workmanship it produces. Personnel testing enables employers to screen in the most skilled, motivated, and cooperative employees available. Hence, the company controls defect and error rates, and satisfied customers continue to buy.
- *Enhanced management skills.* A rising trend in personnel testing is the development of tests for management potential and ability. Spotlighting such aspects as knowledge of procedures, problem solving, supervisory skills, and even ethics, these tests help to ensure that an organization is sound, right through to the boardroom. An intelligent and highly motivated management team will be better prepared to make the tough decisions that will increase revenues while containing costs.

Cost Containment (Expenses)

- *Reduced turnover.* By selecting quality employees, a company establishes a more stable workforce that is less likely to have extensive turnover. This stability will reduce the cost of training new employees. Retaining key employees is especially important in tight labor markets.
- *Reduced stress-related losses.* Studies demonstrate that stress is strongly related to incidents of counterproductivity (for example, chronic lateness, increased absenteeism, more accidents, poor-quality workmanship). Unscreened employees are more likely to experience job-related stress, since they might not have adequate skills and work orientation for their position.
- *Reduced theft.* With reduced profit margins and inflated replacement costs, theft of inventory by workers is a more costly concern than ever before. Research indicates that

anywhere from 20 to 40 percent of employees engage in costly acts of insider theft. This is nowhere more true than in the retail sector, where layoffs have reduced floor staff but not floor space, thereby increasing the potential for employee theft.

Impact of Multipurpose Testing on Financial Performance

The following information comes from a study I conducted based on four years of financial statements from eight major multimillion-dollar corporations (see Jones, 1991). Four of these corporations were test users—they used no paper-and-pencil personnel testing during the first two years studied, then implemented such a program for the second two years. The other four corporations were nonusers—they had considered using personnel testing after the initial two years, but chose not to.

The results were evaluated using three key financial indicators:

1. Income as a percentage of sales (higher numbers indicate a more productive, more cost-efficient company)
2. Earnings per share of stock (higher figures reflect revenue growth and expense control)
3. Return on equity for 1989 (higher numbers reflect greater return on investment)

Both companies registered similar numbers with regard to these indicators during the two-year pretest phase. In fact, with an average of $2.97 earned per share, test users actually fared less well in the pretest phase than nonusers, who averaged $3.02 per share (see Tables 8.2 and 8.3). Following the implementation of multipurpose personnel testing for such qualities as integrity, productivity, and salesmanship, the differences became pronounced. Note that the average change from the pretest to the posttest phase was positive for the test-users and negative for the nonusers.

The average return on investment in 1989 for nonusers was barely more than what money would earn in a basic money

Table 8.2. Test-Users' Financial Performance.

Type of Company	Pretest Phase*		Posttest Phase*	Percent of Change
Financial	(I)	8.46%	10.63%	+26%
	(E)	$1.65	$2.39	+45%
	(ROE)		3%	
Retail	(I)	4.65%	5.25%	+13%
	(E)	$2.42	$3.39	+40%
	(ROE)		25.2%	
Petroleum	(I)	1.35%	1.4%	+4%
	(E)	$2.78	$3.12	+12%
	(ROE)		17.8%	
Grocery	(I)	5.85%	10.85%	+85%
	(E)	$5.03	$10.02	+99%
	(ROE)		29.5%	

Key: (I) Income as percent of sales Average income change = +32%
(E) Earnings per share Average earnings change = +49%
(ROE) Return on equity of Average 1989 returns = 18.88%
investment for 1989

* Each phase represents an average of two years of financial information.

market fund. It is also important to note that the choice to utilize these tests indicates a corporate philosophy that is committed to the search for the highest quality and most productive workforce available. While it would be misleading to say that the comprehensive personnel selection program was totally responsible for the improved financial posture of the test-using companies, it is safe to say that the testing was probably a major contributor to the change. While the control group strategy does not always account for all confounding variables, it does yield meaningful return-on-investment estimates.

Establishing an Employment Testing Program

Proper use of an employment test for making personnel decisions requires careful planning. The following paragraphs pre-

Table 8.3. Nonusers' Financial Performance.

Type of Company	Pretest Phase*		Posttest Phase*	Percent of Change
Retail	(I)	3.15%	2.75%	−13%
	(E)	$3.56	$3.51	−1%
	(ROE)		10.6%	
Grocery	(I)	1.05%	.5%	−52%
	(E)	$3.99	$2.96	−26%
	(ROE)		10.4%	
Department store	(I)	2.15%	1.5%	−30%
	(E)	$.96	$1.04	−8%
	(ROE)		0%	
Petroleum	(I)	7%	5%	−29%
	(E)	$3.57	$3.14	−12%
	(ROE)		9.7%	

Key:	(I) Income as percent of sales	Average income change = −31%
	(E) Earnings per share	Average earnings change = −12%
	(ROE) Return on equity of investment for 1989	Average 1989 returns = 7.68%

* Each phase represents an average of two years of financial information.

sent a seven-step strategy for ensuring that the testing program is effective. These steps are relevant to most personnel strategies.

Step One: Conduct a thorough job and risk analysis. A job analysis is a breakdown of general job functions into distinct activities essential to performance on a specific job. Each activity is analyzed to determine which human behaviors or characteristics critically affect successful completion of the job activity. A risk analysis identifies any job-related exposures or hazards that could lead to a financial loss. For example, a risk analysis might reveal that an employee has access to company cash and merchandise and therefore a theft exposure exists, or that an employee is exposed to safety hazards and therefore a risk of industrial accidents and insurance losses exists.

Step Two: Select the appropriate employment test. Choose employment tests that assess attitudes, behaviors, experiences, and characteristics relevant to the job. These may include vocational preferences, past work experiences, job knowledge and skills, specific mental abilities, work attitudes, and other personality characteristics. The relevancy of the test you select should be supported by the results of the job analysis and/or risk analysis.

Step Three: Properly administer the testing program. It is essential to follow all instructions for administering and scoring the instruments (these instructions are typically included in a test manual or administrator's guide). It is especially important to adhere to any time limits indicated and to provide identical instructions and test-taking conditions to all persons tested.

Step Four: Standardize testing conditions, especially decision-making rules. Apply cut-scores (lowest acceptable passing scores) consistently when using tests for employment decisions. If you are using a test for personnel selection, apply the measure to all applicants consistently. Changing cut-scores or varying testing procedures makes it difficult to determine the effectiveness and fairness of the selection test.

Step Five: Monitor the testing program. Monitoring the testing program will help determine whether more accurate and useful personnel decisions actually result from test use. In addition, monitoring will reveal whether the testing program is unbiased with regard to race, sex, and age. If adverse impact is ever suspected, a company must either eliminate the adverse impact or ensure that the testing program is definitely job-relevant and thoroughly validated, and that no alternative assessment procedure exists that would yield fairer results.

Step Six: Ensure that the test is valid. While this step is technically required by law only if test use leads to adverse impact, it is nevertheless always sound testing practice to use thoroughly validated employment tests. To validate a test means to conduct a systematic comparison between test scores (the predictor) and relevant job performance (the criterion). Validation provides a measure of the predictive power or accuracy of the test in identifying successful performers. Validation also establishes the range of scores typically obtained by high- and low-performing employees. Professional assistance should be sought when evaluating test validation research, or when attempting to locally validate a test within a particular organization.

Step Seven: Make sure the test complies with professional and legal standards. Use the following resources as general guides for proper test selection and use:

- *Standards for Educational and Psychological Testing* (1985). Available from the American Psychological Association, Washington, D.C.
- *Principles for the Validation and Use of Personnel Selection Procedures* (1987). Available from the Society for Industrial and Organizational Psychology, Arlington Heights, Illinois.
- *Code of Fair Testing Practices in Education* (1988). Available from the Joint Committee on Testing Practices and the American Psychological Association, Washington, D.C.
- *Model Guidelines for Preemployment Integrity Testing Programs* (1990). Available from the Association of Personnel Test Publishers, Washington, D.C.

Conclusion

HSM managers use employment tests and other assessment strategies to objectively and fairly identify the best person for the job. It is the goal of any good manager to hire qualified and productive employees, and to do so as accurately as possible. Hiring mistakes are costly and can seriously affect the bottom line. A valid assessment tool is a key component in achieving this goal — validity means accurate, sound selection decisions. HSM managers want to quickly select or place a job candidate in a position in which the candidate has a high probability of being both successful and satisfied. Using an effective personnel-selection program typically leads to a win-win situation for both the organization and the job applicants.

Chapter Nine

Know Your Competitors

HSM managers use competitive intelligence systems to overtake and outdistance their opponents. Competitive intelligence can be used to surprise competitors, to establish offensive and defensive positions with competitors, and to direct and motivate personnel. For example, if a competitor is financially over-extended, an HSM manager might develop a plan to offer higher-quality new products and services to the competitor's key accounts, knowing that the competitor will not be able to quickly block such a move. Similarly, if an HSM manager learns that a competitor's product quality is slipping, she will confirm the value and quality of her own company's products and quickly yet tactfully offer these products and services to the competitor's key accounts.

HSM managers never enter a market without first study-ing the industry and their competitors. They know exactly who they will be competing against, what sequence of competitive strategies their opponents will use against them, and what strat-egies they personally will use. HSM managers know they must monitor and counter both existing and future competitors.

HSM managers use knowledge of their toughest com-petitors to improve planning, enhance product designs, devise more competitive pricing strategies, lower production costs, develop more effective selling tactics, and improve advertising and public relations campaigns. Moreover, HSM managers covet other companies' customers. When total market growth in new customers is slow, sometimes the only way to increase market share is to win over a competitor's customers. HSM managers are committed to gaining market share by exploiting weaknesses in competitor's strategies, selling tactics, products, and services.

The Basic Competitive Intelligence System

There are five major steps in gathering competitive intelligence. The first step is to clearly establish your company's intelligence needs. Determine what specific information has to be collected and how often. Target the most relevant competitors. Establish who within your company is responsible for managing the com-petitive intelligence system and who will use the competitive information.

The second step is to collect raw data. Once the most fruitful sources of data have been identified, research strategies need to be devised to collect timely and accurate information on a regular basis. Data can be collected from the field staff, from trade publications, and so on.

The third step is to compile and analyze the raw data. The accuracy of the data needs to be established so that both misin-formation and disinformation are eliminated. Data should be combined with other sources of relevant information from a competitor's file. The compiled data should then be analyzed so that conclusions can be drawn about a competitor's business goals, strategies, successes, failures, and weaknesses.

The fourth stage is to communicate the findings in an understandable and useful manner. An in-depth yet succinct report on a competitor or group of competitors should be presented to senior management on a regular basis. The information shared should be labeled as confidential, and all reports should be kept in secure files.

The last and most important step is to use the results. HSM managers know that competitive intelligence findings need to be integrated into a company's overall decision-making and planning process. Gathering intelligence data is a waste of time unless they are used to have an impact on strategic and or tactical business plans and activities.

Useful Competitor Information

HSM managers are committed to getting the most relevant and timely information for their cause. Companies consistently indicate that the most useful information they can have about their competitors includes the following:

1. Expansion plans
2. Key customers
3. Market share changes
4. New product plans
5. Pricing and sales figures
6. Strategic plans

When analyzing their competitors, HSM managers need to know all relevant information. The following is a list of examples of strategies and tactical information managers need to collect, analyze, and respond to:

Strategic Information	*Tactical Information*
History in marketplace	Pricing strategy in designated markets
Current goals and strategies	
Priority market niches and market share	Knowledge of price posturing and promotions
Satisfaction with current market share	Advertising efforts
	Sales and marketing tactics

Method of defending markets
Research and development
   expenditures
Growth strategies (internal
   and acquisitions)
Potential strategy shifts
Financial status and goals
Management style and
   commitment
Legal situation
Personnel relations
Strengths and vulnerabilities
Organizational structure
Diversification plans
Ability to keep up with
   market demands

Merchandising programs
Deployment of sales staff
Customer loyalty
Costs to compete
Production capabilities
Public relations activities
Comparative quality of
   products/services
Recent personnel changes in
   key positions
Technological capabilities
Responses to technological
   trends

HSM managers are also aware that competitive knowledge can be gained from both internal and external sources.
Some of the most useful sources of information include the
following:

- *Sales and marketing staff* can gain information from trade
  shows, catalogs, and customers.
- *Market research firms* can analyze electronic data bases, trade
  publications, scientific journals, and other information
  resources.
- *Service technicians* can gain information about a competitor's
  products when servicing accounts and when training
  distributors.
- *Purchasing agents* can gain competitive facts from suppliers.
- *Research and development professionals* can interact with competitor's technical staff at scientific conferences.
- *Financial staff* can obtain information about competitors
  from their financial and government contacts.
- *Legal staff* can learn about competitors from sources such as
  legal data bases, court records, and congressional reports.
- *Manufacturers* can learn of competitors' plant capabilities

and labor relations from subcontractors, suppliers, consultants, unions, and regulators.

- *On-line data bases* can provide updated information on competitors' financial stability and key executives' activities.
- *Competitors' communications* (such as promotional materials, newsletters, press releases, speeches, publications, patents filed, federal compliance reports, and annual reports) can be obtained.

HSM managers know they must control the unauthorized release of valuable information about their own company to their competitors. That is, competitive intelligence works both ways! HSM managers must pay special attention to two primary areas of exposure: (1) company publications and publicity, and (2) trade shows, conventions, and conferences. The following strategies can be used to defend against competitor intelligence gathering:

Company Publications and Policy

- Review and approve articles in newsletters, journals, magazines, technical papers, and press releases.
- Warn staff against divulging critical information in interviews, news stories, and speeches.
- Limit distribution of internal publications and reports to employees only.
- Mark documents "company confidential" if they include information that is not for outside consumption.

Trade Shows, Conventions, and Conferences

- Do not disclose sensitive information to employees attending a trade show unless they are warned about confidentiality issues in advance.
- Instruct employees not to take sensitive information that can be duplicated and distributed to a trade show.
- Brief key employees on what to say when they talk to competitors.
- Warn your key employees that when they interview with a

competitor, interview a competitor themselves, or are encouraged to disclose key data about their company, they
should not violate a code of conduct that says *no* confidential
or proprietary information can be shared. Ideally, non-
disclosure contracts should be signed to legally enforce such
an agreement.

Understanding the Major Competitive Forces

HSM managers must understand both their major competitors
and the industry in which they are competing. In other words,
they must analyze all the forms of competitive pressure their
company experiences. Michael Porter, a Harvard business professor who specializes in the science of competitive business
strategies and author of *Competitive Strategy: Techniques for Analyzing Industries and Competitors*, has delineated five competitive
forces that must be monitored, analyzed, and dealt with effectively. They are as follows:

1. *Rivalry among competitors.* How are current competitors jock-
   eying for position in areas such as price competition, advertising, product features, customer service, and warranties?
   Are there too many or too few competitors, and are the
   competitors small or large firms? Is slow or rapid industry
   growth to be expected? Are competitors similar or different
   in their competitive strategies?
2. *Threat of new entrants.* Are the barriers to entering a market—
   that is, economies of scale, customer loyalties, capital requirements, customer-switching costs, access to distribution
   channels, and any form of cost disadvantage—too high?
   How severe and effective a retaliation would be forthcoming
   from the established companies? Does the industry require
   scarce resources?
3. *Threat of substitute products/services.* Are substitute products a
   viable and less costly alternative? Are there many or few
   substitute products that can perform the same functions?
   Are substitute products currently being advertised as alter-

natives? Are there any substitutes that cost less and out-perform the industry's main product?

4. *Bargaining power of buyers.* Do purchasers play competitors against each other? Can a buyer develop the product or service in-house, and therefore demand a sizeable price concession? Does the buyer face few, if any, switching costs?

5. *Bargaining power of suppliers.* Are suppliers able to justifiably raise the prices or lower the quality of their goods and services? Are there a few or many potential suppliers? Is the supplier able to quickly develop the industry's product? Does the supplier perceive the industry as an important source of business? (Adapted from Porter, 1980)

Porter also reports that nearly all companies use one of three major competitive strategies: (1) overall cost leadership, (2) product innovation and differentiation, and (3) targeted marketing. A brief description of each strategy follows.

Overall cost leadership means offering the lowest cost relative to the competitors. The requirements for this strategy include tight cost control; cost minimization in research and development, advertising, and selling; continual cost reductions from increased experience; intense supervision of labor; and utilization of a low-cost distribution system. Companies using this strategy must avoid product-line proliferation, outdated manufacturing processes and technologies, and a failure to creatively develop new products when absolutely necessary.

Companies that base their competitive strategy on *product innovation and differentiation* continually try to offer the most unique products and services. They continually differentiate their product features, brand image, customer service, dealer network capabilities, and overall quality. Their products, since they are one of a kind, are less vulnerable to low-priced competitors. They are also better insulated against substitute products.

To compete with innovation and differentiation strategies requires extensive research, product redesign, high quality procedures, and intensive customer support. There is a heightened need to attract highly skilled and creative employees. HSM managers using this strategy cannot allow low-cost competitors to outbid them by too much, however, since brand loyalty could be jeopardized. In addition, users of this strategy must stay ahead of the imitators.

Targeted marketing — focusing on a particular buyer group, geographic market, or segment of a product line — is the third major competitive strategy. Users of this strategy are able to serve their narrow strategic targets more effectively than competitors who serve broader markets. It is preferable to select targets that are least vulnerable to substitute products and where the competition is weak.

Users of this third competitive strategy must guard against competitors finding submarkets within the users' targeted markets. Also, one must always make sure that the targeted group perceives that the products they purchase are truly unique in meeting their needs. If not, the targeted group will start buying lower-cost products that are typically sold to the general population.

A firm stuck in the middle of these three strategies is in a poor strategic position. Hence, companies are encouraged to develop and sustain only one of the three strategies. Rarely is a company suited for all three or even two of these approaches. It is almost mandatory that HSM managers identify which strategies are being used by their competitors, and then develop effective plans to counter these strategies.

Conclusion

HSM managers rely on streamlined and effective competitor information systems. They frequently participate in competitor update meetings to ensure that both competitive opportunities and threats are clearly understood and dealt with. HSM managers are willing to spend time and money defending against competitors in the marketplace. And when competitors' mistakes and vulnerabilities offer opportunities, HSM managers seek to immediately capitalize on them for market share gain.

Chapter Ten

Speed Up Product Development

Companies are experiencing increased pressure to shorten the time it takes to move from conceptualizing a new product idea to actually distributing a profitable product. In addition, companies are placing greater emphasis on new product releases as a major source of sales and profits. For example, the 3M company requires that products less than five years old account for approximately 25 percent or more of their total sales, and more than 30 percent of Apple Computer's annual sales are based on relatively new products.

Companies are finding that it takes more than high quality, low cost, and innovative differentiation to have a successful product. It also takes "speed to market." HSM managers are especially concerned about speed to market because shrinking product lifecycles are forcing them to speed up product development to remain competitive. By thinking in terms of time to market, a manager gets all of his people focused and working together on a common goal. HSM managers try to develop their products significantly faster than the industry average, and significantly faster than their company's norm for developing a comparable product.

Rapid Product Development: A Case Study

Hewlett-Packard attributes much of its recent success to rapid new-product development (see Dumaine, 1989). John Young, chief executive officer of the company, is obsessed with speed. He insists that his company develop and deliver products faster than they have before and faster than the competition. For example, Hewlett-Packard has recently reduced the length of time it takes to conceptualize and develop a desktop laser printer from four and a half years to twenty-two months or less. Young insists that product quality also improve, because high-speed development forces a work team to do it right the first time.

Young uses a number of different HSM strategies at Hewlett-Packard to speed up product development. First, he insists that his company conceptualize, develop, manufacture, and deliver computer and electronics products faster than ever before. To that end, Young encourages all of his engineers to use an expert artificial-intelligence software system that both analyzes product design and recommends changes that can make new products easier and quicker to manufacture. Over the past three years, this system alone has helped to cut failure rates by nearly 85 percent and manufacturing time by more than 80 percent.

Young encourages the use of computer networks to speed all communications among his managers and other personnel. Engineers receive fast solutions to their design problems from colleagues around the world who are part of the information-sharing network. Productivity managers are required to oversee all research and development laboratories and act as information experts, trying to solve unique product development problems and to cross-pollinate their laboratories with the intelligence and wisdom of other engineers. The productivity managers do not act as bureaucratic middle managers. This would only slow the process down.

Finally, Young shaped the company's high-speed culture by announcing a companywide program called "BET"—break-even time. A major objective of BET is to encourage managers to redesign and speed up the product development process, and to establish multidisciplinary, fast-moving product development teams. Break-even time is the interval between the conception of a new product or service and the point at which it becomes profitable. All research, manufacturing, and marketing costs feed into this equation. High-speed companies like Hewlett-Packard try to reduce break-even time with a wide range of strategies, especially faster product development.

Table 10.1 summarizes how several other time-based companies are successfully winning the product development race. HSM managers at these companies typically strive to have their next-generation models in the design and development stages as soon as a new model is introduced into the market. HSM managers constantly set very ambitious goals. For instance, they might inform their product development teams that a new model needs to be completed 20 percent faster and considerably better than the last one. Then they delegate to the product development team both the responsibility and the authority to achieve these goals.

The following list presents some of the benefits of speeding up product development:

- Break-even time can be drastically reduced.
- Higher prices are often paid to the products with the newest features incorporating the latest technology. (As competitors incorporate these features into their products these prices typically decline.)
- Market share should increase since the company's product would be the first of its kind to meet customers' needs.
- Inventories of finished goods shrink because they are not necessary to ensure quick delivery—that is, the fastest manu-

Table 10.1. Speed-Based Companies.

Company	Product	High-Speed Management Strategies	Development Time	
			Old	New
AT&T	Phones	Provided multidisciplinary team with tough deadlines and sufficient authority to meet the deadlines.	2 years	1 year
Navistar	Trucks	Established interdisciplinary team that included suppliers. All team members worked simultaneously, not in a relay-race fashion.	5 years	2.5 years
General Electric	Circuit breaker boxes	Established an interdisciplinary team and streamlined the manufacturing process. Management layers were reduced to speed up decision making.	3 weeks	3 days
Motorola	Pagers	Set clear deadlines. The time-based culture did not tolerate delays. A disciplined management team did not deviate from the established schedule.	3 weeks	2 hours
Brunswick	Fishing reels and outboard motors	Increased spending authority of division heads to speed up approval system. Reduced layers of management to facilitate communication with workers. Reduced paperwork.	3 weeks	1 week

Source: Adapted from Dumaine, 1989.

facturers can make and ship an order shortly after the order is received, rather than having to stock up on the product in order to deliver it on time.

- The odds that a sudden change in market conditions will force management to rework the design of the product are reduced; thus costly delays, additional expenses, and missed opportunities are avoided.
- Internal gains also occur, because faster product development increases the number of new products, thus increasing the odds of releasing a winner.

- Employees become more satisfied because they know they are working for a more responsive organization and because speeding up operations usually gives them more responsibility and authority.

In summary, fast product developers continually gain on slow ones. Slow developers rationalize their pace by arguing that speeding up the process can reduce quality, increase defects, lead to accidents, and/or limit the number of product features that can be carefully added to the new product. No evidence exists to support their arguments.

Old Versus New Product Development Strategies

Takeuchi and Nonaka (1986) were the first to point out that the old approach to product development is sequential rather than holistic. That is, the product moves sequentially from one phase to the next—from concept development to feasibility testing, product design, pilot production, final production, and redesign. A bottleneck in one phase could slow down or even stop the entire development process. Moreover, since each step in the development process is largely dependent on the others, changes made at any postdesign stage, especially after production starts, cause major disruptions. Last-minute adjustments and fixes ripple back through the product, causing almost everything that has gone before to be reworked as well.

The relay race metaphor has been used in management literature to describe the old mode, by which the majority of products are still being developed. One group of functional specialists passes the baton (the product) to the next group, and so on. The functional groups are very segmented and specialized: the marketers assess customers' needs, the engineers design the product, the manufacturers develop a prototype.

HSM managers take a new, more holistic approach to product development. A rugby metaphor could be used to describe this model. That is, an interdisciplinary team of workers tries to develop the product as a unit, constantly passing the ball (the product) back and forth so that they can work concurrently on the product. The following sections discuss the major characteristics of this holistic approach.

HSM Culture

Managers realize that if they come up against a fast, effective company unprepared, their own company can experience both revenue and earnings declines, and possibly even go out of business. Companies that do not speed up their product-development process can lose their competitive advantage. HSM managers find solutions to these business challenges now, not tomorrow. HSM managers realize that putting speed into the corporate culture can be fun and rewarding, and that a lack of speed can be devastating to a company's morale.

Supercharged Team

Top management needs an interdisciplinary project development team to quickly develop a new product or service. The ideal team typically consists of hand-picked members from such departments as design, manufacturing, research, sales, marketing, computer services, and production. Suppliers and expert consultants also are sometimes added. The team needs to work within a culture that emphasizes high-speed product development and to think in terms of minutes, not hours; weeks, not months; months, not years.

The fastest companies routinely establish these interdisciplinary teams, which become the epicenter of authority for product development. The teams are given tough deadlines yet sufficient authority to meet them. They are allowed to work relatively free of bureaucracy, yet are held fully accountable by senior management for meeting all deadlines. All team members consistently strive to work as an integrated unit with shared goals, objectives, and rewards.

While top management provides a broad goal or general strategic direction, each project team is granted a wide measure of freedom. Team members are sometimes relieved from most of their other day-to-day activities. The project team must develop an agenda and take all necessary initiatives and risks. The team is responsible for conceptualizing and implementing product development strategies to transcend the status quo and complete the new product in record time.

Senior management is limited to providing moral support, guidance, money, and other essential resources. Top management acts as a venture capitalist to a start-up company. However, management should accept only extremely challenging goals, and supply an element of constructive tension to the project team. The team must be subtly pressured to succeed in its quest to develop a new product in record time without sacrificing quality.

Most managers will be unsuccessful if they try to speed up product development by simply working employees harder. Employees will just burn out. Instead, management needs to rethink all business practices relevant to product development. A diverse team of experts needs to determine which time intervals should be reduced and which HSM strategies should be implemented to best speed up the overall development process.

Concurrent Development

Product development team members must synchronize their individual efforts to meet the aggressive deadlines. They must work in unison. They must constantly share relevant information among themselves during all phases of the project. Cross-fertilization of ideas occurs when the team interacts in this way, and if a bottleneck occurs during any phase of the development process, the whole process will not come to a halt.

With the old relay race model, developmental phases did not overlap. The production department would not work on a prototype until the design engineer was totally finished. The marketing department would not work on any promotional literature or pricing schedules until the production department was completely finished, and so on. If a delay occurred at any phase, the entire process became seriously stalled.

With the new concurrent model, however, overlapping activities typically take place among the different departments participating in the development process. For example, a representative of the production department might sit in on meetings with the designer to better anticipate what equipment and resources need to be available to quickly develop the new product. Similarly, a representative of the marketing department might work closely with a representative of the production team so that she can immediately begin to establish a clear understanding of the new product. She could pick the brains of the production representative so that she knows which features might be best received in the marketplace.

The overlap might extend across many different departments, and could actually extend across several phases. For example, the entire product development team could schedule weekly team meetings to get an overview of what each member is doing during the current phase of development and plans to do in future phases. This would allow the marketing representative to share any late-breaking competitive intelligence with the design representative. A design could then be quickly altered if a competitor comes out with a new product with similar features.

With the old relay race method problems occur at hand-off points. The new rugby approach avoids these problems by keeping all functional specialists informed and involved in all phases of the product development process. By working concurrently, the team acquires broad knowledge and diverse skills, which help them become a versatile and flexible work unit. The team becomes capable of solving problems quickly, and can respond to rapidly changing market conditions. There is always the risk that the rugby approach can lead to more interpersonal conflict than the relay race approach because the entire team is working on the project at once. However, the team needs to realize that such conflict is part of the high-speed development process.

Subtle Management Control

In the holistic approach to product development, senior management must anticipate and tolerate some mistakes, but establish enough checkpoints to prevent chaos. Moreover, senior management must not overcontrol the product development team. Overcontrol can impair the team's creativity and spontaneity. The emphasis needs to be on team control through peer pressure.

HSM managers should attempt to reduce the number of times a new product requires internal approval before it reaches the customer. Requiring many internal approvals lengthens the development process. Red tape, complicated bureaucracies, and restrictive policies do more to slow down the development process than any other factors.

Ultimately, the customers, not the product development team, will judge the success of the new product. Therefore, HSM managers must constantly encourage members of the development team to go out into the marketplace and listen attentively to what dealers and customers have to say about the new product. The product design and development process should immediately be revised if a diverse group of dealers and customers consistently provides feedback that is in opposition to the product development plan.

Meet All Deadlines

An HSM manager accepts no excuses for missing a deadline. The HSM manager provides the leadership, resources, and occasional monitoring to ensure that deadlines are continually met or beaten. Moreover, the HSM manager must establish overall time-related goals for the team so they know what is expected of them. For example, one goal imposed by management might be to have a team reduce by half the time it takes to develop a new product. It is up to the team to determine how that goal can be creatively and successfully reached.

Everybody, including team members and senior management, should respect the development schedule. Employees should be constructively disciplined if deadlines are missed. There should be no exceptions without extremely good reasons. For example, the needs of the support staff should be anticipated so that they are never allowed to slow down the development process. Also, the product specifications should be frozen once they are thoroughly studied and approved, so that people do not have second thoughts, an occurrence that almost always slows down or stops the process.

Streamline the Distribution System

No matter how fast a product is developed, a company will not gain a competitive advantage if the product is delayed in marketing and distribution. Speed is needed at all points in the distribution channel. Sales agents electronically linked to their customers can keep track of reorder points. Customers can use the electronic linkups to continuously access information about product updates and price schedules. Sales agents linked to both the manufacturing plant and the warehouse can make sure that sufficient units of the product are in stock for quick delivery.

Some management experts feel that the holistic approach might not be appropriate in all cases. For instance, some companies might not have the personnel or the financial resources for this rapid development process. If a team wants to work longer hours to meet a tight deadline, management has to have the funds to pay overtime. Breakthrough projects that require a totally revolutionary invention masterminded by a genius might not work either, unless the genius happens to be part of the product development team. The holistic approach seems most appropriate when the team needs to quickly differentiate an existing product and/or devise new ways to reduce the break-even time.

Also, the product development team needs to realize that no one functional specialist should dominate all phases of the development process. For example, early in the process a design engineer might emphasize product differentiation as the way to achieve the desired outcome. Later in the process, the marketing representative might need to focus on how to effectively integrate the product into the existing product lines and into the company's overall advertising campaign. Both areas of emphasis are important, and both need to be strongly encouraged and coordinated.

Fast Innovation

HSM managers live by the rule that fast innovation can quickly put competitors on the defensive, and can also ensure the long-term success of their own company. Slow-response managers typically expend a great deal of time and energy searching for a major breakthrough. Yet major breakthroughs are very rare. HSM managers have learned that the secret of rapid innovation is to incrementally increase the newness of a company's existing products and services on an ongoing basis, improving them in a variety of small yet meaningful ways rather than always trying to develop breakthrough products.

More products are being incrementally differentiated by embedding larger information systems into the physical product itself. For instance, it used to be that the typical hand-held electronic organizer would hold only five hundred names, addresses, and phone numbers. Now, in response to the growing demand for such informationalized products, electronic organizers have unlimited information-management potential. The Sharp Wizard, for instance, includes the following features and capabilities:

Features	*Applications*
Size: 7 × 3 ⅞ × ¾ inches	Daily, weekly, monthly
Weight: 10.6 ounces	calendar
Raised keyboard	Expense tracking
Seventy-five well-spaced keys	Three-part phone book
Liquid-crystal display	Memo pad and outliner
Eight forty-character lines	Calculator
Touch-screen commands	Three-dimensional
Multiple data search modes	spreadsheet
Memory expansion cards	Organizer
Lithium-cell battery	Business-card files
Modem adaptability	Spell-checking and thesaurus
Links to computer	Facsimile

Multiple editing features   Book disks
Easy to store   Games
On-line service

     The Japanese firm Mitsubishi Electric Company used an incremental improvement strategy to differentiate and improve a three-horsepower heat pump at least eleven times in a fourteen-year period. Some business strategists estimate that Mitsubishi's American competition is now ten years behind and losing ground fast. The following list (adapted from Stalk & Hout, 1990) chronicles the major milestones of Mitsubishi's rise to dominance with their heat pump:

- *1975–1979.* Improved sheet metal work and reduced material costs.
- *1980.* Improved energy efficiency ratio by adding integrated circuits to control the heat pump cycle.
- *1981.* Augmented the integrated circuits with microprocessors, for easier installation and use; added quick-connect freon lines, eliminating the need for expensive technicians to install copper tubing. The pump could now be sold through general distributors and installed by local contractors.
- *1982.* Replaced the reciprocating compressor with a rotary compressor, further improving the energy efficiency ratio.
- *1983.* Again, improved energy efficiency ratio, by adding more sensors and computing power.
- *1984.* Added an inverter to convert AC to DC then back to AC again in a new wave form.
- *1985.* Added shape-memory alloys to allow the air louvers to better position themselves depending on whether hot or cold air blew through the unit.
- *1986–1987.* Added more advanced electronics (such as optic sensors and remote control devices) to improve efficiency and convenience.
- *1988.* Added learning circuitry to improve both self-

defrosting and differential regulation of temperature throughout the day.

- *1989.* Added air purifiers to its top-of-the-line models.

Peter Drucker (1985) identified the following seven sources of innovation that managers can use to recognize and seize opportunities to be more innovative.

1. Unexpected success, failure, and outside events
2. Incongruity between reality as it is and as it should be
3. New societal or business needs
4. Changes in industry or market structure
5. Demographic changes
6. Changes in customers' perceptions, moods, and meanings
7. New knowledge (both scientific and nonscientific)

Ensure Product Quality

Almost everyone has an opinion about the definition of product quality. In business, multiple definitions have made product quality appear to be a difficult thing to achieve. For the HSM manager in charge of product development, quality means the timely and successful achievement of all product performance requirements. Defining quality as the successful achievement of all product performance requirements makes quality a very specific element. HSM managers use a variety of strategies to ensure the rapid development of quality products, including the following:

1. All employees are required to conform to all performance objectives and requirements, without exception.
2. All employees must try to eliminate opportunities for error *before* problems occur. They must be committed to identifying new and improved ways to achieve quality.
3. All employees must recognize that the performance standard is zero defects. They must continuously try to meet this

high performance standard and never settle for "that's close enough."

4. All employees must realize that the measure of quality is the difference between the cost of doing something right and the cost of doing it wrong, and that the cost of doing something wrong needs to be quickly eliminated.

5. Customers, suppliers, and all company personnel must always be fully aware of all quality improvement activities.

When traditional product development managers are asked what control systems are involved in quality management, they immediately think of the more familiar ones, such as inspections, tests, and audits. Unfortunately, these activities all have a common failing: they are aimed at finding errors or defects *after the fact*, then fixing them. Such traditional quality management systems are based on a philosophy of appraisal and control. The HSM manager believes that the best approach for ensuring ultimate quality is *prevention*.

Prevention means identifying opportunities for error and taking direct action to eliminate those opportunities *before* a problem occurs. Unfortunately, prevention is rarely a planned activity. It is often considered illogical to spend time and resources on situations that have not yet occurred. A prevention-oriented approach to quality involves getting it all straight up front.

The common standard used by many slow-response companies is acceptable quality level, or "that's close enough." This performance standard can easily be misunderstood, because it leads people to believe that nonconformance or subpar performance is sometimes expected and tolerated. The answer to "How often do you want me to do things right?" should always be "All the time." Therefore, the standard that HSM managers must communicate is *zero errors*.

HSM managers also measure quality. They know that what gets measured gets done right. The best way to measure quality is to calculate what it costs to do things wrong—the money wasted due to lost time, redesign, rework, repair, reprocessing, client reconciliation, and other correctional efforts.

All companies can benefit when both the frequency and the cost of poor quality products decrease and are eventually eliminated for good.

Link Research to Corporate Strategy

HSM managers know that research and development (R&D) must be used as a key strategic weapon if a company is to succeed in quickly offering high-quality products ahead of its competitors. This means that a company's R&D efforts must always be closely connected to the company's overall business strategy. HSM managers continuously strive to merge the research department's plans with the company's overall plans since the research unit plays an extremely important role in developing new products, ensuring product quality, rapidly modifying current products, reducing production costs, keeping up with new technologies, and basically guaranteeing the company's future viability.

HSM managers also know that R&D strategies, initiatives, and expected outcomes must be approached differently in the 1990s than in previous years. While these managers never question the relationship between a company's long-term profitability and the amount of support given to its research department, the increased global competition of the 1990s will require more strategic and efficient deployment of R&D investments. In addition, a company's researchers must become more focused on commercial applications of their research, since the rapid introduction of high-quality, innovative, and cost-effective new products has become the status quo in the marketplace. Research also needs to play a bigger role in helping companies shorten their product development cycles. The list that follows outlines a number of trends emerging within corporate research units that should help companies better translate their research efforts into viable new products for targeted groups of customers.

Slower-Paced R&D Focus	*Emerging High-Speed Focus*
	Strategy
• Science first, business second	• Science closely linked to business objectives

- R&D's plans not integrated with companywide plans

- Research treated as a costly overhead

- Research not always linked to products and services

- Major scientific break-throughs sought

- Satisfaction with simply publishing articles in scien-tific journals

- R&D's plans integrated with company's strategic plans

- Research viewed as a strate-gic investment

- Research designed to accel-erate the introduction of innovative new products

- Incremental yet meaning-ful scientific gains sought

- Dedication to quickly translating ideas and re-search into profitable products and services

Integration

- R&D's value to company unclear

- Executives lack scientific literacy

- R&D isolated from rest of company

- R&D not closely linked to top management

- R&D constantly faces back-log of projects

- R&D repeatedly contrib-utes profitable products, services, technologies, and processes

- Executives are scientifically literate

- R&D tied to strategic busi-ness units

- R&D represented in execu-tive suite

- R&D prioritizes and stays either on or ahead of schedule with projects

Technological Dominance

- R&D is underfunded

- R&D is not a technological leader

- R&D staff has little talent

- R&D is adequately funded

- R&D is perceived by indus-try to be a technological leader

- R&D staffed with talented researchers

- R&D is constantly in catch-up mode with competitors
- R&D rarely establishes a new direction for an important line of research

- Competitors are always trying to keep up
- R&D known for setting new, innovative directions for key areas of research

Arno Penzias, vice president of research at AT&T's Bell Laboratories, is in the process of transforming Bell Labs into a more high-speed research unit. He comments in a recent *Scientific American* article that he is initiating a sweeping reorganization at Bell Labs to speed the flow of products that have their origin in his laboratories (see Corcoran, 1991). As he mentions in the article:

> [T]he challenge is finding a way to spin research into products faster and yet preserve the environment that led to so many breakthroughs in basic science. . . . The structural changes that [I have] undertaken are straightforward: (1) slashed duplicate research efforts by consolidating projects into 15 laboratories divided among four divisions. Over the past year [I have] also begun sliding the balance of funding away from high-cost and relatively low-payoff work, such as basic physics and materials science, toward the more lucrative software and information technologies. Finally—and most important—[I have] been nudging almost half of [my] 1,200-person research staff into supporting business unit projects. . . . [I have also] assigned each of [my] 19 business directors the task of working with one of the business units. (Corcoran, 1991, p. 138)

Penzias makes a number of other important observations about the changes going on at Bell Labs. He points out that researchers originally felt that their job was complete when the scientific results of their project were written up and published. Now the research staff must carry those ideas further than the publication phase and more quickly into product development. He also points out that traditional researchers used to derive most of their joy from publishing their results and advancing science. The advances that researchers helped to bring about in the area of commercial applications were hardly celebrated— nor were they well-rewarded in terms of salary or bonuses.

Penzias indicates that his managers want to have their staffs continue to advance basic science, yet their primary goal is to develop commercial applications that benefit humankind. He points out that "managers now find they must continually be looking sideways to spot the product possibilities for [their staffs'] research efforts" (Corcoran, 1991, p. 139). This vigilance in order to shorten the idea-to-product cycle will surely pay off for AT&T in the near future.

Finally, Philip Roussel, Kamal Saad, and Tamara Erickson review what industry needs from modern-day R&D teams in *Third Generation R&D: Managing the Link to Corporate Strategy.* Their book is highly recommended for any prospective HSM manager. They distinguish among three basic types of R&D: (1) incremental, (2) radical, and (3) fundamental. HSM managers tend to prefer incremental research due to its faster payoff.

Incremental R&D

Roussel, Saad, and Erickson referred to this type of R&D as "small *r*" and "big *D*." The goal of incremental R&D is to make small yet continual advances in products and technologies that are based on established scientific principles. This approach usually carries a lower risk of failure. Incremental R&D can be characterized as the clever application of existing scientific knowledge and know-how to existing products. HSM managers have discovered that the small incremental gains typically yield large strategic results. That is, although each incremental improvement in a product may be small, in the aggregate the small changes typically create tremendous value.

Radical R&D

Referred to as "large *R*" and "*possible* large *D*," this type of R&D requires the discovery of totally new knowledge. That is, the development of a new product rests on discovering or learning something not already known. This involves substantial risk, cost, and time delay. And even though the goal is to translate the new knowledge into a profitable commercial application, there is little assurance that the requisite knowledge will be acquired to ensure timely commercial success.

Roussel, Saad, and Erickson report that 80 percent of all radical R&D projects fail. Many companies engage in this mode of R&D, however, hoping to develop one of the few successful breakthrough projects. Successes usually provide the high-margin products that evolve into totally new industries (for example, nuclear energy, or superconductors). These successes truly distinguish a company from its competitors. Yet since success is so elusive, it seems safe to conclude that this radical R&D focus should only be used in conjunction with incremental R&D.

Fundamental R&D

Finally, the third approach to R&D is characterized as "large R" and "no D." The research goal is to learn more about the unknown. New discoveries will probably have no immediate commercial application, yet they might have relevance to future technological and product advances. Fundamental R&D forces management into a very tough strategic decision, since it will not provide a payoff for many years — if ever! Usually, HSM managers drastically limit their staffs' involvement in fundamental R&D, and instead rely on strategic relationships with productive universities and research centers.

In summary, HSM managers know that highly focused research is needed to (1) support and expand existing business, (2) create and drive new business, and (3) broaden and strengthen a company's technological capabilities. Therefore, R&D must always use resources efficiently, while attracting only the top scientists who feel comfortable with a basically incremental approach to research and development. All research efforts must also be fully integrated with a company's strategic goals and initiatives. This will be the formula for success in the 1990s.

Summary

HSM managers strive to develop new products and services as fast as possible. They are aware of the competitive advantages that accompany fast product development, including larger market share, the ability to charge higher prices, and a more satisfied working group. HSM managers use a holistic, or concurrent, model of product development as opposed to the old sequential approach that simulates a relay race. That is, HSM managers appoint supercharged teams of functional experts, encourage concurrent product development efforts, and monitor the development effort without stifling the creativity and initiative of the product development team. Most importantly, HSM managers always ensure the development of high-quality products even when they are implementing a rapid product development plan.

Chapter Eleven

Dominate Market Niches

While high-caliber competition is rapidly increasing, most markets are not. New technologies have shortened product development life cycles, and excess manufacturing capacity has led to strong price cutting in many industries. Profit margins are declining as the unit cost of servicing many markets is up. Success in this tough business climate is usually related to a company's ability to focus on and serve a very specific market niche that offers attractive growth opportunities.

HSM managers try to quickly identify and dominate profitable market niches. Niche marketing is defined as a highly integrated effort to create, discover, arouse, and satisfy the needs of a targeted group of customers with very similar and specific needs. HSM managers are aware that advances in product development technologies and marketing science have made it possible for their companies to rapidly create high-quality product solutions for ever-narrower segments of the marketplace.

Customers also have more products than ever before to choose from; therefore they can afford to be less loyal to a particular product or brand name. Customers are crying out for an end to uniform products that historically companies have mass-marketed. Instead, customers want products that look, feel, and perform as if specifically developed for them. Rather than pushing generic products into the marketplace without regard for customers' specific needs, HSM managers acquire a complete understanding of these needs, and they only offer products and services that are responsive to them. By relying on niche marketing, HSM managers can

- Establish an in-depth understanding of the requirements of a specific customer group, realizing that one company cannot be all things to all customers.
- Target advertising, public relations, and direct mail to a specific group of customers. These promotional efforts improve a company's chances of quickly educating customers about how the product will meet their needs.
- Position their products and services to stand out in a very crowded marketplace, thus facilitating the sales process.
- Develop stronger customer relations, because the entire company is focused on and committed to servicing the needs of a clearly delineated market niche.
- Analyze competitors' performance to determine their relative strengths and weaknesses within the niche and to quickly block competitors' threats.

How to Dominate a Market Niche

Presented here is an eight-step model that informs prospective HSM managers how to quickly dominate a market niche.

1. *Think small.* For big results in today's fragmented, fast-moving marketplace, the key to success is to quickly identify, understand, and stay close to very specific customer groups.

Smaller companies, or smaller strategic business units within a larger company, often are leaner and swifter than their bigger competitors — they can more easily zero in on and respond to targeted customers' needs. Large companies have access to more resources, yet if they are competing against smaller, fast-moving teams they lose some of their advantage. The smaller the company, the easier it is to strike first and dominate a market niche. This is the way of the guerrilla marketer.

It is often easier for smaller companies to service their customers within the niche. In small companies, decisions are made and implemented by fewer people. In large firms, getting everyone to buy into a strategy can take years. Big companies are simply not as flexible.

2. *Define the niche.* Problems can occur if the targeted market niche is not narrow enough. For example, a company that sold a high-quality knitted scarf initially defined its market as anyone with a throat who lived where it snowed. Sales did not take off until the company targeted only skiers and other cold-weather sports enthusiasts. In brief, if a company's market is everybody, then it is not committed to niche marketing.

The HSM manager determines what characteristics, needs, and purchasing idiosyncrasies the prospects in a targeted market niche have in common. He polls the most successful suppliers, distributors, and market researchers to understand the niche. He uses a computer to analyze data bases that contain a wide variety of customer demographics and purchasing preferences. He researches the market size and determines whether the niche has enough money to justify the product's entry. Finally, the HSM manager identifies and studies the competition in the niche, and their strengths and weaknesses. The HSM manager must know the answers to the following questions:

- How do I define my niche in the best way possible?
- What competitive advantage do I derive from targeting this niche?
- Have my major competitors achieved an advantage by segmenting the market differently?

- Which niches offer the most attractive growth opportunities?
- How will the product quickly gain recognition?
- What network of distributors can best handle my product?
- What kinds of special support will this customer base require?
- How can I continually improve my relationship with this targeted customer group?

Many companies do not segment narrowly enough. If a company does not narrow their focus enough, the competition will do it for them.

3. *Conduct research.* HSM managers continually study the marketplace. They analyze the niches they currently serve and they try to identify opportunities for developing new ones. Market research helps the HSM manager better understand how a particular market is structured. Market analysis reduces over-reliance on the trial-and-error approach. By utilizing high-level market and consumer behavior research, managers can more easily pinpoint the ideal market niche, identify the most desirable product-positioning strategy for this niche, and design truly effective pricing, promotional, and distribution strategies. At a minimum, HSM managers should conduct the following types of research:

- *Gather demographic information.* Who are the prospective customers? How big is the market? Is there a more promising niche than the one we are currently focusing on? Can the niche be defined even more narrowly?
- *Assess customers' reactions.* HSM managers use both qualitative feedback (such as focus groups) and quantitative feedback (such as customer preference surveys) to answer the following questions: How do customers feel about several different products and product features? Will customers develop product loyalty? Are they satisfied with the support and service they are receiving? What would force them to buy a competitor's product? Are there any substitute products that the customers are currently considering?

- *Know the competitors.* HSM managers must know their competitors' strengths and weaknesses. What marketing strategies do the competitors use? What percentage of market
  share do they have? What aspects of the competitors' products do customers like and dislike? What new products do
  competitors have in the pipeline? Are there any competitors
  that can totally redefine the industry or create totally new
  market niches or subniches?

Most importantly, HSM managers always remember that
research is merely a tool, not an end product. They know that
research results need to be transformed into strategic plans,
action steps, and eventually higher sales before the research
contribution has been fully realized.

4. *Position the product.* A great product at a fair price is
simply not a sales guarantee in the 1990s. HSM managers must
ensure that customers perceive their products as superior to
competitors' products. They must educate customers about any
unique product features and capabilities that set their products
apart from the competition. HSM managers must skillfully and
repeatedly communicate how their products' performance will
meet their customers' unique needs. HSM managers must establish the fact that their product is indeed better than any other
competitor's product, both in perceived value and in actual
product performance.

5. *Build a reference system.* HSM managers make it a priority
to get an endorsement from important people, key companies,
and influential distributors within a niche. This loyal network of
business contacts becomes a reference system for product promotion. HSM managers start with a narrow reference system
and continually educate people in this network about their
product as their reference system gradually grows.

For example, HSM managers can create advisory panels
of eminent specialists within the niche. They can also build
alliances with leading distributors. Through word of mouth, the
reference system will quickly establish a product's reputation.
Moreover, a reference system can be quickly activated at any time
to help extend information about a product past the media to all

of the influential people and companies within a niche. In essence, the reference system helps to promote, sell, and sustain the life of the product.

6. *Customize the product's identity.* HSM managers pay special attention to the product's name, logo, labeling, trademarks, and the overall reputation it has developed in a particular niche. A product's name is particularly important because it can quickly establish a feeling about what the product stands for within the targeted customers even before they use it. A high-impact name should:

- Be developed or at least reviewed by linguists who specialize in naming products and services
- Have the symbolic properties the company wants to communicate (that is, elicit favorable associations)
- Be easy to say (and not sound overly technical)
- Be differentiated enough that it can be legally trademarked
- Be differentiated enough in appearance that it can occupy a unique position in a customer's mind
- Support a worldwide brand identity, if relevant, and yield no negative associations in the global market

Most importantly, the market niche should always be taken into account when naming and packaging the product. For example, if a videotape training product is being offered to the banking industry, the product's name should probably reflect its targeted industry and the packaging should be very appealing to this group of customers. HSM managers know that the product's name and packaging can serve as its best advertisement.

7. *Promote the product.* HSM managers know that both advertising and public relations are essential in order to quickly reach all the customers within a niche. Advertising objectives can include educating the market about the value of a new product, or about new uses for one that is already available; about how the product works, its current and future availability, an upcoming price change, and where the product can be purchased. Advertising can persuade customers to prefer one

brand over another, to switch brands, and to drop false impressions about a product or change their perceptions of a product's capabilities.

Ad agencies offer a wide range of services, from media strategies to creative product positioning to account management. Unfortunately, a high-caliber advertising campaign is usually very expensive. Company-initiated public relations campaigns are typically less expensive. A low-cost public relations campaign might include an article about the product in a key trade magazine or journal. Press releases can also be used to describe both the need for and the benefits of a product in a particular niche. The best times to use press releases are when

- Your company has conducted a survey and is announcing results that clearly support the use of your product.
- You have a business trend prediction to make that is based on interviews with leading experts from your reference system.
- Your company has introduced a new line of products or has made an improvement in your current line.
- Satisfied customers describe how your product helped them to contain costs, enhance profits, and/or improve the bottom-line indicators.
- Your company wants to communicate a position on a key economic or legislative trend.
- You need to quickly address a rumor that can hurt the reputation of your company.

Descriptions of the product's benefits can be presented in the form of well-documented testimonials by satisfied customers or a well-designed scientific study. Most importantly, any positive publicity about the product can be immediately routed through the reference system described earlier so that the reference system always maintains a very high level of enthusiasm about the product.

HSM managers also know they must promote their company's image along with their product's image. If two products are perceived by prospects as being basically identical, then customers will probably buy from the company with the better reputation. Therefore, HSM managers make sure that all employees, including sales, marketing, research, and customer service professionals, do everything in their power to promote and sustain the strong reputation of their company.

In *Relationship Marketing: Successful Strategies for the Age of the Customer*, Regis McKenna describes how a company can benefit by being properly positioned in the marketplace as a well-respected leader. Areas of gain include the following:

- *Faster market penetration.* Everyone — including customers, lenders, the media, and policy makers — prefers to work with industry leaders.
- *Higher retention rates.* A strong corporate position helps companies retain clients longer, even when competitors begin to surface with effective new products.
- *Better access to information.* Everyone wants to interact with the leader in order to review new products, discuss new ideas, or form an alliance. Information will thus be shared about new and established markets, technology breakthroughs, and legislative movements.
- *Higher price.* Industry leaders can sometimes charge higher prices for their products, since it is assumed they are of the highest quality.
- *Quicker sales.* The market more readily accepts a leader's products because they are associated with the company's strong name and reputation. In essence, the company's sales people do not have to work as hard promoting the product, and this leads to lower cost of sales.
- *Strong investor relations.* Wall Street analysts are attracted to industry leaders with a history of success. Investors are more likely to accept a higher price-earnings ratio for a company with a strong corporate reputation.
- *Increased employee loyalty.* Employees are more focused and more determined when they work for a leading company. Employees identify with the company's success and are less likely to quit.
- *Stronger recruiting.* The best available talent prefers to work

for the best companies. They want to be where the action is, and gravitate toward well-positioned companies.

8. *Establish distribution channels.* HSM managers choose distribution channels that directly feed into their niche. They constantly survey their market for information about the most effective and efficient channels. They find out how, when, and where their prospects prefer to buy, and what they require in the way of timely delivery and support. Nothing is left to chance. Distribution decisions are an integral part of the niche marketing plan. The next three sections describe customized approaches to niche marketing.

Implement Bottom-Up Marketing

Al Ries and Jack Trout's outstanding book *Bottom-Up Marketing* describes a time-based management approach to niche marketing that encourages companies to properly position their products and services in the minds of prospects and customers. Companies must view the targeted markets they want to dominate as being within the customer's mind. Ries and Trout explain this point as follows:

> When you look for [an advertising] tactic, you are looking for an idea. But the notion of an idea is a nebulous one. What *kind* of idea? *Where* do you find one? In order to help you answer these questions, [you must realize that] a tactic is a *competitive mental angle*. A tactic must have an element of differentness. It could be smaller, bigger, lighter, heavier, cheaper, more expensive. It could be a different distribution system. [The] tactic must be competitive in the total marketing arena. . . . In other words, the battle takes place in the mind of the prospect. Competitors that do not exist in the mind can be ignored. (1989, pp. 8–10)

Traditional managers believe companies must develop their strategies first, then decide on which tactics to use. That is, managers must create a planning committee to decide *what* they want to do (the strategy), then the committee must determine *how* they want to do it (the tactics). This top-down model is a deeply ingrained tradition in business.

Unfortunately, top-down marketing places too much emphasis on untested strategies. First, it is difficult to accept tactical failure since usually so much time, talent, and money has gone into the strategic planning process. If problems do surface, management minimizes them, by saying that only minor adjustments are needed.

Another significant problem is the failure to quickly capitalize on unplanned success. This phenomenon usually provokes such sentiments as, "We had the idea first, but we did not capitalize on it like our major competitors did. The novel concept just didn't fit into our strategic vision, and we are now suffering from our lack of action in the marketplace."

A third important downfall is that top-down companies are slow responders in the marketplace. Their strategies take a long time to develop, and implementation takes too long to succeed, if it succeeds at all. The top-down company is usually far removed from its customers. Traditional managers try to change the marketplace through their top-down strategies without even knowing what their customers are thinking. Finally, the traditionalists prefer to fight over existing markets, rather than create new niche markets.

Ries and Trout point out that bottom-up marketers believe the planning process should be reversed. That is, the tactics should come first, then the strategies. This process seems to lead to the quickest and most successful discoveries. The bottom-up strategy must evolve from a deep understanding of the preference for the actual business tactic, not vice versa. The following case study from Ries and Trout (1989) illustrates how bottom-up marketers try to find tactics they can quickly exploit in the marketplace.

After a long research phase, Vicks developed a strong cold medicine, but the medication put people to sleep. This was very bad for daytime users who had to work, drive, think clearly, and so on. The traditional manager might have written off the project at this point, losing the invested time and money in the process. But Vicks used bottom-up marketing to discover an effective tactic — the idea of the first *night-time* cold remedy — and then developed a strategy to exploit the tactic — a full-scale plan to introduce a new cold medicine called NyQuil. NyQuil be-came the most successful product in Vick's history and the best-selling cold remedy in the country, even though it was not initially included in any strategic plan.

Ries and Trout spent a lot of time defining a *tactic*. A tactic is an idea that provides a product or service with an element of differentness. A tactic must provide a competitive mental advan-tage, and it should be the definitive point of attack. Ries and Trout point out, for example, that the Volkswagen Beetle was the first car to occupy the "small" position in consumers' minds. (Ries and Trout provide a number of effective techniques for identifying a winning tactic in their book *Bottum-Up Marketing*.)

Yet tactics must be supported by strategies. While a tactic offers a competitive advantage, a strategy must provide an effec-tive way to exploit that advantage. The strategy should deliver a *coherent marketing direction*. It should describe how to best com-pete for the mind of the customer. Ries and Trout describe a strategy as follows:

> [A] strategy. . . is a *coherent* marketing direction that is focused on the tactic that has been selected. [A] strategy encompasses coherent *marketing* activities. Product, pricing, distribution, advertising — all the activities that make up the marketing mix must be coherently focused on the tactic. . . . [And once] the strategy is established, the direction shouldn't be changed. . . . [Finally], in marketing as in war-fare, the safest strategy is rapid exploitation of the tactic. Rest is for losers. Winners keep the pressure on. (1989, pp. 11–12)

Ries and Trout (1989) provide many examples of time-based companies that are benefitting from bottom-up marketing. For example, detergent manufacturers are constantly looking for the winning tactic. Tide gets clothes "whiter," Cheer delivers "whiter than white," and Bold gives us "bright." Domino's Pizza succeeded in a crowded pizza market because their leader, Tom Monaghan, selected a sufficiently novel tactic—home delivery of pizza in thirty minutes or less, guaranteed—that was supported by a well-thought-out strategy (a nationwide chain of home-delivery-only units, no frills, bare-bones menu, informing customers they were buying speed and not premium pizza, and so on).

Part of the success of Japanese companies is their bottom-up approach to marketing. They build many of the same products as American companies, yet they try to build them better, cheaper, and smaller (the tactics), then utilize proven strategies to ensure the success of their tactics.

Ries and Trout make a number of other important marketing observations in *Bottom-Up Marketing*. For example, they believe that today's managers must go down to the front lines to find their company's competitive mental angle. Marketing is just too important to be turned over to junior staff. Yet the senior managers must realize that the front line is in the mind of the customer, not in a store.

Ries and Trout feel that managers of large companies are more out of touch with the front line than managers of small companies. Small companies have fewer management layers and are therefore less insulated from the marketplace. Poorly performing companies can have in excess of eight layers, which filter out too much important information. The quickly responding companies usually have four or fewer layers. Finally, large companies usually try to be all things to all customers. Their efforts get diluted and slowed down. Managers of small companies are able to keep their attention focused; they do not try to sell everything to everybody, and they are able to quickly move with changing market conditions.

Ries and Trout believe that marketing today is as much a battle of ideas as it is a battle of products and services. Therefore,

HSM managers must always be on the lookout for new and effective mental angles (tactics) that can be supported with streamlined, cost-effective strategies. HSM managers must make sure that their products are the first to move into the minds of their customers. And since their products will be the first, these managers have to be prepared to create the new niche market, since there is by definition no current market for the newly conceived product. The following section describes how to handle the process of new market creation.

Creating New Niche Markets

Traditional managers typically have a market share mentality, while HSM managers also adopt a market creation perspective. Regis McKenna, one of America's top marketing consultants, makes a distinction between these two strategies in his book *The Regis Touch: New Marketing Strategies for Uncertain Times*:

> Most people in marketing have what I call a "market-share mentality." They identify established markets, then try to figure a way to get a piece of the market. All [advertising and merchandising] strategies are aimed at winning market share from other companies in the industry. In fast-changing industries, however, marketers need a new approach. Rather than thinking about *sharing* markets, they need to think about *creating* markets. Rather than taking a bigger slice of the pie, they must try to create a bigger pie. Or better yet, they should bake a new pie. (1986, p. 21)

McKenna points out that the more traditional market share strategies are common in slow-moving industries (such as consumer goods). These industries usually require a strong emphasis on advertising, pricing, distribution, and availability. Yet market-creating managers are constantly challenged to quickly turn their creative ideas into novel products. The goal with the market-creation approach is to rapidly conceptualize

and develop high-quality new products, quickly educate targeted customers about the value of the new products, and establish a supportive industry infrastructure (the niche market,
prestigious customers, retailers, distributors, financial analysts,
the media, trade associations, luminaries, alliances and so forth)
that will endorse and continuously promote the product.

In addition, market-creating managers often try to revise
and upgrade the standards for an industry. For example,
McKenna points out that part of Apple Computer's early success
was establishing a new set of standards for their computer's disk
operating system:

> Rather than simply producing a "clone" of the pop-
> ular IBM personal computer, Apple wanted to de-
> velop a new computer that was radically easier to
> use. To do that, Apple decided to establish its own
> operating system rather than be tied to the limita-
> tions of the industry standard MS-DOS. The risks
> were great, but to do otherwise would mean that
> Apple would be completely at the mercy of IBM's
> control over the standard. (1986, p. 25)

HSM managers realize that in the 1990s, products will
move from the drawing board to the marketplace with lightning
speed. In addition, customers will prefer to buy more diverse
and customized products rather than mass-manufactured products. Therefore, in order to stay one step ahead of their competitors, and thereby retain dominance in any of the niches they
create, McKenna (1989, 1991) points out that market-creating
managers will need to:

- Build solid relationships with targeted customers instead
  of just promoting and selling products to them. This will
  ensure that customers will continue to buy products even
  when some competitors offer lower price and/or better
  alternatives.
- Continually attempt to improve their understanding of the
  market niche, move with it, and adapt to the niche's new

form if necessary. This could include repositioning the product and the company.

- Uniquely position their product and company in the minds of the targeted consumer group. The positioning should always be in relation to the key competitors, and should enhance the product's and the company's overall image in the marketplace.

- Always be prepared to create new markets. With rapid technology advances and with heightened competition, cutting-edge products can soon become outdated, and products that were once perceived to be inexpensive could soon become too expensive.

- Skillfully sell intangible factors (such as quality, leadership, innovation, service, and support) rather than only technological specifications. As McKenna states, "Technological leads are usually short-lived. . . . Companies that live by specsmanship often die by specsmanship. . . . In fact, most customers are not interested in narrow technical differences between products." (1991, p. 42)

- Always be willing to experiment. Market-creating companies are usually breaking new ground with their products. Therefore, they must view their new-product launches as experiments, that often must be quickly modified and adjusted in order to successfully meet the needs of a targeted customer base.

Achieving Hypergrowth Through Niche Marketing

In *Hypergrowth: Applying the Success Formula of Today's Fastest Growing Companies*, H. Skip Weitzen isolates the unique niche marketing strategies of the fastest growing companies in America. The companies he studied reached his "hypergrowth" standard "when they each quickly generated sales of one billion dollars or more within a decade of incorporating or emergence from relative dormancy" (1991, p. 3). Companies that experience hypergrowth have achieved one of the major milestones of success in business. Here is his general description of the hypergrowth phenomenon:

> Hypergrowth begins with the search for early signs
> of change [in the marketplace]. Sometimes the mar-
> ket initiates that change and creates the demand
> for new products. At other times, the product
> drives the change in market behavior. In both cases,
> hypergrowth companies transform themselves
> quickly from entrepreneurial phenomenons into
> mature market leaders. (1991, p. 15)

The following is a list of some of the hypergrowth companies that Weitzen thoroughly discusses in his text:

Compaq	Introduced the first portable com-puter. Compressed development cy-cles. Went from $0 to $2.9 billion in less than a decade.
Reebok	Exploited new exercise niches for athletic footwear. Rapidly grew from 3 shoe designs to 250 models in 12 categories. Sales grew from $1 mil-lion to $1.8 billion in a decade.
Home Depot	Capitalized on the do-it-yourself home improvement niche that was created by double-digit inflation. Trained employees to educate and service do-it-yourself homeowners. Sales grew from $22 million to $2.8 billion in a decade.
Apple Computer	Developed a user-friendly computer and managed to keep its product offerings streamlined. Exploited out-standing marketing and service strat-egies. Went from $117 million to $5.3 billion in a decade.
Federal Express	Created a hub-and-spoke air cargo delivery system to ensure timely de-livery of high-priority packages.

	Grew from $415 million to $5.2 billion in a decade.
Tele-Communications, Inc. (TCI)	Purchased a vast network of existing cable television franchises (over 150 cable companies) to avoid the cost and delays associated with new construction. Became the largest cable enterprise, with sales growing from $135 million to $3.0 billion in a decade.
MCI Communications	Developed a telecommunications network to compete with AT&T on service and price in the long-distance market. Sales revenue grew from $234 million to $6.5 billion in a decade.
Liz Claiborne	Categorized women's fashion year into six seasons to ensure innovative offerings every season. Became so fast and flexible when designing, producing, and merchandising fashions that the company was able to deliver a new line of clothes every other month. Went from $79 million to $1.7 billion in a decade.

Weitzen notes that hypergrowth companies utilize high-level conceptual models to direct their efforts to change the marketplace. The better the company's model, the more likely it is to achieve hypergrowth. The following paragraphs describe Weitzen's six-step hypergrowth formula.

Step One: Anomaly. Weitzen defines an anomaly as any new activity that creates a gap between actual and perceived reality. Anomalies typically represent newness, and they offer clues to potential hypergrowth opportunities. All anomalies challenge the status quo—an example is Compaq Computer's identification of portability as a very important productivity factor in the emerging computer industry.

Step Two: Metonymy. A metonymy describes the potential impact of the anomaly on different businesses and industries — it sheds light on who will be the winners and losers if the anomaly eventually brings significant changes to the market-place. For example, Compaq's development of a portable computer led to the creation of a whole new niche known as the portables market, due primarily to the productivity gains that the portable computer offered. This new market niche obviously threatened the desk-top market.

Step Three: Inference. The entrepreneur thoughtfully studies the relationship of the anomaly to the metonymy. This is a time when the hypergrowth game plan gets fully developed. Weitzen (1991) notes that "[i]nference is a conclusion based on a premise that links cause and effect. ⋮ . . . To confirm an inference's accuracy, [one must] be sure to find several observations that lead to the same conclusion" (p. 17). For example, executives at Compaq inferred that software developers would not rush to design software programs specifically for a new, unknown computer. Therefore, Compaq brilliantly designed an IBM-compatible portable computer to address the aforementioned inference.

Step Four: Penetration. This step requires sound planning to reach and influence trendsetters who will eventually fuel the hypergrowth phenomenon. Trendsetters must be constantly exposed to the new product so they can promote it by word of mouth. The media also need to sing the praises of the new product. Finally the distribution channel needs to get excited about the product. Compaq skillfully penetrated and educated both the media and the dealer network about the value of portability. Compaq also hired away key marketing personnel from IBM's PC team to ensure that their portable computer would get quality air time and shelf space with the dealer network.

Step Five: Trends and Fads. The anomaly provides a new business opportunity that can eventually create a new market direction. Hypergrowth companies want to stay ahead of all trends (technological, economic, social, and political) that can radically transform their industries. Since hypergrowth begins to slow down as a trend matures, a major marketing objective of hypergrowth companies is the continual search for new anomalies. For example, Compaq created a radically new marketing direction when the computing power that previously could only be found in the business office suddenly became portable.

Step Six: Hypergrowth. Hypergrowth companies amass a large fortune rapidly, as Compaq did when it quickly became the world's leading manufacturer of portable personal computers. Hypergrowth companies continually watch for and then seize windows of opportunity. Moreover, they are prepared to stay highly focused on a single major goal for at least a decade. These companies also institute all changes with speed and flexibility. That is, they always accelerate their operating pace. As Weitzen describes:

> Speed will improve your company's strategic position and enhance your management effectiveness. The key is to be different, then fast. Hypergrowth does not require wholly novel products. Some of the fastest growing companies simply provided innovative spins to existing products, then moved with alacrity to build sales, profit, and market share. (1991, pp. 5–6)

A key marketing objective for hypergrowth companies is to quickly identify anomalies. Anomalies are a starting point since they are the first clues of impending change in the marketplace. Weitzen discusses in depth how anomalies typically emerge as "pressure points that lead to pattern breaks in the market" (p. 27). Companies that quickly identify an anomaly can offer a better product or service to exploit this pressure point, thus initiating the hypergrowth process.

Weitzen discovered that anomalies that fuel hypergrowth typically emerge among one of the following fourteen pressure points:

1. *Niches.* Finely segmented customer groups that can be quickly dominated and expanded.

2. *Standards.* Adherence to and then advancement of product norms for an industry.
3. *Inflation.* Economic climate that encourages new markets, such as the do-it-yourself and the self-help markets.
4. *Flaws.* Inadequacies, such as defective products and inadequate service, that lead to continual customer complaints.
5. *Needs.* Preferences that can be filled at a fair price.
6. *Laws.* Legislative changes can be a company's biggest ally or foe, depending on which side of an issue one supports. Hence, be poised to capitalize on issues that are in your favor.
7. *Competition.* Identification of weak points in a competitor's business strategy, followed by an immediate attack on this competitor with creative products and marketing campaigns.
8. *Innovations.* Capitalizing on a new product by quickly converting it into a marketable entity that can be rapidly diffused into the marketplace.
9. *Pareto's Law.* Determining the needs of the 20 percent of customers who provide 80 percent or more of the revenue. Never ignore this important customer group.
10. *Time floats.* The gap between when a customer makes a request for a product or service and when the request is fulfilled. The goal is to continuously reduce this gap.
11. *Defects.* Design and performance problems in a competitor's product that can be isolated in order to legitimately discredit the competitor's product line.
12. *Monopolies.* Monopolies can be challenged on quality, price, and service since they are usually sluggish and not used to aggressive competition.
13. *Integration.* Creatively meshing different technologies and business practices (such as AT&T's Picture Phone).
14. *Intermediaries.* Manufacturing intermediaries can sometimes stimulate innovation in the product development process. (Adapted from Weitzen, 1991)

One must always remember that pressure points are very difficult to quantify early on. This is why most analysts overlook potentially lucrative anomalies. Yet once an anomaly is thoroughly and quantitatively documented, the trend has already emerged and the hypergrowth window of opportunity has begun to close. Weitzen's book *Hypergrowth* is must reading for all HSM managers. Like Regis McKenna, Weitzen clearly illustrates that market-creation strategies are one of the major dimensions of the hypergrowth phenomenon.

Winning Back a Market Niche

Even when a niche is created and dominated by one company, it sometimes will be challenged and fought over by other companies. For example, stories that made the news during the past few years described how Zelco Industries develops innovative products known for their design excellence, usefulness, and reliability. Two of the company's leading products are the shirt-pocket-size fluorescent lantern and the "itty bitty" book light, whose sales zoomed from approximately $2.5 million in 1982 to $10 million in 1983. Since the book light typically yielded a 70 percent profit margin during this period, Zelco was favored with enormous cash flow. Unfortunately, competitors were quick to enter this lucrative market niche. The following high-speed strategies were used by Zelco executives to develop and retain this niche.

Creating a Niche

Zelco's founder, Noel Zeller, started out selling cheap imported flashlights through gift shops. One day he realized that if he went the way of the Japanese and made small, innovative, and well-designed lighting products, his company could create and dominate a whole new market niche.

The first product he created following this vision, a miniature lantern for travelers, was a smashing success. It fit in the car glove compartment, near bedside tables, even in a shirt pocket. This was followed by a lamp that was just big enough to fit inside a book, so that a person could read at night without disturbing a nearby sleeper. Zeller was in a strong position to prosper from his well-defined market niche, which he created by combining in his lighting products the concepts of miniaturization and useful application.

Strategic Pricing

The "itty bitty" book light was immediately successful. The product was designed with a tiny white fifty-hour bulb placed on a tiny arm that was attached to a large paper clip. The light clipped easily onto a book. The product was creatively packaged in a hollow book-shaped box.

The book light would have been more successful had it not been for over seventy competitors, who quickly offered imitation products. While the book light's initial success was built around its innovative design, its survival was ultimately determined by strategic pricing. The original Zelco book light cost approximately $30 and came with a rechargeable battery pack, an AC adapter, and a spare bulb. In order to match the price of the competitors, Zeller quickly lowered the price to $20 for an "abridged edition" of his product. He included only an adapter with this second version. He then came out with a "paperback" version that contained only a battery pack and sold for $15.

By 1989, Zeller had established an 80 percent share of the overall book light market, up from a low of 30 percent. Over seven million book lights had been sold as of 1990, approximately seventy percent in the United States and 30 percent in Canada, Europe, and Japan. Zeller wisely and quickly resorted to strategic price cutting to defend his niche.

Slowing Down Competitors

Competitors can quickly copy products like the Zelco book light. With new technologies, knock-off products can be brought to market within a few months. In order to protect his innovation, Zeller launched a number of lawsuits against competitors, alleging that they had copied his book light. Many cases were successfully settled out of court, with Zelco eventually collecting royalties.

Zelco did win one case in court, yet the company being sued declared bankruptcy and Zelco received nothing for its efforts. However, the legal action, although frustrating, time-consuming, and costly, sent a very clear message that Zelco was willing to fight to save its innovation. Some competitors were probably slowed down by the threat of legal action, and some would-be competitors probably never launched a copycat product. Moreover, Zelco did receive some royalties that it would not have received without a legal fight. Although Zelco's profit margins surely shrank because of the increased legal expenses, the most important point is that it is still a profitable and viable company.

Conclusion

Customers can never be taken for granted. HSM managers never forget that their best customers can be lost to the competition if their needs are not continually met. Only by being slightly insecure about the permanence of a customer base will a manager be totally responsive to his customers' needs. Niche marketing is consistent with a company's goal of being very responsive to customers' needs. However, it is never enough to merely identify potentially profitable market niches. HSM managers must also move fast enough to capture, dominate, and retain these market segments. Fast response time from market identification to product delivery is the key to this effort. HSM managers must stay very close to rapidly changing market conditions, and they must quickly identify and seize new marketing opportunities if they plan to consistently outperform their slower competitors.

Chapter Twelve

Close Sales Faster

HSM sales managers are committed to establishing a quick-response sales culture at their companies. They use state-of-the-art personnel assessment systems to hire, train, and retain a highly successful sales force. They use training, motivation, goal setting, timely feedback, coaching, performance appraisals, and strategic compensation plans to ensure that their sales personnel close sales more quickly than their competitors. HSM sales managers continually teach their staff the most important sales skills—relationship building, sales negotiation, and time management. Finally, HSM managers utilize computer technology to establish highly efficient and well-coordinated sales information and account management systems.

In contrast, slow response sales managers often communicate unclear, overly complicated, and unrealistic goals and objectives to their sales force. They sometimes hire "any warm body" to attempt to sell their products and services. They rarely use scientifically proven personnel-assessment instruments to hire the most motivated and skilled sales team. Finally, slow response sales managers rarely or inappropriately use computer-based information systems to identify market niches, process sales leads, assign accounts, focus their staff's efforts, maintain ongoing client contact, and analyze customer satisfaction and purchasing trends.

Quick-Response Sales Models

Sales theorists are starting to conceptualize a wide variety of quick-response sales models, which usually are characterized by very streamlined, highly focused, and/or automated approaches to selling. I will briefly describe three of these models.

Streamlined Selling

Quick-response sales theorists do not feel the sales process needs to be overly complicated. Spencer Johnson and Larry Wilson present a streamlined model in *The One Minute Sales Person.* These sales consultants base their model on the experiences, insights, and advice of thousands of successful sales people from more than one hundred major corporations. Their bare-bones model consists of five basic steps, which novice sales representatives can quickly learn.

Step One: Selling on purpose. Top sales professionals always sell with a purpose, which usually means helping buyers get the specific feelings they want when they make a purchase. The most successful salespeople only want to make money if they add value to and create good feelings in their customers. By helping customers solve problems, seize new opportunities, and feel better, an effective sales professional develops clients who trust him, continually give him profitable referrals, and stay with him for the long haul. Johnson and Wilson state that successfully selling on purpose is like swimming downstream.

Step Two: Preparation. Top sales professionals constantly study the features and benefits of what they sell. In addition, they rehearse before their sales presentations. They try to understand the buyer's point of view by visualizing the buyer benefitting from and getting the feelings he wants from the purchase. Such visualization allows the salesperson to anticipate and skillfully respond to key phases of the sales call. These "one minute mental rehearsals" are kept positive and upbeat, and happy endings are always visualized. In brief, successful salespeople set the stage for their success by preparing for it mentally. This preparation leads to more sales, with considerably less stress. (Similarly, many top athletes practice visualizing successful performance in their sports competitions.)

Step Three: The sales call. Top sales people know that prospects hate to be sold to, but they love to buy. These salespeople thoroughly understand their buyers' needs, know how their products can successfully meet these needs, and are convinced their customers will feel satisfied with their purchases. Major obstacles that must carefully be overcome during sales calls include customers' (1) not trusting the salesperson, (2) not feeling a need for the product or service, (3) not believing the product is better than a competitor's, and (4) not feeling any urgency to buy immediately. Therefore, the salesperson must use a mix of exemplary listening, paraphrasing, and questioning skills to accurately and truthfully relate the product or service to the way prospective customers want to feel. When buyers feel they can get their needs met and achieve good feelings with the purchase, they will ask for the sale. The salesperson does not need to resort to any manipulative closing tactics. Customers will close sales themselves because they perceive their needs will be met without incurring a high level of risk.

Step Four: After the sale. The successful salesperson routinely checks with clients after the sale to make sure they feel good about their purchases. The sales professional never gets upset when he receives bad news from a buyer; he just sees it as an opportunity to quickly make things right. If a customer is happy, the salesperson sincerely praises the decision to buy and recaps some of the highlights of the sales process. Finally, the sales professional asks for referrals, and for permission to use the customer's name as a recommendation.

Step Five: Self-management. Top sales professionals are exemplary self-managers. They write out their sales goals in one page or less, and they constantly practice visualizing the successful attainment of their goals. These sales professionals praise themselves whenever they do anything that gets them closer to their sales goals. They also reprimand themselves whenever they engage in unacceptable sales behavior. They do not put themselves down, only their unproductive behavior. By learning how to be a one minute salesperson, a sales professional adopts a very streamlined sales model that is built around the essentials of successful selling.

Niche Selling

William Brooks's main premise in *Niche Selling: How to Find Your Customer in a Crowded Market* is that, due to an incredibly crowded marketplace, sales professionals will have to have a razor-sharp focus on their customers' needs if they are to succeed. In other words, the top sales professionals will have to be niche sellers. Moreover, their customers' preferences for technical superiority, high quality, stylish design, flexible service, and outstanding value at a fair price will change on a more frequent and unpredictable basis. Hence, it appears accurate to say that successful sales professionals must keep a vigilant focus on a constantly moving niche. Following are eight key aspects of Brooks's niche selling system (adapted from Brooks, 1992).

Sell Value. The key to success in a crowded marketplace is to quickly determine what a targeted group of buyers value most and then to point out the unique ways your product or service reliably addresses those values. Slow-response sellers typically focus more on the product and not on the customers' needs. By quickly focusing on exactly what customers want (not what the seller thinks they need), the quick-response sales professional creates perceived value that makes his product stand out in a crowd. This ability to quickly showcase a product by highlighting unique value leads to more positive buying decisions.

Application Selling. In the 1990s, the most successful sales professionals will conduct a needs analysis to accurately and thoroughly assess a customer's needs. Application selling then occurs by using easy-to-understand language to show a buyer how a particular product or service can fulfill the buyer's critical needs. Mere demonstration selling is typically avoided because it focuses exclusively on the product and not on the customer.

The Pareto Principle. The Pareto Principle, or the 80/20 Rule, applies to the niche selling system. Brooks discovered that approximately 80 percent of salespeople conduct presentations that focus exclusively on their product or their company. Yet these salespeople typically account for only 20 percent of the sales made in the marketplace. Conversely, the remaining 20 percent of sales professionals, who have a laser-tight focus on the exact needs and wants of their customers, account for 80 percent of all sales in the marketplace. Therefore, the more sales revenue a company wants, the more its sales staff will have to focus exclusively on the needs of targeted customers.

Stay Within Your Niche. Quick-response sellers must avoid wasting excessive time by meeting with prospects who have no need or sense of urgency to buy. They should avoid prospects who have no authority or ability to buy. Prospects whose demographic characteristics are far outside one's targeted selling niche should also be avoided. Finally, the shotgun approach to prospecting should be abandoned. Instead, sellers should focus on key decision makers within their niche who have both a real need for the product or service they are selling and the authority to buy.

Be Very Knowledgeable. Quick-response sales professionals need to be far more knowledgeable about their niche than more traditional sales representatives. They must know the

- Needs of their targeted customers, which their product can meet better than any other
- Demographics, geographics, and economics of their niche
- Products, services, and pricing offered by their competitors
- Formal and informal networks within the niche that influence product preferences and purchasing decisions
- Future needs of the market niche
- Most crucial mistakes (such as poor service) made by competitors within the market niche
- Potential customers within the niche who are most profitable, recession-proof, price-sensitive, and so on
- Trade journals, associations, and other marketing and public relations outlets that are most relevant to the niche

Raise Customer Value. Brooks (1992) has developed a simple yet creative formula to measure the value that a product or service brings to a customer. The formula is:

$$V = \frac{PB}{PP}$$

V equals *value.* A positive value is desirable. The prospective customer realizes that your product is worth more to him than what it costs in terms of money, time, effort, and risk. Sales are closed more quickly when the value of *V* is substantially greater than one. *PB* equals *perceived benefit.* This is the perceived advantage or benefit that a particular product offers to fulfill prospective customers' needs. The perceived benefits are estimated, however, since each customer will determine the benefits differently. *PP* equals *perceived price.* This is the true cost of the product, which is different for each prospective customer. The true price is more than a dollar amount; it often includes some risk, such as a threat to a key decision maker's reputation. This price also includes training, set-up, and monitoring costs.

Slow-response sales professionals usually try to increase value (*V*) by lowering the price of the product. Hence, they focus on only one part of the equation. Quick-response sales professionals, on the other hand, focus on both increasing the perceived benefits (*PB*), by communicating all the ways their product will bring value to the customer, and lowering the perceived price (*PP*) if absolutely necessary. Most importantly, they are able to find and promote a key benefit to their prospect, that is, the single, most critical benefit, which is usually the "hot button" that leads to an immediate sale.

Top sales professionals never emphasize the product *features* (attributes or qualities that make a product distinctive) over and above the product *benefits* (advantages that a feature brings to the customer). For example, a major feature of automobile antifreeze is its ability to work at minus 20 degrees Fahrenheit. However, the ultimate benefit to the customer is the health and safety of the driver and passengers during dangerously cold weather.

Align Sales and Marketing. Brooks points out that sales will suffer if a company's sales and marketing strategies are not aligned. The marketing strategy quickly gets a salesperson to the prospect's door in the best possible light, while the sales strategy is what happens once a salesperson meets with the prospect. Quick-response salespeople try to work in Cell D of the following matrix, while slow-response salespeople are typically doomed to work in Cell A.

		SALES STRATEGY	
		Unfocused	*Focused*
MARKETING STRATEGY	*Unfocused*	Failure A	Marginal Success B
	Focused	C Marginal Success	D Ongoing Success

Source: Adapted with permission, from Brooks, 1992.

Cell D reflects a situation in which both the marketing strategy and the sales strategy are well thought-out and clearly defined, well-known to all relevant employees, and, most importantly, accepted by all. Long-term success is expected when the two strategies are in full alignment. Conversely, Cell A reflects a situation where both the marketing and sales strategies are poorly conceptualized, unclear, unknown to all parties, and more than likely unacceptable to many key players. Failure is inevitable.

Strategic Sales Plans. Without a strategic sales plan for each account, salespeople will be assigned general goals; they will push hard to attain them, yet they will usually fall short of reaching them. An account's sales plan should be simple, effective, precisely followed, and revised if necessary. The sales plan needs to align perfectly with the values and needs of the accounts that fall within the salesperson's niche. The plan should be firmly grounded in the following value-based selling principles:

- Prospects will only take time to buy something they definitely need or value; it is easier to sell to a prospective customer who perceives that he needs the product.
- The need to clearly and unequivocally differentiate one product's value over another's is absolutely essential with niche selling, because competition becomes very intense within a narrowly defined niche.
- A value-based sales plan needs to be very creative and must successfully connect with the deepest hopes and aspirations of every prospect called upon.
- A well-conceptualized plan that is focused on the most qualified prospects within a niche will yield the highest closing rates.

Automated Selling

American Hospital Supply was an early pioneer in automated selling (see Porter, 1985). They installed supply-order terminals in over three thousand of their client hospitals and health care centers. This strategy facilitated inventory checking and ordering and resulted in quicker deliveries. Competitors were almost completely blocked out. Now American Hospital Supply's competitors are also automating various aspects of their sales process, so new innovations in automated selling are necessary to retain a competitive advantage.

Some companies are electronically linked to their customers' computers via a modem. Their customers are typically subscribers to an on-line shopping service where they can browse, study, and even make purchases without ever having to visit a store or a showroom. H. Skip Weitzen, author of *Infopreneurs*, referred to this automated selling paradigm as the *Information Triangle*, which integrates the three most important requirements for rapid selling in the Information Age: (1) the computer, (2) the telephone, and (3) electronic funds transfer. This powerful sales paradigm has emerged as one of the main drivers of the Information Age, as Weitzen concludes:

> The Information Triangle offers business its next productivity breakthrough. As [managers] integrate the Information Triangle into traditional business functions, they can do more for less, increase the value of information, and *instantly* turn data into dollars. (1988, p. 12)

The Information Triangle is a unique way to penetrate, expand, and dominate a market niche. It takes competition to a new level by offering a streamlined and efficient sales distribution channel and a reliable and instant method of payment. For example, the major on-line information vendors provide access to unlimited computerized shopping. Customers can examine and order tens of thousands of items, often at discount prices. They can order instantly, pay for the selected items with their credit card, then choose from several rapid-delivery options.

One company that capitalizes on the Information Triangle is PC Flowers, which can be accessed on-line twenty-four hours a day through the Prodigy service. Customers can use PC Flowers to order seasonal flowers, balloons, fruit baskets, and the like by charging them to a major credit card. These gifts typically cost anywhere from $20 to $60. They are delivered the next day to almost any place in the United States. Purchasers can also request to send a card with a personalized message along with the gift.

Computerized shopping will probably create a major revolution in retailing because many Americans own a personal computer, nearly all have access to telephones, and most are holders of one or more credit cards. Moreover, electronic transactions lower the cost of entering and processing an order. When these costs shrink to almost nothing, smaller orders become more economical. The electronic transaction means greater precision in ordering, shorter response time, significant overhead reduction, and a savings in working capital.

Reducing Time Lags in the Sales Process

HSM sales managers must continually monitor and reduce the critical time intervals in the overall sales process. Some of the most common time intervals that I have identified are summarized in the following list. A brief review of this summary will reveal that there are many opportunities for HSM sales managers to speed up the overall selling cycle.

Initiating Events: (Beginning Point)	*Concluding Events:* (End Point)
1. Marketing promotions and sales campaigns are planned.	Promotions and campaigns reach prospective customers.
2. Corporate promotions are fulfilled and field-generated leads are received.	Leads are qualified and entered into a sales information management system.
3. Leads are assigned to the proper sales representative.	Leads are analyzed and a sales strategy is formulated.
4. Initial contact is made with a prospect and preliminary information is sent.	A meeting is scheduled with key decision makers authorized to buy.

5. A formal sales presentation is made.	Remaining unresolved prospect issues are identified and the next steps are agreed upon.
6. A follow-up meeting (by telephone or in person) is held.	Final obstacles to closing the sale are identified and resolved.
7. The prospective client decides to purchase the product or service.	Negotiations on price, follow-up services, and the like are successfully concluded.
8. The product or service is ordered.	The product or service is delivered.
9. The client uses and evaluates the product or service purchased.	Repeat sales and referrals ensue and service is provided when necessary.
10. The client develops new needs and encounters new problems to be solved.	New selling opportunities are identified and new sales activities are initiated.

A critical time lag is the number of minutes, days, hours, months, and so on between an initiating sales event and a concluding event. By establishing the average time lags for each of these eight stages of the sales process, the HSM sales manager takes the first step toward the goal of reducing these critical time intervals. If time-lag reductions occur in just a few of these steps, the sales staff moves closer to embracing a quick-response model.

For example, HSM sales managers can establish benchmarks for how long it usually takes their staff to (1) enter leads into a sales data base once they are received, (2) schedule a meeting with a potential customer once the initial contact has been made, (3) negotiate a successful price and service plan once the decision to purchase is made, and so on. The HSM sales managers can then work with staff to develop strategies for shortening these critical time lags in the future without jeopardizing the quality of the relationship with the prospects. In fact, it is very likely that customers will appreciate shortening the sales process, since their time will be saved and they will also benefit sooner from the product they purchased.

Hiring Successful Sales Professionals

HSM sales managers realize that they need to hire a high-caliber sales force if they plan to close sales faster. This is probably one of the quickest, most cost-effective strategies for developing a quick-response sales culture. Evaluating the effectiveness of a salesperson is always easy six to twelve months *after* the decision to hire is made. It's all in the sales revenue numbers. But predicting, before making a hiring decision, which candidate will be a top producer, benefit from sales training, and stay with the company long enough to make a difference is much more difficult. Therefore, most seasoned sales managers and human resources specialists have learned the hard way that they cannot rely on intuition when hiring a sales force. They need a more objective and scientifically based approach to hiring, such as professionally developed employment tests.

HSM sales managers use employment tests to help them eliminate the guesswork associated with hiring. Employment tests allow HSM sales managers to objectively screen candidates who possess the ambition, knowledge, and skills to successfully close sales in the shortest amount of time. One of the leading tests for hiring successful sales professionals—the *Sales Professional Assessment Inventory* (London House, 1992)—is described here to illustrate how a highly ambitious, skilled, and service-oriented sales force can maximize sales performance.

The Sales Professional Assessment Inventory

The Sales Professional Assessment Inventory (SPAI) provides a standardized measure of potential for success in sales, and is an ideal instrument for selecting outside or inside salespersons. The SPAI was primarily designed for personnel selection and placement, as well as for the identification of training needs. The SPAI assesses a candidate's interest, motivation, and skills necessary for success in the sales profession.

The SPAI provides HSM sales managers with a quick yet comprehensive assessment of a person's sales orientation and potential. Each subscale measures behavioral and psychological characteristics that have been found to be valid predictors of successful sales performance. Still, SPAI scores are usually interpreted in conjunction with other sources of information, such as past sales experience, work history, performance appraisal ratings, and job knowledge. The HSM sales manager never relies on just one source of information when making a hiring decision.

The SPAI accurately assesses all of the personality traits and motivational styles needed by successful sales professionals. The following list provides a brief description of low and high scorers on the SPAI. A description of a high scorer on the overall SPAI composite score is also provided. HSM sales managers prefer to hire sales professionals who score at the higher end of all the subscales and on the overall composite. The overall composite, the Sales Potential Index, summarizes the results from the twelve SPAI diagnostic scales and is used for making the final personnel selection or placement decisions.

Subscale Titles and Interpretation Guidelines for the SPAI

Low Scorers	*High Scorers*

1. Sales Work Experience

Have less sales education and training	Have more sales education and training
May need special training to reach sales potential	More likely to have previous sales experience

2. Sales Interest

Low interest in sales-related activities	High interest in sales-related activities

3. Sales Responsibility

Blame others for problems	Responsible for actions

Pessimistic   Optimistic
Believe in luck and fate   Believe in skill and hard work

4. Sales Orientation

Confused about goals   Self-knowledgeable
Low drive   Highly ambitious
Immature   Emotionally mature

5. Energy Level

Low energy   High energy
Low productivity   High productivity
Procrastinators   Get the job done

6. Self-Development

Inattentive in training   Very attentive in training
Little respect for trainers   Much respect for trainers

7. Sales Skills

Socially ill at ease   Socially at ease
Weak communication skills   Strong communication skills
Low self-confidence   High self-confidence

8. Sales Understanding

Lack awareness of typical   Good grasp of typical sales
  sales practices   practices
Unattuned to buyer needs   Appreciate logic behind stan-
                                  dard sales policies

9. Sales Arithmetic

Minimal math skills   Basic math skills for suc-
                                  cessful performance

Likely to make mistakes in   Handle account paperwork
  paperwork, particularly in   accurately
  totaling orders and other
  math-related tasks

10. Customer Service

Feel customers are demand-   Glad to be of assistance
  ing and ignorant

| Rude | Friendly |
| Avoid customers | Approach customers |

11. Business Ethics

| Feel that breaking company business policies is acceptable | Feel that breaking company business policies is unacceptable |
| Think that sales gains justify unethical or illegal business practices | Think there are no valid reasons for unethical or illegal business practices |

12. Job Stability

Easily dissatisfied with job	Tend to remain satisfied with job
Frequently plan to change jobs	Like the security of a stable job
Often think about quitting	Generally content with job conditions

Sales Potential Index

Low sales interest	High sales interest
Undependable and unproductive	Dependable and productive
Weak drive for success	Strong drive for success
Slow workers	Fast, energetic workers
Poor sales skills	Strong sales skills

Research Support

The SPAI is the product of extensive research by industrial psychologists and business consultants (see Behrens, 1992). The accuracy of each SPAI scale as a predictor of successful performance has been supported through a series of scientific studies. The SPAI also adheres to the Federal Uniform Guidelines, all state regulations, and the American Psychological Association's Standards for Educational and Psychological Testing. Summaries of a few of the major SPAI validation studies follow. These studies clearly highlight the benefits of using valid tests to hire top sales professionals. While these particular studies are specific to the SPAI, HSM sales managers typically will refuse to use *any* employment test or personnel selection procedure that is not well-grounded in scientific research.

Retail Electronics Industry. In this study, seventy-seven currently employed sales counselors at a chain retail electronics equipment company completed the SPAI. The Sales Potential Index was validated against supervisory ratings made at the same time and against employment outcomes and sales performance measures gathered over the following six months. The following results were obtained:

- The Sales Potential Index was significantly and positively related to better supervisor ratings in ten performance dimensions: courtesy and tact, customer service, job interest, responsibility, maturity, adaptability, energy level, sales knowledge, product knowledge, and sales performance.
- The Sales Potential Index was significantly related to four employment outcomes: higher retention rate by supervisors, better records of attendance, better records of punctuality, and lower turnover rates.
- Sales counselors recommended by the SPAI had gross revenues almost $30,000 higher for a six-month period, on the average, than those not recommended. Also, the recommended group had over $3,000 more in average service contract revenues for the same period than the group not recommended.
- The top 10 percent of recommended sales counselors had gross revenues over $70,000 higher on average, and about $6,500 more in service contract revenues, than the group not recommended. These results are summarized in Figure 12.1.

Retail Super Stores. In this study, 160 currently employed salespeople at a Super Store retail chain completed SPAI. Salespeople were drawn from store departments specializing in furniture, large appliances, and personal computers. The com-

Figure 12.1. Retail Electronics Industry Average Sales Revenue by SPAI Status.

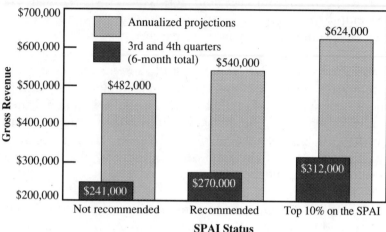

posite Sales Potential Index was again validated against monthly individual sales figures and supervisory ratings of performance. The following results were obtained:

- The Sales Potential Index was significantly related to higher average gross profit revenues and higher average commission earnings.
- The Sales Potential Index was significantly related to better supervisor ratings on three performance dimensions: sales performance, customer service, and job interest and motivation, as well as on a combined supervisor rating of general sales effectiveness.
- Salespeople recommended by the SPAI had average gross profit revenues over $7,000 higher than those not recommended during a four-month period. The expected annual gain in gross profit revenue for each new salesperson hired with the SPAI is estimated at $3,900 annually. These results are summarized in Figure 12.2.

Food Distribution Company. In this study, fifty-one currently employed territory managers at a national food distribution com-

Figure 12.2. Retail Super Stores Average Gross Profits by SPAI Status.

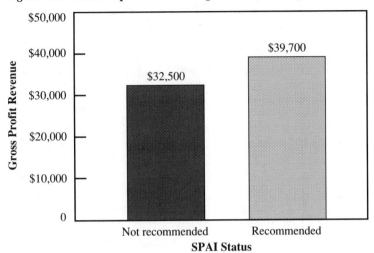

pany completed the SPAI. The composite Sales Potential Index was validated against year-to-date sales revenues through ten months and also against supervisory ratings of performance. The following results were documented:

- The Sales Potential Index was significantly related to better supervisory ratings of overall sales performance.
- Territory managers recommended by the SPAI generated over $350,000 more in year-to-date sales revenues, on the average, than those not recommended, which was a significantly greater amount.
- Territory managers in the top 10 percent of those recommended by the SPAI generated 100 percent more in total sales revenues, on the average, than those not recommended. These findings are summarized in Figure 12.3.

Developing High-Speed Selling Skills

HSM sales managers realize that the most successful salespeople have different levels of skills and abilities from the less successful sales personnel. More importantly, these managers realize that

Figure 12.3. Food Distribution Company Average Sales Revenue by SPAI Status.

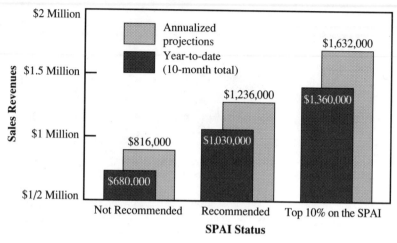

nearly all of the critically important sales skills can be taught, and any unsuccessful sales habits can usually be avoided or unlearned. The following list cites examples of sales styles used by both fast-responding and slow-responding salespeople. The HSM sales manager makes sure that his staff knows about, endorses, and implements these attitudes and skills at all times.

Fast Responders	*Slow Responders*
Attitudes and Abilities	
Study sales strategies	Avoid self-development programs
Enjoy selling	Feel selling is just a job
Highly responsible and energized	Undependable and lazy
Strong business math skills	Weak business math skills
Strong service orientation	Dislike customer contacts
Quickly establish trust and rapport	Manipulative and untrustworthy
Exemplary questioning and probing skills	Awkward interviewers and communicators

Fast learners	Slow learners
Excellent listening skills	Inattentive and interrupt customers
Sell value	Sell pure price instead of value

Sales Skills

Use streamlined and focused selling systems	Use complicated and confusing selling systems
Prospect targeted customer groups	Use unfocused prospecting strategy
Use effective phone selling skills	Use phone inappropriately
Avoid job stress and burnout	Cannot cope with sales pressure
Assertively take charge of sales process	Are intimidated by customers
Quickly determine customers' needs and preferences	Do not know clients' needs or how product could provide value
Use a strategic sales plan	Do not plan effectively
Are prepared for all sales calls	Are unprepared and disorganized
Are able to diplomatically and persuasively overcome objections	Are intimidated by objections and argue with or withdraw from customers
Keep all appointments and follow up on commitments	Fail to follow up and miss appointments
Have strong closing skills	Have weak closing style
Utilize computer-based sales tools and software	Do not utilize computer-based sales technology

Create a Buying Climate

In 1990, Saul Gellerman published research in the *Harvard Business Review* that proved the seller must create an optimal buying climate to better ensure the success of a sales call. Gellerman identified three important factors that create an optimal buying climate and that ultimately determine whether a customer is predisposed to buy.

1. *Appropriate discussion focus.* Gellerman found that if the customer takes the seller seriously, then the customer will engage in less small talk, and focus his discussions on purchasing. When the seller exhibits both competence and usefulness to the purchaser, she creates a climate in which she is taken seriously. Strong salespeople learn how to quickly establish their credibility during the first few contacts with the buyer in order to be taken seriously at all times. In addition, skilled sales professionals know how to steer the conversation back to the sales task whenever it drifts for any length of time into the area of small talk.

2. *Time management during sales calls.* Gellerman discovered that for successful salespeople time management during the sales call is very different than for less successful salespeople. Time management while on a call has a profound impact on the buying climate. Customers who are ready to buy allow no interruptions during the sales call, do not waste time with excessive small talk, and do not keep the salesperson waiting. The successful salesperson will reschedule a sales presentation if she experiences constant interruptions, long waits, and a continual steering of the conversation to small talk. Less effective salespeople will tolerate the interruptions, wait for long periods of time, and accommodate small talk. It is no surprise that they typically fail to get orders during such nonproductive visits. High producers know that it is usually better to immediately move on in search of interested customers who are currently eager to buy, and to return to the distracted prospects at a later time. However, top producers make sure that they courteously withdraw from the distracted customers to avoid burning bridges and missing future opportunities.

3. *Sticking to the fundamentals.* Finally, Gellerman points out that the seller's job is extremely difficult and full of rejections. Gellerman found that top salespeople are able to cope with rejection, while weaker salespeople are often unable to repeatedly bounce back. Slow-response sellers try to maladap-

tively cope with rejection by working at half speed, taking excessively long lunches, and cutting corners by neglecting the fundamentals of their craft. Top salespeople persevere, stick to their fundamentals, and confidently wait out a run of bad luck. HSM sales managers realize that they must continuously coach their people to persevere in the face of rejection, so that buyers are not forced to interact with a disillusioned and burned out sales representative.

Establish Trust

Successful salespeople know how to develop trusting, long-term relationships that are beneficial to both the seller and the buyer. Effective sellers repeatedly communicate the message that it is good business to trust them, and then they do everything in their power to never let their clients down. They avoid deceptive tricks of the trade, since prospective clients can quickly see through them and would lose trust and respect for them as sales professionals. The most trusted salespeople follow through on everything they say and promise. Salespeople win respect, repeat sales, referrals, and trust when they consistently deliver what they promise.

Ask for Referrals

Referrals are the key to a successful career in sales. High-performing salespeople do not base their success solely on the leads generated by their company's marketing and advertising efforts. Instead, they rely on additional sources of leads, such as satisfied customers. Successful salespeople boldly and confidently ask their customer base for leads, and then they ask those leads for leads, and so on. For example, if ten extremely satisfied customers each give a salesperson five potential leads, and if 50 percent of these new referrals each in turn provide five leads, then the salesperson has quickly generated seventy-five leads as promising sources of new revenue and referrals. This is how sales professionals can rapidly build their client base exponentially. Quick-responding sales professionals carry 3×5 index cards or very small electronic organizers or palmtop computers at all times to immediately record any referrals they receive from clients, prospects, friends, and chance acquaintances.

Develop Persuasive Phone Skills

The most successful sales professionals see the phone as a major competitive resource. These professionals have developed persuasive phone selling skills. They consistently and tirelessly make their calls one after another and avoid any form of procrastination. The following is a list of some of the phone techniques used by successful and less successful salespeople. (Special personnel selection tests, such as the London House Telemarketing Applicant Inventory, 1991, help companies hire people with promising telephone selling skills.)

Successful Salespeople

- Plan ahead for each phone call
- Talk to the right person(s)
- Speak clearly and use common words
- Are always courteous
- Quickly build rapport
- Set goals for their call (such as to get an appointment)
- Have effective sales scripts to fall back on
- Take succinct and meaningful notes
- Are relaxed and unhurried
- Want results now, yet are willing to make callbacks
- Call back prospects and clients at the times they suggest
- Take few breaks between calls

Unsuccessful Salespeople

- Are very unorganized
- Do not have an outline of their goals for the call
- Argue with prospects/customers on the phone
- Extend negative conversations
- Are unable to establish rapport
- Procrastinate between calls

- Forget details of their calls
- Speak unclearly and use jargon
- Come across as pushy
- Annoy customers with their impatient manner
- Want results now but ignore callback requests

Avoid the Stress of Selling

HSM sales managers know the importance of teaching their sales staff to avoid the major stressors in selling. *Stressors* are typically defined as unpleasant and extremely trying situations that lead to feelings of discomfort, upset, anger, and anxiety. The sales professional often encounters stressors that are different from those of other professions. For example, losing an old and valued customer and having very few active prospects are two of the most distressing events a sales representative can experience.

If the stress of selling is not properly handled, the sales professional begins to slow down due to the extreme emotional and physical exhaustion known as burnout. The following is a list of some of the most commonly identified sales stressors that need to be confronted:

Job-Related Stressors	*Customer-Related Stressors*
• Losing an important sale	• Losing an old and valued customer
• Arguing with sales manager or colleagues	• Losing a key new sale
• Working excessively long hours	• Prospect being late for or missing a meeting
• Being late for or missing an appointment	• Making a sales presentation to nondecision makers
• Making errors in judgment (such as quoting wrong price)	• Customer repeatedly requesting price concessions
• Preparing for a tough sales call	• Inattentive prospect
	• Client complaining about slow deliveries

- Poor personal production
- Being assigned a new sales territory
- Receiving a very tough sales quota
- Strong competition
- Learning a new product line
- Inadequate support
- Low company morale
- Insufficient sales training
- Excessive paperwork
- Being asked to engage in unethical behavior
- Getting a territory with low potential
- Job-related family pressures

- Inadequate service provided to your accounts
- Customers continually complaining about your products
- Customers making unrealistic demands
- Having major misunderstanding with a customer

Computerizing Sales Management

HSM sales managers know they must skillfully adapt to using the latest advances in computer hardware and software if they are to optimally manage their sales staff. In fact, most traditional sales managers already use software for such applications as budgeting, forecasting annual sales, making interim sales analyses, tracking expenses, and determining commissions. Most traditional sales managers also use some basic form of account management software. However, HSM sales managers try to use a computer for more than just the basic sales applications just mentioned. They might also use computers to better profile and categorize prospects, plan and estimate the future earnings contributions of different sales strategies, determine the profit margins by account for different product mixes, and analyze and improve their staff's time management skills. In brief, while traditional sales managers might use computers to merely keep track of sales and related account activity, HSM sales managers are more concerned with using computers for strategic purposes, to ultimately improve corporate earnings.

Thayer Taylor, senior editor of *Sales and Marketing Management*, published a six-month study in 1991 in which he interviewed scores of sales and marketing software users and software vendors. He also reviewed over eight hundred sales and marketing software packages. This application software could be grouped under the following general categories:

Sales Software	*Marketing Software*
Account management	Advertising
Electronic mail	Direct marketing
Expense tracking	Market analysis
Remote order entry	Market research
Contact management	Marketing management
Hiring and training	Marketing planning
Lead tracking	Product management
Territory mapping	Telemarketing
Time management	Trade show marketing
Sales negotiations	Zip code tracking
Pricing and bidding	Charting
Sales analysis	Desk-top publishing
Sales forecasting	Graphics
Sales management	Meeting planning
Sales planning	Project management
Sales presentations	Statistical analysis
Territory management	Word processing

Taylor and his staff found that sales professionals were more likely to use software if it would quickly lead to greater sales productivity. That is, salespeople want software that helps them to make more sales immediately, not software that slows them down by turning them into data entry clerks for other departments. Sales professionals do not get excited about gathering input data for the entire corporation.

Currently, one of the most successful software packages for sales professionals is contact management software. This software primarily provides sales assistance and customer support. Contact management software stores and instantly retrieves all of the sales professional's most critical day-to-day information, such as prospects and clients he is currently working with, key presentations he needs to make, summaries of what happened at the latest sales presentations and why, and a description of the next steps in the sales process. If a sales representative gets a call from a prospect, he can courteously put that person on hold for twenty seconds, call up the prospect's record on the computer screen, and have all of the important account information at his fingertips (for example, the caller's position, degree of influence, purchasing plans, and product preferences). Having this crucial information at one's fingertips increases the odds of quickly meeting the prospect's needs. Some of the major features of the leading contact management software packages are summarized as follows:

Administrative Features

- Word processing
- Prewritten memos, letters, proposals, and contracts
- Day-at-a-glance and week-at-a-glance calendars
- Calculator and graphic functions
- Activity planner and "to-do" lists
- Miscellaneous accounting windows (order entry, inventory tracking, accounts payable)
- Auto mileage diary and expense tracker
- On-line product catalogs and sales support literature
- Lead and quota tracking
- Billing and collection tracking
- Spell checkers

Client Contact Features

- Prospect files
- Comprehensive client contact records (call reports)
- Sales records and forecasts
- Rolodex-type screen displays
- Automatic phone dialers
- Electronic mail access
- Alarms tied into scheduled phone calls, meetings, and appointments
- Mailing list manager and envelope generator
- Client logs and "scratch pads" for note taking
- Tickler files
- Record linking
- Precall plans

- Mainframe interfaces
- Security functions
- User-definable fields
- Remote order entry

The HSM sales manager also tries to equip his sales staff with a very fast laptop, notebook, or palmtop computer. In fact, Taylor reported that in 1991 36.2 percent of the 1,700 salespeople he surveyed in a national study used laptop computers, while only 11.4 percent used desktop computers. Approximately 11.2 percent used both. Therefore, the preference seems to be for the small computers. In addition, approximately 80 percent of the salespeople reported productivity gains attributed directly to their computer skills and resources. The computers helped sales professionals provide more timely answers on the status of orders and shipments, professional-looking sales presentations, faster turnaround in written sales proposals, timely and accurate call reports and expense reports, and frequent and accurate sales forecasts for their accounts and territories.

Conclusion

HSM sales managers strive to establish quick-response sales cultures at their companies. They gravitate toward streamlined, niche-oriented, automated models of selling, instead of overly complicated and time-consuming systems. They try to meet their prospects' needs and expectations by selling value over specific product features. HSM sales managers try to ensure that their sales plan is tightly aligned with the marketing plan, and they always try to reduce manageable time lags in the sales process.

HSM sales managers also use professionally developed sales tests to accurately select the most qualified sales candidates. They utilize the latest sales management software packages to budget, forecast sales, track sales finances (such as expenses and commissions), profile markets, and establish optimal sales strategies. Finally, they equip their staffs with laptop, notebook, or palmtop computers with contact management software installed on the system. HSM sales managers utilize the latest advances in technology with one goal in mind — to establish a sales staff that generates more sales, at less cost, in a shorter amount of time.

Chapter Thirteen

Retain Satisfied Customers

The most successful companies stay ahead of their competitors because they adopt the attitude that the customer is supreme. Companies that place nearly all their emphasis on attracting new customers typically fail to give the necessary attention to their loyal customer base. And this misplaced emphasis hurts where it counts the most, the bottom line. HSM managers know that it costs five times as much to acquire a new customer as it does to service and retain an existing one. Many traditional managers fail even to acknowledge the cost of losing an existing customer. The following summary illustrates the financial impact of losing customers at a superstore that sells food, clothes, appliances, and pharmaceuticals. The estimates are based on a formula developed by Laura Liswood, a management consultant who specializes in customer-retention strategies, and author of *Serving Them Right: Innovative and Powerful Customer Retention Strategies*.

1. Total superstore clients lost per year   1,000
2. Average annual purchases per customer $2,500
3. Total revenue $2,500,000
4. Profit lost: $2.5 million × 15 percent
   profit margin $375,000
5. Related administration costs $20,000
6. Total bottom line cost $395,000

Never Neglect Customers

Tom Peters, well-known author and business consultant, opens a chapter of his book *Thriving on Chaos: A Management Revolution* with the following message from Fred Smith, founder of Federal Express:

> The United States has been terrible as it applies to customer service. When the history of American business is written, I think that's going to be the most incredible part of the historian's view of what we did during the sixties and seventies. I mean, we killed the goose that laid the golden egg. Somehow, management let employees believe the customers weren't important. (1987, p. 89)

Smith's contention that management minimized or even neglected the concerns of the customer did not go unnoticed by the buying public. Every day, all across the United States, millions of consumers talk about those companies with whom they do business. For companies that consistently satisfy their customers' needs, this is good news. But for those businesses that cut corners on customer service, this is bad news indeed, for the following reasons:

- The average customer who feels wronged will tell eight to sixteen people. About 10 percent will tell more than twenty people about their bad experience.
- About 95 percent of those who have negative experiences will not buy at that establishment again, unless something is done to make things right.
- About 90 percent of wronged customers will stay with the business if an attempt is made to resolve their problems. (Adapted from Cleary, 1991)

Consumer research has found that the vast majority of dissatisfied customers will talk to just about anyone *except* the company itself. Only one in twenty-six customers will actually complain to management about bad service. When a disgruntled customer walks out the door, the company may never see that person again—and management will probably never know why. HSM managers strive to provide quality products and services that are backed by strong customer service, so they can avoid this disgruntled customer syndrome.

Establish Service Standards

HSM managers are committed to building a winning customer service team. They design service-oriented jobs, they select job applicants who have strong service orientations, they train their staffs to provide exemplary service in a timely manner, and they ensure full management support for all service-related activities. Most importantly, they develop and communicate written service standards that employees can use to focus their efforts. Service standards provide a sense of purpose, they keep employees focused on service goals, and they lead to fair performance reviews. HSM managers strive to set service goals in the following areas:

1. *Timing.* Prompt service is needed at all times, yet the customer should never feel rushed. Service providers should learn to anticipate customer needs, so they are never caught off guard by a customer's request.

2. *Flow.* There should always be a smooth flow of products and services to customers. Backups and breakdowns should be avoided at all costs.

3. *Flexibility.* Service delivery systems should never be overly rigid. They should be convenient to customers and flexible enough to accommodate unusual requests from time to time.

4. *Communication.* Effective communication is needed between service-oriented employees and their customers. Service-related messages need to be communicated in a timely, accurate, and consistent manner.

5. *Feedback.* Service providers must assess what their customers are thinking at all times. This customer feedback must be routinely and effectively collected, analyzed, and acted on. Strategies for obtaining feedback include brief person-to-person meetings, phone calls, focus groups, mail surveys, suggestion boxes, newsletters, and feedback forms.

6. *Style.* Strong service providers are attentive, exhibit a well-groomed personal appearance, and have a positive attitude toward customers in general. They work well under pressure and are outstanding problem solvers. They are tactful and avoid behaviors that can alienate customers. Finally, they know how to sell their company's services, so they can retain and expand their customers' business.

In brief, HSM managers establish clear and specific service standards. They set standards that are concise, realistic, and measurable. They use standards that are agreed upon by all affected employees. HSM managers establish service standards that come as close as possible to zero problems. Finally, employee compensation is tied into successful adherence to these standards, and no deviation from them is accepted.

Clients Must Perceive Quality Service

HSM managers know that providing good service is simply not enough. In order for a transaction to be successful, the customer must *perceive* that he is receiving good service. Customers come to a company because they have needs. It is up to that company's employees to determine what their customers need and then to successfully meet those needs according to the customers' expectations.

Customers will remain loyal to the company only as long as they believe the level of service being offered meets their needs. No longer satisfied, they will quickly go elsewhere. Therefore, HSM managers constantly train and motivate their staffs to use the following procedures to reinforce the customer's perception of strong service (see Bowen, Chase, & Cummings, 1990).

1. *Prompt attention.* Customers do not like to wait or feel as though they are being ignored. For instance, if a customer is ignored at a checkout counter while the service representative chats with coworkers, the customer feels unimportant. If the employee is too busy when a customer walks up, he should simply smile and say, "I'll be with you in just a minute."

2. *Reliability.* Customers want their shopping experience to be as convenient and hassle-free as possible. They want to know that when they walk into a store they will find what they need or quickly get directions on where to find it. They also expect that if a company representative makes a promise, he will keep it. If he is unable to keep the promise, he should let the customer know ahead of time, so the customer will not be inconvenienced.

3. *Personal attention.* No one likes to feel like a number, or just another customer; but with today's technology, that can sometimes be a problem. For example, customers who receive mass-produced letters in the mail that read "Dear Friend" usually do not read them. But the same customers will rarely throw out original letters that begin with "Dear Mrs. Smith" or "Dear Mike."

4. *Customer appreciation.* Customers like to feel as though their business is appreciated. And that is exactly what a service employee communicates to customers when he responds to their needs enthusiastically. Again, if a customer is ignored, he feels unappreciated, and he will probably take his business elsewhere.

5. *Knowledgeable staff.* Customers expect service-oriented employees to be very knowledgeable about the products and

services they are selling. For example, in today's high-tech industries, customers must often rely on service employees to help
them make choices. A customer calling a travel agent must rely
on the agent to know how to get the best price on an airline
ticket from a reliable carrier. If the travel agent does not get the
best price, then his relationship with the customer can be seriously damaged.

6. *Empathy.* Customers want to be listened to and understood. This is particularly true when they have a problem or are
confused. If the customer service employee acts as though he
could care less, the customer will leave feeling that the company
does not really care. When a customer explains a problem, the
service provider must always respond with something like, "I
understand why you might feel that way. Let's explore how we
can jointly resolve this issue to your satisfaction." HSM managers
know that empathic listening skills can quickly turn a dissatisfied customer into a loyal one.

The Service Promise

HSM managers communicate clear service messages to their
customers so that they know exactly what level of service they
will receive. For example, Jill Cleary (1991) reported that an
owner of a dairy store in Norwalk, Connecticut, has what he calls
his "rock of commitment." He chiseled the well-known service
slogan "The customer is always right" into a three-ton rock next
to the front door of his store. His customers are not confused
about his service promise. In fact, the owner quickly built his
business from a mom-and-pop operation to a company with
annual sales close to $100 million. He attributes the bulk of his
success to his unusually well-executed customer service policies
that start, literally, with the promise on the rock at his front door.

If this is the era in which the customer is supreme, it is also
the era of the "we care" service promise. The promise implied
behind these marketing slogans is quality service. Consider
these messages:

- "A special little hotel at a comfortable little price," from
  Courtyard by Marriott, emphasizes the unique atmosphere

at a line of moderately priced rooms offered to business travelers and families.

- "Your satisfaction is our goal," says J.C. Penney, giving the impression that service is the major focus.
- "Carry the caring card—the card that cares for the Olympic team," from Blue Cross/Blue Shield, attempts to convey several meanings of "care" in only a few words.
- "We'll keep the light on for you," from Motel 6, sends the homey message that budget-class hospitality can also be high quality.
- "You're in good hands at Allstate" has worked well for many years to give consumers the impression that their worries are over.
- "At Radisson Hotels you're worth waiting for" implies that reservations are held no matter how late the customer arrives.

HSM managers encourage the use of personalized service messages that effectively communicate to customers that they will receive individualized attention. Messages that imply each customer will be treated as an important individual are fast becoming the norm in all service businesses. Customers expect to immediately receive the quality service the company promises or else they will quickly become dissatisfied. So the company's image as a strong service provider rests not only on whether it can clearly communicate its promise, but also on whether it can deliver.

Some organizations deliver on their service promises so well they have become known as customer service superstars (see Cleary, 1991). American Express, for example, retains a loyal and profitable customer base despite intense competition from other credit providers. Many experts contend that American Express's customer service policy is the primary reason. Similarly, L.L. Bean, based in Freeport, Maine, built a mail-order empire by providing outstanding service. Fidelity Investors Centers of Boston is a service leader because of its policy that any customer's problem can be solved, and they will go to any length to do it. Marriott, long known as a service superstar, opened their Courtyard division after surveying frequent business travelers. They designed these moderately priced hotels to meet service requirements specifically expressed by these targeted customers—rather than on requirements they assumed the targeted customers wanted.

The Service-Oriented Mission Statement

HSM managers have long known that customer service depends on the high-level performance of those who actually deal with customers on a front-line, day-to-day basis. While the commitment to excellence may begin at the top, it must be implemented by all employees at every level. For example, in 1983, senior staff at Embassy Suites, a subsidiary of Holiday Inns, developed a service-oriented mission statement (see Cleary, 1991). In addition to clearly defined objectives for superior service, the mission statement promised, "We will be the easiest hotel company to do business with."

At Embassy Suites, almost all day-to-day decisions are made on the basis of keeping that promise. All positions are filled by people who receive in-depth customer service training. The breakfast cook, the housekeepers, and the front desk employees all deliver the Embassy Suites commitment to service. And when employees do a good job they are recognized in tangible ways. A fast-promotion track is only one way employees are rewarded for service. Embassy Suites also established a special recognition program to single out employees who give outstanding service. Outstanding employees are chosen by their peers, so the recognition is even more significant. Finally, all employees are trained to make quick decisions to keep guests happy. HSM managers are aware that needing to overcome a lot of bureaucratic red tape to solve small customer problems only leads to delays and a continuous chain of disgruntled customers.

Land's End, a highly successful mail-order business, builds its service philosophy around the fact that most customers never talk with anyone at top management levels (see Cleary, 1991). Therefore, the service-oriented mission statement prepared by Gary Comer, the entrepreneur who started Land's End, is based on the idea that quality service begins with management, yet ultimately depends on the in-depth training given to the hundreds of phone agents who are on duty every day.

Every Land's End phone agent has approximately seventy-two hours of service-related training before going to work on the phones. Each agent participates in an additional twenty hours of supplemental service training every year thereafter. Phone agents quickly learn that the mechanical job of taking orders over the telephone is only a small part of what they can do to establish a loyal and profitable customer base. Comer's attitude is that Land's End is in business to do whatever it takes to satisfy a customer, and therefore he wants his company to build a long-term relationship with a customer, not simply make a one-time sale.

Handling Customer Complaints

Paradoxically, customers who immediately complain about a problem, even if it is never fully resolved, are more likely to do business with the company again than those who never voice their complaints. Most customers who voice their complaints will do business with the company in the future if they feel a good-faith effort has been made to resolve their problem. The most common complaints that need resolution in business today include:

- *Poor service/apathy.* The service representative does not live up to the customer's perceived performance standards, or projects an attitude that he does not care about the customer.
- *Long waits.* The customer is forced to wait too long in lines, is put on hold for too long, or has to wait for a service representative who is simply doing other things. Not having products in stock is another form of making customers wait.
- *Rude service providers.* The customer encounters service providers who are not helpful and who may even be sarcastic or hostile.
- *Billing problems.* When the customer receives his bill, he

discovers that it is not for the amount that the salesperson quoted. Other errors can also be present.

- *Poor communications.* Customers are not kept informed in language they can easily understand. Customers are not listened to.
- *Unknowledgeable service people.* The service provider does not know enough about his company's products or services to resolve a customer's problem promptly and properly.
- *Untrustworthy employees.* The customer interacts with a dishonest, unreliable, or overly manipulative employee.
- *Difficulty with returns.* The service employee is uncooperative when the customer attempts to return or exchange merchandise.
- *The runaround.* When the customer tries to get help, he is passed from employee to employee without getting quick attention or ever getting ultimate satisfaction.
- *Poor return on investment.* The customer realizes that the product or service he purchased never had the impact that it was supposed to have.

Quickly Resolve Customer Problems

All customers want the same thing: to find a solution to their needs. They also want to have a positive relationship with the company that provides the solution. If customers did not care, they would not even bother to tell the company that they had a problem with a product or service; they just would never return. Therefore, HSM managers know the importance of teaching their people how to solve customer problems by using the following techniques:

- *Prize the customer.* Customers who voice a complaint or problem must always be prized by the service provider. These customers are actually providing the company with an opportunity to strengthen itself by improving quality and fine-tuning the operations.
- *Listen empathically.* Let the customer explain exactly what the problem is. Do not interrupt unless it is to clarify a point or

to gain additional information. Let the customer know that you understand how he feels about the service issue. The customer will be reassured and encouraged to believe that you could possibly help solve his problem.

- *Be open.* Do not begin the discussion thinking that the customer is wrong. He may or may not be! Do not say anything that may be interpreted as resistance or that would only aggravate the customer. Instead, say something like, "I'm sorry you've experienced this problem. Let me get some additional information from you so that we can quickly resolve this matter to your satisfaction."

- *Identify the problem.* Question the customer until you understand exactly what is wrong. Find out what the customer would like to see happen. You may discover that what he wants is actually less than the settlement you are willing to offer.

- *Be prompt.* If you have the authority to make a settlement and if what the customer is asking for is fair, do not delay with your offer. The quicker you settle the problem, the more likely the customer is to come back. If possible, settle the problem during the first contact. Prolonging the situation only makes the customer feel more frustrated. If the solution takes a long time, be sure to keep the customer fully informed.

- *Say thank you.* No matter how difficult the customer's transaction, it is always a good idea to say "Thank you." By thanking the customer, you let him know that you care and you want to be helpful. Also, let the customer know that the company will try to prevent the same mistake from happening in the future.

Service Recovery

Ron Zemke, co-author with Karl Albrecht of *Service America,* explains that if a customer's experience with a business deviates from expectation, a customer quickly notices it—and remembers. When the service received is less than what was promised,

Zemke labels it a *breakdown*. However, there is usually a chance to make things right; Zemke calls this *recovery*.

According to Zemke, there are two distinct levels of service breakdown. The first is the stage he calls *annoyance*. It is characterized by the mild irritation customers feel when service is slightly below what was expected. The second level, however, is *victimization*. A victimized customer feels that he or she has been seriously inconvenienced by the service short-fall. Both degrees of service breakdown can lead to lost customers if they are not handled properly.

Fortunately, HSM managers have learned that if the business responds quickly and with a strong effort to remedy the service problem, then full service recovery is possible. Zemke delineated five critical dimensions of a successful service recovery plan.

1. *Immediate apology.* Obvious? Maybe so. But, according to Zemke, this simple gesture is often overlooked. Furthermore, an apology means more when it is personal and comes from the service provider in the form of an "I" statement rather than the editorial "we." An apology acknowledges that the breakdown in service occurred.
2. *Urgent reinstatement.* Customers must believe that those delivering the service are doing everything possible to put things right. A sense of urgency along with an apology is often sufficient if a customer is merely annoyed.
3. *Empathy.* According to Zemke, mere sympathy is a sign of insincerity, whereas empathy implies that the dissatisfied customer is being dealt with, not just the problem. When service personnel are effectively empathetic, customers will feel that their needs and concerns are being heard. Customers will sense that the business cares about the consequences of the service breakdown.
4. *Symbolic atonement.* This is a way of telling the dissatisfied customer that the company wants to make amends — for instance, with complimentary drinks on a delayed flight or a special discount on future purchases. Such gestures may cost far less than the permanent loss of the customer.

5. *Follow-up.* A follow-up gesture or phone call to the customer after the company has resolved the problem is a way of providing closure. It puts the matter to rest and affirms the message "We care." (Adapted from Albrecht & Zemke, 1985)

Provide Team-Oriented Solutions

In order to get a customer's problem resolved quickly, a service provider must usually work closely with other people in his company. How he interacts with these people will determine how quickly and successfully the problem gets resolved. In dealing with others, the HSM managers should use the following guidelines:

- *Explain what solving the problem means to the customer.* Tell the other company employees everything you know about the problem and what the implications are to the customer. For example, telling someone in your order department that Mr. Jones needs the item shipped immediately for health reasons will probably get the order clerk to respond a little more quickly than simply saying, "The customer wants it delivered now." If the order clerk understands the exact nature of the problem, he can respond to it better.
- *Do not be accusatory.* Regardless of the situation, never approach another employee and accuse him of causing the problem with the customer, or even imply that it is his fault. The HSM manager knows that his main goal is to satisfy the customer's complaint, and pointing the finger is not going to help in the long run.
- *Say thank you.* Being courteous to the people you work with is just as important as being courteous to your customers. All employees like to be treated with respect. It is also essential if you expect their full, timely, and ongoing cooperation in the future.

Account Retention

One of the most important duties of service professionals is to retain accounts. This is especially important for companies that

expect substantial repeat business from their current customers. It is typically the service professional's responsibility to
quickly identify dissatisfied accounts who are at greatest risk of
dropping a program, discontinuing a service, or eventually
changing vendors.

Unfortunately, most service representatives have only limited information or "gut feelings" about whether serious trouble
is brewing on an account. Most service professionals do not use
an objective, standardized, and accurate procedure for predicting the likelihood that an account is at risk of being lost. Yet if
service professionals could quickly and accurately determine
the risk level of an account, they could begin to immediately
address the problem areas and perhaps save the account in the
process.

I developed the Account Retention Index (ARI) for this
exact purpose. The ARI (see Jones & Werner, 1988) is a twenty-
eight-item checklist designed to quickly identify those accounts
that may be experiencing difficulties with a vendor's product or
service. Service representatives are asked to truthfully complete
the ARI based on their perceptions of and experiences with a
particular account. The ARI prompts service professionals to
acknowledge the presence of twenty-eight signs and symptoms
that usually characterize problematic, unstable accounts, and
that are not present with trouble-free, stable accounts.

The twenty-eight ARI items basically assess three dimensions of account stability: *product effectiveness,* through a series of
questions that assess how effective and valuable a product has
been for the customer; *client commitment,* through an assessment
of how pleased a client is with the vendor's product, staff, and
overall methods of doing business; and *client enthusiasm,* through
a set of questions that assess whether a customer is still excited
about a product or product boredom has set in. A few sample
items from the ARI are presented in the following list.

ARI Sample Subscale Items

Product Effectiveness

- The account is not sure if the product is impacting their
  bottom line.

- The client complains that the product is not working.
- There are increasing complaints about support services in general.
- Client begins to share specific incidents about where the product failed.

Client Commitment

- The company is looking at other vendors' products.
- There is a decrease in product usage at some units but not at all units.
- The account is resisting paying bills.
- Client begins to question or raise issues regarding the price of the product.

Client Enthusiasm

- The account does not agree to be a reference.
- Critics or nonsupporters of the program begin to be identified.
- Client becomes more impersonal on the phone.
- Client is not returning phone calls.

The service provider's responses to the twenty-eight ARI items are then computer-scored. This overall score is called the *Stability Quotient* and ranges from 0 to 100. This score reflects the level of confidence that the service provider has about whether an account is in good standing. In one study with sixty accounts, the ARI score was approximately 96 percent accurate in differentiating a group of unstable accounts from a group of stable ones. HSM managers can use systems like the ARI to accurately assess and resolve a client's problems before it is too late. These managers must make sure the product is providing the expected return on investment, and that the client remains highly enthusiastic about and committed to the vendor and its products.

Making the Service Vision a Reality

HSM managers know that as markets tighten up and competition increases, the success of a business often depends on how well it delivers on its service promise. HSM managers diligently implement a winning customer service plan by:

- Being aware that service is everyone's job and that the service message starts at the top.
- Developing and keeping a service promise; making sure that their employees constantly convey service as the Number One value of their organization.
- Putting a plan in place for quick recovery from service breakdowns.
- Finding a way to quickly satisfy the needs of all customers within a targeted market niche.
- Making efforts to hire service-oriented employees by screening applicants carefully.
- Providing ongoing customer service training programs that work.
- Assessing employee and customer attitudes. (Nothing gives HSM managers a more accurate picture of employee morale and customer satisfaction than a professionally developed survey. The survey should be conducted regularly and managers need to respond to the results.)
- Recognizing and rewarding employees who provide exceptional customer service; letting them know that their efforts are extremely important to the company.
- Looking at ways that certain service functions can be automated and computerized to improve convenience, increase reliability of service delivery, and eventually contain costs.
- Using standardized questionnaires to determine the odds of retaining or losing key accounts.

Conclusion

The era in which the customer is supreme is likely to be with us for a long time. Therefore, HSM managers will need to develop, implement, and constantly upgrade effective customer service programs. The service programs should be based on sound hiring, training, and motivational practices and should lead to a more satisfied group of employees. The HSM manager's ultimate goal is to maintain an established customer base as well as to attract new customers who are seeking reliable, service-oriented companies.

Chapter Fourteen

Keep Financial Score

Managers who understand finance often make better business decisions than their less knowledgeable counterparts. Time-based managers understand basic financial terms and concepts. They understand how to analyze and interpret an income statement and balance sheet, according to the terms in the following list:

Income Statements and Balance Sheets:
The Basic Accounting Equations

Income Statement
Net sales – Expenses = Net income (Net loss)

- *Net sales.* Cash or credit sales, minus returns and allowances that result in an increase in assets (cash or accounts receivable).

- *Expenses.* The cost of doing business that results in a decrease in assets or an increase in liabilities (such as cash or accounts payable).
- *Net income.* The excess of net sales revenue over expenses for the accounting period. (An excess of expenses over revenues is referred to as a net loss.)

Balance Sheet
Assets = Liabilities + Owner's equity

- *Assets.* Economic resources (such as cash, merchandise, equipment) that a company owns.
- *Liabilities.* Debts that a company owes to a creditor.
- *Owner's equity* (Net assets). Excess of a company's assets over its liabilities. Residual value available to the owners in a company. Undistributed net income is a component of owner's equity.

High-speed managers know how to perform cash-flow analyses to maintain adequate liquidity. They know the importance of performing expense analyses in order to quickly cut unnecessary expenditures. Most importantly, HSM managers vigorously monitor their companies' key financial ratios or indicators in order to adjust operations, investments, and/or financing, if necessary, and to seize new profit, growth, and investment opportunities.

The Income Statement

The basic income statement summarizes net sales and expenses for a period of time (a month, a quarter, a year). Sample income statements for 1989 and 1990, presented in Tables 14.1 and 14.2, are from a fictitious small company that sells word processing software. (Note: Ms. Lyn Soo-Hoo, CPA, provided input on the proper formatting of the financial tables in this chapter.)

The first line on the basic income statement is net sales. This amount is the gross sales minus any discounts. The next line is cost of sales expense, which typically includes such costs as labor, materials, and other related manufacturing costs. Cost of sales subtracted from net sales yields the gross profit.

Table 14.1. ABC Software Corporation, Income Statements for Years Ended 1989 and 1990: Horizontal Analysis.

	1990	1989	Horizontal Analysis Dollar Change	Horizontal Analysis Percent Change
Net sales	$468,547	$395,595	$72,952	18.4%
Cost of sales expense	90,825	68,676	22,149	32.3%
Gross profit	$377,722	$326,919	$50,803	15.5%
General and administrative	$256,981	$192,759	$64,222	33.3%
Selling	37,253	27,984	9,269	33.1%
Total operating expenses	$294,234	$220,743	$73,491	33.3%
Operating income	$83,488	$106,176	($22,688)	-21.4%
Interest expense	3,614	3,258	356	10.9%
Earnings before taxes	$79,874	$102,918	($23,044)	-22.4%
Income tax expense	20,949	30,875	(9,926)	-32.2%
Net income	$58,925	$72,043	($13,118)	-18.2%

Table 14.2. ABC Software Corporation, Income Statements for Years Ended 1989 and 1990: Vertical Analysis.

	1990	1989	Vertical Analysis 1990 % of Total Sales	Vertical Analysis 1989 % of Total Sales
Net sales	$468,547	$395,595	100%	100%
Cost of sales expense	90,825	68,676	19.4%	17.4%
Gross profit	$377,722	$326,919	80.6%	82.6%
General and administrative	$256,981	$192,759	54.8%	48.7%
Selling	37,253	27,984	7.9%	7.1%
Total operating expenses	$294,234	$220,743	62.7%	55.8%
Operating income	$83,488	$106,176	17.9%	26.8%
Interest expense	3,614	3,258	.8%	.8%
Earnings before taxes	$79,874	$102,918	17.1%	26%
Income tax expense	20,949	30,875	4.5%	7.8%
Net income	$58,925	$72,043	12.6%	18.2%

The next lines on the basic income statement are operating expenses not directly associated with the manufacturing of the product. These general and administrative expenses include items such as rent, office expenses, wages, and insurance. Selling and general and administrative expenses are usually listed separately in most income statements.

The total operating expenses are subtracted from gross profit to yield the operating income. Interest expense is subtracted from operating income to yield earnings before taxes. Finally, income tax expense is subtracted from earnings before taxes to yield net income.

Very simplified income statements and balance sheets are used in this chapter to illustrate the basics of managerial finance. Readers are directed to the recommended readings in order to gain a better understanding of all the financial terms, statements, equations, and analyses covered in this chapter. And again, this chapter is intended primarily for nonfinancial managers.

The Balance Sheet

The balance sheet is a snapshot of how a business stands at any given point in time. Sample balance sheets for 1989 and 1990 are summarized in Tables 14.3 and 14.4. These balance sheets are also based on the fictitious software company.

Assets can be broken down into two main categories: current and long term. Liabilities can be broken down into the same two categories. Items classified as current assets or liabilities are expected to be utilized or realized within the company's net operating cycle—typically, one year. The difference between assets and liabilities equals net worth, or equity. Net worth is the residual available to the owners of the company once all the liabilities have been paid. Net worth consists of capital stock and retained earnings (cumulative undistributed net income of the company).

Financial Statement Analysis

The HSM manager routinely reviews monthly financial statements in an analytical manner. Annual financial statements are

Table 14.3. ABC Software Corporation, Balance Sheets
as of December 31, 1989 and 1990: Horizontal Analysis.

	1990	1989	Dollar Change	Percent Change
			Horizontal Analysis	
Current Assets				
Cash	$172,433	$164,909	$7,524	4.6%
Accounts receivable	56,972	45,541	11,431	25.1%
Inventory	11,273	9,210	2,063	22.4%
Prepaid expenses	7,430	5,665	1,765	31.2%
Total current assets	$248,108	$225,325	$22,783	10.1%
Long-Term Operating Assets				
Building, equipment and furniture	$142,435	$93,116	$49,319	53%
Accumulated depreciation	− 55,482	− 41,196	− 14,286	34.7%
Net book value	$86,953	$51,920	$35,033	67.5%
Other assets	25,183	40,408	− 15,225	− 37.7%
Total Assets	$360,244	$317,653	$42,591	13.4%
Current Liabilities				
Accounts payable	$39,491	$31,685	$7,806	24.6%
Accrued expenses	34,756	27,021	7,735	28.6%
Income tax payable	7,231	19,168	− 11,937	− 62.3%
Short-term notes payable	14,441	7,736	6,705	86.7%
Total current liabilities	$95,919	$85,610	$10,309	12%
Long-Term Debt	$75,400	$30,000	$45,400	151.3%
Stockholders' Equity				
Capital stock (13,000 shares outstanding)	$130,000	$130,000	0	0%
Retained earnings	58,925	72,043	− 13,118	− 18.2%
Total equity	$188,925	$202,043	− $13,118	− 6.5%
Total Liabilities and Stockholders' Equity	$360,244	$317,653	$42,591	13.4%

compared and analyzed over a minimum of a two-year period.
The HSM manager can then compare the current fiscal year to
the previous years for each line item on the income statement
and balance sheet. HSM managers are cautious when analyzing
balance sheet information. That is, since the balance sheet is

Table 14.4. ABC Software Corporation, Balance Sheets as of December 31, 1989 and 1990: Vertical Analysis.

	1990	1989	Vertical Analysis 1990 % of Total	Vertical Analysis 1989 % of Total
Current Assets				
Cash	$172,433	$164,909	47.9%	51.9%
Accounts receivable	56,972	45,541	15.8%	14.3%
Inventory	11,273	9,210	3.1%	2.9%
Prepaid expenses	7,430	5,665	2.1%	1.8%
Total current assets	$248,108	$225,325	68.9%	70.9%
Long-Term Operating Assets				
Building, equipment and furniture	$142,435	$93,116	39.5%	29.3%
Accumulated depreciation	– 55,482	– 41,196	– 15.4%	– 13%
Net book value	$86,953	$51,920	24.1%	16.3%
Other assets	25,183	40,408	7.0%	12.7%
Total Assets	$360,244	$317,653	100%	100%
Current Liabilities				
Accounts payable	$39,491	$31,685	11%	10%
Accrued expenses	34,756	27,021	9.6%	8.5%
Income tax payable	7,231	19,168	2%	6%
Short-term notes payable	14,441	7,736	4%	2.4%
Total current liabilities	$95,919	$85,610	26.6%	27%
Long-Term Debt	$75,400	$30,000	20.9%	9.4%
Stockholders' Equity				
Capital stock (13,000 shares outstanding)	$130,000	$130,000	36.1%	40.9%
Retained earnings	58,925	72,043	16.4%	22.7%
Total equity	$188,925	$202,043	52.4%	63.6%
Total Liabilities and Stockholders' Equity	$360,244	$317,653	100%	100%

only a snapshot of a company's financial position, it may not by itself provide significantly meaningful information. Two strategies are initially used to examine financial statements: horizontal and vertical analysis.

Horizontal Analysis

When conducting a horizontal analysis, the HSM manager compares the changes from one year to the next for each line on the financial statements. Two changes are typically examined: (1) the *total dollar change* from one year to the next, and (2) the *percent change* from one year to the next.

Horizontal analyses of both the income statement and the balance sheet are presented in Tables 14.1 and 14.3, respectively. Such analyses can be used to detect and examine important financial shifts and operating trends. For example, the HSM manager would note that net income *dropped* $13,118, or 18.2 percent, in 1990 compared to 1989, despite the fact that net sales *increased* $72,952, or 18.4 percent, for the same period. More detailed analysis shows that total operating expenses increased $73,491, or 33.3 percent. The HSM manager would move swiftly to identify negative spending trends and control unnecessary expenses.

A horizontal analysis of the balance sheet also yields useful information. For example, an examination of assets in Table 14.3 shows that accounts receivable have increased by 25.1 percent from 1989 to 1990. The vigilant HSM manager will quickly determine if he needs to speed up his collections process and/or rethink his credit and follow-up policy. Inventory has also increased 22.4 percent, alerting the HSM manager to examine reasons for the inventory build-up. The HSM manager might need to address overstocking or an accumulation of obsolete items, which ultimately result in poorer cash flow. Finally, it is obvious that the company is expanding its facilities (buildings, equipment, and furniture) by 53 percent. The HSM manager needs to make sure that all aspects of the expansion are warranted given a decline in overall profitability.

A horizontal analysis of liabilities and stockholders' equity yields useful information as well. For example, long-term debt increased by 151.3 percent. This finding coincides with the company's expansion of facilities. Retained earnings *decreased* by $13,118, or 18.2 percent, while total equity decreased by 6.5 percent. The HSM manager is aware that net worth can be improved even more if he improves profitability by controlling expenses and increasing net sales.

Vertical Analysis

Vertical analysis of the balance sheet and the income statement are presented in Tables 14.2 and 14.4. When analyzing the income statement, the HSM manager determines what percent of total net sales each line item equals. When analyzing the balance sheet, the objective is to determine what percent of total assets or total liabilities and stockholders' equity each line item represents.

Examination of the income statements in Table 14.2 reveals that the cost of sales as a percentage of net sales was 17.4 percent in 1989, versus 19.4 percent in 1990. Moreover, total operating expenses as a percentage of net sales was 55.8 percent in 1989, compared to 62.7 percent in 1990. These findings would suggest that the 1990 expenses need to be better controlled. The HSM manager needs to gain a better understanding of why net income as a percentage of net sales (18.2 percent in 1989) slid to 12.6 percent in 1990.

A vertical analysis of the balance sheet in Table 14.4 also yields useful information. An examination of the assets reveals that cash as a percentage of total assets slipped from 51.9 percent in 1989 to 47.9 percent in 1990. Part of this shift is because the accounts receivable figure as a percentage of total assets grew from 14.3 percent in 1989 to 15.8 percent in 1990, while inventories grew from 2.9 percent in 1989 to 3.1 percent in 1990. A detailed cash flow analysis would also reveal these negative trends.

A vertical analysis of liabilities and stockholders' equity is also useful. While total current liabilities as a percentage of total liabilities and stockholders' equity was reduced from 27 percent in 1989 to 26.6 percent in 1990, long-term debt as a percentage of total liabilities and stockholders' equity increased considerably, from 9.4 percent in 1989 to 20.9 percent in 1990. Retained earnings as a percentage of total assets slipped from 22.7 percent in 1989 to 16.4 percent in 1990. These findings are consistent with the findings from the horizontal analysis.

Trend Analysis

The comparison of three or more years of financial statements is called a trend analysis. Trend analysis is an extension of the two-year horizontal and vertical analyses. The purpose of trend analysis is to identify a pattern of financial activity over more than two years.

In trend analysis, the earliest year is frequently selected as the base year. The base-year figure is equal to 100 percent, and each subsequent year is expressed as a percentage of the base year. The following equation is used: trend percentage = (current-year figure/base-year figure) × 100.

An example of a trend analysis for five years is presented in Table 14.5. The 1989 and 1990 net sales, costs of goods sold, and gross profit figures from Table 14.1 were compared to these same line items from 1986, 1987, and 1988. Table 14.5 reveals the following five-year trends:

- Except for 1989, net sales, cost of goods sold, and gross profit have steadily increased.
- The financial outcomes for 1989 are similar to 1988, suggesting a flat trend.
- The increases in net sales have tended on average to exceed the increases in the costs of goods sold, yielding very favorable gross profits.

Ratio Analysis

After initially interpreting the financial statements with horizontal and vertical analyses, the HSM manager can then use ratio analysis to gain a deeper understanding of the company's financial performance and status. These ratios highlight the strengths and weaknesses of a company's financial condition. To gain additional insight, the HSM manager will compare ratios between years to identify trends. One company's ratios can also

Table 14.5. ABC Software Corporation, Gross Profit
and Five-Year Trend Analyses.

	Gross Profit Analysis				
	1986	*1987*	*1988*	*1989*	*1990*
Net sales	$198,025	$295,000	$405,000	$395,595	$468,457
Cost of goods sold	47,525	55,000	70,000	68,676	90,825
Gross profit	$150,500	$240,000	$335,000	$326,919	$377,632
	Trend Analysis				
	1986	*1987*	*1988*	*1989*	*1990*
Net sales	100%	149%	205%	200%	237%
Cost of goods sold	100%	116%	147%	145%	191%
Gross profit	100%	159%	223%	217%	251%

be compared to the ratios of other companies in a similar line of business. Industry ratio averages are often published by trade associations and financial service organizations. Such cross-company comparisons supplement a company's analysis of annual financial statements. If interested in these types of comparisons, the reader should consult the recommended readings listed at the back of this book.

There are four major classes of financial ratios that can be examined:

1. *Liquidity ratios.* These ratios assess the firm's ability to maintain adequate operating capital, which is a primary objective of sound financial management. The HSM manager strives at all times to have adequate, yet not excessive, amounts of cash or asset equivalents that can readily be turned into cash to meet the obligations of the current accounting period.
2. *Profitability ratios.* These ratios assess management's overall effectiveness, as shown by the returns generated on sales and assets. Profitability is also a primary objective of sound financial management.

3. *Efficiency ratios.* These ratios measure how effectively a company is using its assets and resources. These ratios indicate, for example, how successfully a company collects on its sales and how often inventory turns over in a given period of time.
4. *Leverage ratios.* These ratios measure the extent to which a company has been financed by debt. Highly leveraged companies are a greater credit risk for lending institutions (such as banks), which may result in the company's inability to obtain additional funds or lower interest rates on loans.

The following sections describe some of the more commonly used liquidity, profitability, efficiency, and leverage ratios. The formulas for computing the various financial ratios are summarized in Table 14.6. The ratios that were computed from the 1989 and 1990 financial statements summarized in Tables 14.1 and 14.3 are included as examples.

Liquidity Ratios

Current ratio measures a company's short-term solvency or ability to meet short-term obligations. It indicates the extent to which the claims of short-term creditors are covered by current assets, and is one of the best-known quick measures of financial strength.

A higher current ratio is preferred. A low ratio suggests a company may not be able to pay off bills on a timely basis. Too high a ratio indicates that perhaps excess cash is available for long-term investment or purchase of fixed assets that will yield greater return (such as new machinery). A general standard of excellence for the current ratio is 2 to 1 or higher. Therefore, the ratios in Table 14.6 are acceptable. Had the current ratios been too low and if a serious downward trend were detected, the HSM manager might have attempted to increase liquidity by obtaining a loan, refinancing liabilities, or obtaining new equity capital.

The quick ratio (or acid test) is almost the same ratio as the current ratio except it eliminates inventory and prepaid ex-

Table 14.6. ABC Software Corporation Ratio Analyses.

Major Category	Ratio Title	Formula	1990 Ratio	1989 Ratio	% Change*	Trend**
Liquidity	1. Current ratio	Current assets/current liabilities	2.59 to 1	2.63 to 1	-1.5%	D
	2. Quick (acid test) ratio	Cash + receivables/current liabilities	2.39 to 1	2.46 to 1	-2.8%	D
	3. Turnover of cash ratio	Sales/working capital	3.1 times	2.8 times	10.7%	I
Profitability	1. Gross margin	Gross profit/net sales	80.6%	82.6%	-2.4%	D
	2. Net margin	Net income/net sales	12.6%	18.2%	-30.8%	D
	3. Net profit ratio	Earnings before interest and taxes/net sales	17.8%	26.8%	-33.6%	D
	4. Return on investment	Earnings before taxes/net worth	42.3%	50.9%	-17%	D
	5. Return on assets	Earnings before taxes/total assets	22.2%	32.4%	-31.6%	D
	6. Earnings per share	Net income/shares of common stock	$4.53	$5.54	-18.2%	D
Efficiency	1. Accounts receivable turnover (days sales outstanding)	(Accounts receivable/annual net credit sales) × 365 days	44 days	42 days	4.8%	D
	2. Inventory turnover Days sales in inventory	(Inventory/costs of goods sold) × 365 days	45 days	49 days	-8.2%	I
	How often inventory turned in year	365 days/days sales in inventory	8.11 turns	7.45 turns	8.9%	I
	3. Total operating cycle	Days sales outstanding + days sales in inventory	89 days	91 days	-2.2%	I
	4. Total asset turnover ratio	Net sales/total assets	1.30 to 1	1.25 to 1	4.4%	I
Leverage	1. Debt to equity ratio	Total liabilities/net worth	.91 to 1	.57 to 1	58.5%	D
	2. Debt to assets ratio	Total liabilities/total assets	.48 to 1	.36 to 1	30.7%	D

* Change percentages based on raw values, not rounded values.   ** I = Improved, D = Deteriorated.

penses, so that only cash and accounts receivable, the most liquid assets available, are counted. (Some analysts encourage companies to reduce the accounts receivable figure by 20 percent to 25 percent before computing this ratio to adjust for bad debts or receivables unlikely to be collected.)

This is a more reliable measure of liquidity than the current ratio. An optimal quick ratio is 1 to 1 or higher. The quick ratios in Table 14.6 are therefore very acceptable. Again, although the HSM manager prefers high current and quick ratios, he does not want idle cash balances. This cash needs to be properly invested to maximize a company's profitability.

Turnover of cash ratio incorporates a net working capital concept. Working capital equals current assets minus current liabilities. By maintaining a positive working capital balance, the HSM manager secures the means to finance his sales efforts without struggling to pay his expenses. A generally accepted standard is that sales should be five or six times greater than working capital. Examination of Table 14.6 reveals that the turnover of cash ratios for both 1989 and 1990 are below the acceptable standard.

Profitability Ratios

Gross margin is a general indicator of the profitability of the sales and manufacturing/production effort. This ratio indicates the percentage of each sales dollar left to cover administrative, selling, and other fixed costs. In 1989 the gross margin was 82.6 percent; it dropped to 80.6 percent in 1990. Higher values are preferred.

Net profit margin indicates the percentage of each sales dollar retained in earnings and ultimately paid out to stockholders. High values are best. The net margin dropped from 18.2 percent in 1989 to 12.6 percent in 1990. This means that in 1990 the company made a profit of 12.6 cents for every dollar of sales, compared to 18.2 cents in 1989. Computing the net profit margin of sales for specific products is also useful and indicates which products are being developed and marketed in a profitable manner.

Net profit ratio assesses the company's operations by filtering out any distortions that may occur because of high debt costs or significant tax expense. A high ratio suggests expenses are being controlled, while a low ratio suggests that expenses are too great or that sales volume is simply too low to maintain fixed expenses. The net profit ratio dropped significantly in 1990, compared to 1989.

Return on investment is one of the most useful measures of profitability. This ratio should be compared with other investment opportunities currently available. For example, a low ratio suggests that a company may have done better investing its money in stocks, bonds, or some other investment outlets. A high ratio typically reflects that management is efficient. However, it could also indicate that perhaps creditors are a source of much of the available funds, or that the company is undercapitalized.

Return on assets reflects the profit that is generated by the use of the company's assets. A low ratio indicates a less effective employment of assets, while a high ratio indicates a more effective use. Table 14.6 highlights a more efficient use of assets in 1989 than in 1990.

Earnings per share represents earnings attributable to each share of stock outstanding. The numerator is net income; the denominator, the weighted average of shares outstanding for the year. The earnings per share decreased in 1990, compared to 1989.

Efficiency Ratios

Accounts receivable turnover indicates whether receivables are being collected in a timely manner. A decreasing trend is preferred. This ratio is also referred to as the number of days sales are outstanding (DSO). Table 14.6 indicates a slight increase in the number of days it takes to collect credit sales. The HSM manager always needs to improve on inadequate collection practices. He might also need to quickly confront bad accounts or an overly liberal credit policy. The following list presents a rule-of-thumb guideline for estimating the probability of collecting from overdue accounts.

ABC Software Corporation
Accounts Receivable Aging Schedule

Past Due	Estimated Probability of Collection
1 month	95%
2 months	75%
4 months	10%
6 months	5%

Inventory turnover highlights the rate at which inventory is being sold. The two figures reported in Table 14.6 are the days sales in inventory figure (DSI) and how many times the inventory turns in the year. Compared to 1989, the number of days the 1990 inventory remained unsold decreased. The standard number of inventory turns in a year largely depends on the type of merchandise, product line, or nature of the industry. Both the 1989 and 1990 figures were acceptable for this company, reflecting a slight improvement.

Total operating cycle represents the number of extra days per year it takes a company to convert a dollar earned from sales into a dollar in the bank. The operating cycle decreased by two days from 1989 to 1990. This trend can always be improved.

Total asset turnover ratio reflects whether a company's sales are commensurate with its assets, that is, whether a company is generating sufficient sales volume for the size of its asset investment. This ratio increased from 1989 to 1990. An increasing trend is preferred.

Leverage Ratios

Debt to equity ratio reflects the amount financed by an outside source rather than by the owners of the company. Companies with ratios of 3 to 1 or higher are viewed to be highly leveraged. The debt to equity ratios in Table 14.6 are acceptable for a company this size. From a lender's point of view, a lower ratio is desired.

Debt to assets ratio reflects the percentage of assets that are funded through debt. A ratio that is too high is risky, while one that is too low usually indicates inefficient use of capital. The ratios in Table 14.6 are quite acceptable.

The HSM manager knows that examination of financial ratios cannot take the place of management experience and sound financial judgment. However, the proper use of ratio analyses can make good managers better. The HSM manager can compute ratios that quickly identify financial trends or potential problems that require immediate investigation and action.

Performing Expense Analysis

The HSM manager always remembers that expenses, whether fixed or variable, must be controlled at all times. A manager must understand what drives a company's expenses and be knowledgeable of current expense levels. Additionally, the HSM manager will pay particular attention to those expenses that have a more concrete impact upon the operation as a whole. Changes in expenses from one year to the next should be compared and justified using both horizontal and vertical analyses.

Expense control helps to maximize profits on the same or even a smaller number of sales. Sales revenue is a function of unit price times unit volume sold. If either the price or the number of units sold decreases, sales dollars will drop. This will eventually lead to a loss of profit unless the HSM manager can quickly adjust expenses or the marketing and sales plan accordingly.

The HSM manager needs to keep the following questions in mind at all times: Can the cost of goods sold be decreased? Are labor expenses, freight charges, and other manufacturing costs too high? Is there more shrinkage due to theft or spoilage? Reduction of these costs can help counteract a decline in profitability due to lower sales.

Fixed expenses (such as salaries, utilities, telephone, rent, office supplies, interest) are typically spread over twelve monthly installments for the accounting year. If sales decrease, then fixed expenses can contribute to greater losses than variable expenses (expenses that are tied to sales) since fixed expenses cannot be easily reduced on a short-term basis. Strategies to quickly control fixed expenses may include the following:

- Negotiating the lowest price for all purchases and always getting competitive bids
- Paying creditors only as much and as often as you need to
- Looking for lower prices without sacrificing quality on purchases
- Renegotiating more favorable payment terms with vendors (such as insurance providers and freight carriers)
- Hiring temporary and/or hourly employees during peak productivity seasons
- Conducting proper space planning (for instance, consolidating work space and subleasing excess space)
- Scrutinizing travel and entertainment expenses

Increasing the Productivity of Investments

After the HSM manager has cut expenses, he should try to increase the productivity of his investments. This can be accomplished in a number of ways. The following list shows managers some ways to increase productivity in the areas of credit policy, payroll, inventory control, and marketing. The list of strategies is for illustrative purposes only, and therefore is not exhaustive.

Credit Policy

- Invoice promptly
- Promptly follow up on delinquent customers
- Check purchasers' credit references
- Consider offering cash discounts for prompt payment

Payroll

- Consider temporary help, freelancers, and part-timers

- Monitor compliance with starting, quitting, and break times
- Reduce downtime caused by equipment failure

Inventory Control

- Teach proper handling and storage skills to prevent damage
- Implement loss-control procedures to reduce theft
- Look into just-in-time inventory maintenance strategies to reduce storage costs, obsolescence, and insurance costs
- Maintain a level of inventory relative to the company's needs

Marketing

- Use advertising targeted to specific customer groups
- Train salespeople to cross-sell and to sell accessory items
- Retain customers through high-quality service
- Have a cost-effective policy on returns and repairs

HSM managers also support all company plans to improve earnings by increasing revenues and/or controlling expenses. The five basic ways that HSM managers can increase earnings are: (1) reduce costs, (2) raise prices, (3) sell more products in old markets, (4) expand into new markets, and (5) drop or revitalize losing operations and/or products. HSM managers know a company that successfully improves earnings almost always has an edge over its competitors.

Planning Cash Position

HSM managers know that they can never afford to run out of cash. Cash is needed to pay creditors and employees. A company without sufficient cash will not be in business very long, even if the company is showing a paper profit. Cash shortages are the major reasons for the failure of many small businesses today.

The HSM manager can create a cash positioning chart to forecast when extra cash will be needed to pay bills, fund expansion, or finance new products. A cash position analysis can help the HSM manager determine when he needs to obtain the necessary cash (for instance, by increasing cash sales, selling stock, borrowing, or speeding up collections) or when excess cash is available for capital expenditures and other investment purposes. The cash position analysis allows the HSM manager to make arrangements for improving cash flow before serious shortages occur.

An example of a five-month cash position chart is presented in Table 14.7. An estimated cash position analysis deals only with cash on hand, cash received, and cash disbursed. (While Table 14.7 presents the *estimated* cash position, it is also beneficial for the HSM manager to keep track of *actual* cash positions compared to the estimate.)

When constructing a cash position chart the HSM manager estimates starting cash in the first line. Projected cash sales and cash to be received from various sales are then listed and summed to equal the total cash receipts. Estimates of cash basis expenses are listed and summed to form the total cash disbursement figure.

By adding the starting cash figure to the total cash receipts figure and then subtracting the total cash disbursements

Table 14.7. ABC Software Corporation Cash Position Analysis.

	Months				
	1st	*2nd*	*3rd*	*4th*	*5th*
Beginning Cash	$4,200	$6,200	$9,925	($375)	$7,750
Cash Receipts					
Cash sales	$72,750	$75,000	$65,000	$72,500	$74,475
Cash received on receivables	11,250	8,750	9,250	12,400	13,495
Total receipts	$84,000	$83,750	$74,250	$84,900	$87,970
Cash Disbursements					
Purchases	$25,500	$24,250	$26,500	$21,250	$22,375
Wages	42,025	42,025	44,025	44,025	44,025
Rent	5,000	5,000	5,000	5,000	5,000
Other	9,475	8,750	9,025	6,500	6,250
Total disbursements	$82,000	$80,025	$84,550	$76,775	$77,650
Ending Cash	$6,200	$9,925	($375)	$7,750	$18,070
Change in Cash Position	$2,000	$3,725	($10,300)	$8,125	$10,320

figure, the HSM manager is able to compute the ending balance. The ending balance becomes the starting cash figure for the upcoming month. The cash position is computed by subtracting total cash disbursement from total cash receipts. The cash position figure only reflects the amount of cash expected to be created or lost during the month.

The cash position analysis summarized in Table 14.7 can be used to effectively plan for future cash needs. For example, cash sales are estimated to decrease $10,000 in the third month, because a major competitor is expected to release a successful substitute product during that month. Wages will be increased by $2,000 per month beginning in the third month, because an addition to the research staff is needed to immediately enhance a product that will be sold against the competitor's new substitute. With estimates of lower sales and increased wages, the HSM manager realizes that he could be looking at a very poor cash position, negative $10,300, at the end of the third month. This would force an ending balance of negative $375, which would be carried over as the starting cash position for the fourth month.

The HSM manager must sometimes make quick financial decisions to keep his company continuously solvent. The cash position chart allows the manager to test out a number of these decisions on paper (sensitivity analysis, or "what if" scenarios). In our example, the HSM manager decided not to borrow. Instead, he planned to offer discounts to customers who immediately paid their bills in cash within thirty days. This was expected to accelerate cash sales by $7,500. In addition, he planned to make a concentrated effort to collect accounts receivable faster. Nonessential purchases and miscellaneous expenses would also be immediately reduced or deferred. The increase in wages would remain so that the company could hire a person to quickly differentiate its product. This would allow the company to stay competitive with the company offering the new substitute product.

The HSM manager determined that with these strategic interventions the monthly change in cash position will equal $8,125 for month four. The ending balance of $7,750 will become the starting cash figure for month five. If the HSM manager continues his financial planning strategies to accelerate cash receipts and delay cash disbursements during month five, a healthy ending cash balance of $18,070 can be projected.

In summary, the HSM manager can use the cash position chart to proactively plan for those times when the company could benefit from additional cash or will have excess cash available. The cash position chart is a forecasting tool that HSM managers can use to keep last-minute surprises to a minimum. When projecting a company's future cash position, the HSM should answer the following questions:

- Will I need additional cash?
- When will I need it?
- How much cash will I need?
- Where can I get the cash?
- How long will I need it?

Preparing a Budget

A company's financial plan is called a budget. A budget can be prepared monthly, quarterly, or annually. A budget is a set of pro forma statements of management's expectations regarding upcoming sales, expenses, production volume, cash needs, and the like. At the beginning of a fiscal period the budget is a plan or standard. However, at the end of the fiscal period, the budget serves as a control device to help management measure the company's performance against its financial plan. The budget allows the HSM manager to be proactive rather than reactive in financial control efforts.

The HSM manager knows that the major reason for having a budget is to provide a company with challenging yet achievable goals. If there were no formalized and quantitative budget, management would have no idea what it hoped to achieve for the month, the quarter, or the year. The HSM manager frequently compares actual sales to budgeted results and investigates any large or unusual discrepancies. The HSM manager also views the budget as an effective communication and coordination tool, a mechanism by which he can measure and evaluate his management staff. Consequently, the budgeting process should involve key individuals from all facets of operation, in order to achieve an appropriate level of buy-in by management.

Types of Budgets

Budgets are generally prepared annually, often using monthly projections. This allows for evaluations at the end of each month, so that any corrections can be implemented quickly. Three types of budgets are commonly used.

The *master budget* contains a forecast of the income statement, the balance sheet, and the changes in cash flows. The master budget is broken down into an operating budget and a financial budget. The *operating budget* includes revenue projections, cost of goods sold projections, administrative expenses, selling expenses, financing expenses, and so on. The information can be combined to prepare a budgeted income statement. The *financial budget* includes the cash budget and any financial statements other than the income statements.

The HSM manager needs to go through the following four basic steps when preparing a budget:

1. *Make assumptions.* A set of assumptions must be adopted before a budget can be developed. What actions will competitors take that might affect sales or pricing decisions? Does the company expect an appreciable increase in market share from existing products? Are new product releases planned? Assumptions about how these events and others could affect the financial performance of the company are necessary before a realistic budget can be planned.
2. *Establish goals.* The HSM manager needs to establish specific, measurable goals. For example, sales should increase by 10 percent, profits by 15 percent. When top management uses a budget to clearly communicate the desired direction of the company, then there is a greater chance that challenging goals can be reached.

3. *Forecast sales and expenses.* Once the assumptions have been
    considered and specific goals have been set, the forecasting
    can begin. Forecasts can be very simple or extremely com-
    plex. A simple forecast may be a projection that what hap-
    pened last year will happen again in the upcoming year. In
    fact, most forecasting is based to a large extent on historical
    patterns. Extremely complex forecasts can be made using
    mathematical formulas and computer modeling. A realistic
    forecast must also consider how the future might be differ-
    ent from the past because of improved technology, infla-
    tion, more or less competition, new government regula-
    tions, and so on. Once forecasts of sales and costs have been
    made, the written budget can be prepared.

4. *Analyze budget to actual results.* Budgets are used to compare
    expected results with actual results. The HSM manager
    particularly monitors unfavorable budget variances (the
    amount actually spent on an expense item is greater than
    the budgeted amount) and discusses these differences with
    management. The HSM manager also maintains very de-
    tailed budgets for more significant expenditures since he
    can achieve a greater degree of control over these items.

    Key aspects of a budget variance analysis are summarized
in Table 14.8. This table reveals that the fictitious company's total
manufacturing costs were $500,000 more than expected for the
month. Yet one needs to examine unit-level variances to gain a
better idea of what has occurred. An analysis of unit variances
indicates that the purchasing unit is responsible for most of the
overspending.

    Still more detail is needed to assist the purchasing unit.
For example, if the budget were analyzed even further, by line
item for each unit, it would become clear why excess costs
occurred. Table 14.8 presents such an analysis for the purchasing unit. It seems obvious that most of the variance occurred in
the area of materials. The HSM manager might find that this
increase is due to an unexpected rise in the price of materials.
He might also discover, however, that some of the rise is due to
poor negotiating between the purchasers and the suppliers.

Table 14.8. ABC Corporation Budget Variance Analysis.

Total Monthly Manufacturing Department Variance

Budgeted Total Costs	*Actual Total Costs*	*Variance Favorable/ (Unfavorable)*
$1,750,000	$2,250,000	($500,000)

Manufacturing Unit Variances

Unit	*Budgeted Costs*	*Actual Costs*	*Variance Favorable/ (Unfavorable)*
Purchasing	$700,000	$1,200,000	($500,000)
Processing	450,000	350,000	100,000
Assembly	300,000	300,000	0
Packing	300,000	400,000	(100,000)
Totals	$1,750,000	$2,250,000	($500,000)

Purchasing Unit Variances

Line Items	*Budgeted Costs*	*Actual Costs*	*Variance Favorable/ (Unfavorable)*
Labor	$350,000	$500,000	($150,000)
Materials	250,000	600,000	(350,000)
Overhead	100,000	100,000	0
Totals	$700,000	$1,200,000	($500,000)

Moreover, some of the rise could be due to excessive damage and waste caused by careless workers. A well-constructed budget serves as an excellent control mechanism, especially when it is monitored at an appropriate level of detail.

Conclusion

HSM managers realize that all their efforts should help to strengthen the financial stability of their company. Hence, they need to skillfully monitor their company's income statement, balance sheet, financial ratios, cash position, and budget status at all times to quickly identify any problems that need immediate attention. By closely monitoring and analyzing all financial reports, the HSM manager is better able to seize new profit enhancement opportunities.

Chapter Fifteen

Lessons and Results of High Speed Management: Fifteen Top Performers

The purpose of this chapter is to profile the fifteen companies that best put into practice the HSM strategies discussed in this book. I have organized them into three groups: *Gold Medalists*, *Silver Medalists*, and *Bronze Medalists*.

I selected the companies from one or more of the following business resources:

1. *Hoover's Handbook of American Business—1992 Edition.* This handbook lists the five hundred leading companies in America, rated from A+ to F, based on approximately ten years of financial data and the current success of the company's overall corporate strategy.
2. *Hoover's Handbook of World Business—1992 Edition.* This direc-

284 High-Speed Management

tory reviews 165 leading companies headquartered outside the United States. These organizations also received an overall performance rating ranging from A+ to F, based on approximately ten years of financial data and the current success of the company's global strategy.

3. *The Strategic Investor's Stock Analyst* (A Prodigy Service). This data base provides up to five years of financial data on over 4,500 individual stocks. Key financial ratios are provided to reflect the company's financial strength, including both income-statement and balance-sheet highlights. The information available in the January 1992 data base was utilized.

4. *Value Line Investment Survey—1991 Edition.* This comprehensive survey provides ten to fifteen years of financial and stock performance data for over 1,700 companies traded on a variety of stock exchanges. *Value Line* rates these companies on their overall investment potential (timeliness and safety of investment) and on their overall financial strength.

The companies were selected and ranked from one to fifteen (one being the top HSM company) based on quantitative scores derived from the following six variables:

1. *Hoover's* overall rating of the company, which ranged from B+ to A+
2. *Value Line's* rating of the company's overall financial strength, which ranged from B+ to A++
3. The amount of business press coverage the company received over the past three years, in which it was described as a HSM company (one = little press coverage, five = much press coverage)
4. A management expert's classification of the company as an effective HSM company (one = no, two = in-between, three = yes)
5. *Value Line's* 1994–1996 projections on the company's future gains in stock prices (an estimate of how the financial experts think the company will perform in the future), rated on a scale ranging from one (0 to 20 percent gain) to eight (141 percent and more gain)

6. Whether the company has recently been rated as one of the best in America or in the world, based on an independent review source, such as *Fortune* magazine's ratings of the most respected companies, Weitzen's rankings of the leading hypergrowth companies, and others

In order to be selected as one of the top fifteen, a company had to exhibit current financial strength, based on key indicators such as sales, earnings and/or dividend growth, key financial ratios, positive stock-price movement, and income and balance-sheet highlights. The company must have received a very high overall performance rating in one of the business handbooks consulted for this study, and it must have received consistently favorable notice in the business press, highlighting that it successfully utilized three or more HSM strategies over the past few years.

It is possible that some of the best HSM companies were not included in this rating because they were not listed in the business directories reviewed. In addition, some companies traditionally characterized in the business press as outstanding time-based competitors might not have been rated in the top fifteen because of recently encountered difficulties, such as failure to meet an important new-product release deadline or unusual financial problems. It is also possible that the inclusion of additional variables would have slightly altered these rankings, so they should not be taken too literally. Above all, they are for illustrative purposes only and should not be used for any investment decisions.

The fifteen companies selected are only briefly described, because the goal of this chapter is to highlight the major HSM strategies they used, rather than to give more extensive general overviews.

The Medal Winners

The following list of the Gold, Silver, and Bronze Medal winners includes each company's name, its primary industry, and its ticker symbol (for those who want to review financial and stock performance).

Company	Primary Industry	Ticker Symbol
Gold Medalists		
1. Merck & Company, Inc.	Drug products	MRK
2. Hewlett-Packard Company	Computer equipment	HWP
3. Minnesota Mining and Manufacturing Company (3M)	Paper and film products	MMM
4. Sony Corporation	Electronic products	SNE (ADR)
5. Liz Claiborne, Inc.	Clothing and cosmetics	LIZ
Silver Medalists		
6. Wal-Mart Stores, Inc.	Retail general merchandise	WMT
7. Apple Computer, Inc.	Computer equipment	AAPL
8. Reuters Holdings PLC	Information and media products	RTRSY (ADR)
9. Microsoft Corporation	Computer services	MSFT
10. Abbott Laboratories	Drug products	ABT
Bronze Medalists		
11. Walt Disney Company	Entertainment	DIS
12. Albertson's, Inc.	Retail food stores	ABS
13. Nintendo Co., LTD	Games and leisure products	NINTY (ADR)
14. Intel Corporation	Electronic equipment	INTC
15. McDonald's Corporation	Retail eating and drinking	MCD

The description of each company includes the 1989 and 1990 financial performance figures. They are provided to give a general indication of the size of the companies. These figures were obtained from reliable sources; the author is not responsible for any errors or omissions contained in them. (The 1991 figures were not available for all companies when this chapter was prepared.) The companies are listed in order beginning with the company ranked number one. Additional information on the strategies used by these companies can be found in the chapters referenced at the end of each section.

The Gold Medalists

The five Gold Medalists are reviewed below. Again, the emphasis is on the major HSM strategies the companies used to gain their speed and dominance.

1. Merck & Company, Inc.

Merck, the world's largest pharmaceutical company, was rated the top HSM company. It is primarily in the business of researching, developing, and marketing health maintenance and restoration products and services. Merck's two major industry segments are human and animal health care products and specialty chemical products. Merck controls more than 9 percent of the very competitive U.S. pharmaceutical market, and more than 3.5 percent of the global market. Merck has more than 36,000 employees and more than 82,000 stockholders. The following paragraphs discuss the HSM strategies Merck has used to achieve its position.

Strong reputation. Merck has established a golden reputation. For six consecutive years it was rated the most admired company in America by approximately eight thousand senior executives, outside directors, and financial analysts. Their ratings were based on Merck's exemplary management efforts, high-quality products, and superior financial performance. The payoffs for Merck's outstanding reputation include (1) being first in the minds of customers (the thousands of doctors who buy their products), (2) easily attracting and retaining top talent, (3) having their products reviewed more quickly by the Food and Drug Administration (FDA), and (4) easier international expansion. (For additional information on this strategy see Chapters 1, 10, 11, and 14.)

Niche focus. Despite its size, Merck has been able to stay highly focused on the pharmaceutical industry. In fact, a full 68 percent of its 1990 sales came from four therapeutic drug classes: antihypertensives and cardiovasculars (41 percent), antibiotics (11 percent), antiulcerants (8 percent), and anti-inflammatories/analgesics (8 percent). This commitment to a

niche helps Merck to optimally target all of its research, marketing, and sales activities. (See Chapters 11 and 12 for additional
perspectives on this strategy.)

Blockbuster products. A number of Merck's products are the
leaders in their class. Some of these include Vasotec (a high
blood pressure medication), Menacor, and Zocor (two
cholesterol-lowering agents). A soon-to-be-released blockbuster
drug is Proscar (a treatment for prostate enlargement). Merck
does not let its future rest on only one or two blockbuster
products. (See Chapters 3, 4, 10, and 11 for additional
information.)

Constant innovation. Merck spends more than 11 percent of
total sales revenues on research and development (R&D). It has
approximately eighteen high-quality drugs that generate more
than $100 million each per year. Merck is committed to
maintaining a steady flow of highly profitable, patent-protected
drugs in the very competitive medical marketplace. (See Chapters 9, 10, and 14.)

Commitment to R&D. Merck's reputation as a leading product innovator is made possible by senior management's strong
commitment to research. P. Roy Vagelos, the current chairman
and a physician and biochemist, has spearheaded Merck's research operations. He is very committed to investing in research
as a competitive weapon, evidenced by his $854 million expen-
diture on R&D in 1990 alone. He only requests that R&D keep
the pipeline continuously filled with new products. Hence, Vagelos prefers *focused research.* Vagelos himself visits six to eight of
the best universities each year (such as Harvard, Yale, and MIT)
to recruit talented scientists (both students and faculty) by sharing his vision of the wonder of discovering new drugs. (See
Chapters 1, 3, 4, 8, and 10 for additional information.)

Financial strength. Value Line gave Merck an A++ rating
for 1991, based on the company's overall financial performance.
Merck's sales continue to grow, and its profit margin is almost
twice as high as the industry average, as are its return on equity
and return on assets. In fact, *Value Line* predicted in its 1994–
1996 projections section that Merck's stock price should gain
anywhere from 70 percent to 105 percent in the next few years.
(For additional information see Chapters 12 and 14.)

Financial Performance of Merck & Company.

Annual Figures	1989	1990
Total sales ($ million)	$6,551	$7,672
Sales per share	$16.57	$19.82
Net profit ($ million)	$1,495	$1,781
Net profit margin	22.8%	23.2%
Earnings per share	$3.74	$4.56
Dividends paid	$1.64	$1.91
Book value per share	$8.90	$9.91

2. Hewlett-Packard Company

Hewlett-Packard designs, manufactures, and services precision electronic equipment for measurement, testing, and computation. It is the world's largest and most diversified manufacturer of such equipment. Hewlett-Packard is also the world's second largest manufacturer of computer workstations, boasting control over 20 percent of the market. This highly focused company primarily operates in a single industry segment and tries to meet the market's demands for high-quality integrated systems. Hewlett-Packard employs over 90,000 people and has approximately 73,000 shareholders. It is the number two HSM company for the following reasons:

Strategic product positioning. Hewlett-Packard will not be outflanked by its competitors by getting stuck in the middle with its product offerings. For example, to avoid losing market share in the fast-growing workstation market, Hewlett-Packard introduced a new, very powerful line of workstations (the Model 700 line) with proprietary architecture, which it claims offers "the best power at fair prices." Analysts estimate that it will take competitors a year or more to catch up. Also, Hewlett-Packard appears to be focusing on workstations in order to move toward this rapidly expanding high-ground market and away from markets in slower-growing fields (for example, minicomputers). (For additional information see Chapters 11 and 12.)

Niche domination. Hewlett-Packard dominates sales in the $3.6 billion PC laser printer market with a 60 percent market share. In fact, its Laser Jet Printer is its best selling product ever in this class. Hewlett-Packard's staff is also tightly focused on three major lines of business: (1) measurement, computation, and manufacturing equipment (37 percent of 1990 sales), (2) peripherals and network products (30 percent of 1990 sales), and (3) service for all equipment and systems (20 percent of 1990 sales). With this intense focus, it will be very difficult for Hewlett-Packard to take its eyes off the ball. (Also review Chapters 11 and 12.)

Constant innovation. Hewlett-Packard is constantly innovating. For example, it has released a low-cost palmtop computer that costs less than $700 (the HP 95LX). This computer even has Lotus 1-2-3 spreadsheet software built in, to make it very appealing to the business traveler. Another source of innovation was to allow the palmtop computer to connect with the desktop computer via an infrared optical link. The palmtop also includes a wireless pager, thus highlighting another way Hewlett-Packard is "informationalizing" its products. Finally, Hewlett-Packard was the first to release a desktop laser-quality printer that could print in either black and white or full color. (See Chapters 3, 10, and 11 for additional information.)

Very strong R&D. The Hewlett-Packard labs, staffed with very talented researchers, are some of the world's largest and most effective electronics research centers. In 1990 Hewlett-Packard spent approximately $1.4 billion on R&D, representing about 10.3 percent of its total sales. Most importantly, in 1990 nearly 50 percent of Hewlett-Packard's orders were for newly developed products introduced in the past three years. (Also review Chapters 8 and 10.)

Timely acquisitions. Hewlett-Packard knows how to save time by capitalizing on strategic acquisitions. In 1989, its $500 million purchase of Apollo Computers, a pioneer in workstations, helped Hewlett-Packard get a successful jump start with sales in this niche; it now ranks second in the world. The company would probably not have this large a share of the market if it had decided to design and develop a line of workstations totally from scratch. (See Chapters 1, 2, 9, 10, and 12 for additional information.)

Faster decision making. In 1990, when Hewlett-Packard was experiencing declining earnings and some delays in the introduction of its new workstation line, it immediately reorganized to simplify its structure, streamline operations, and, most importantly, to speed up a committee-oriented decision-making process. Its 1991 six-month earnings were up more than 20 percent from the same 1990 period, due in large part to this restructuring. (Also review Chapters 1, 4, and 14.)

Financial controls. Hewlett-Packard is financially sound. It received an A+ + financial strength rating from *Value Line*, and it has a rock-solid balance sheet. The company is taking strong measures to end margin erosion by selectively cutting staff (such as employees working on declining products) and by implementing other cost-containment efforts. (See Chapters 1 and 14 for additional information.)

Financial Performance of Hewlett-Packard Company.

Annual Figures	1989	1990
Total sales ($ million)	$11,899	$13,233
Sales per share	$50.07	$54.21
Net profit ($ million)	$829	$739
Net profit margin	7.0%	5.6%
Earnings per share	$3.52	$3.06
Dividends paid	$0.36	$0.42
Book value per share	$22.92	$26.07

3. Minnesota Mining and Manufacturing Company (3M)

Minnesota Mining and Manufacturing Company (3M) is a diversified manufacturer with more than fifty thousand products. Its leading products include pressure-sensitive tapes, magnetic storage media, reflective sheeting for advertisement and warning signs, and fluorochemical products. The 3M Company targets four general areas for product development: (1) electronics and industrial products (including abrasives, adhesives, and protective coatings), (2) information and imaging technologies (such as computer tapes, video and audio tapes, and X-ray films), (3) commercial and consumer products (such as tape, self-stick notes, and cleaning pads), and (4) life sciences products (including dressings, bandages, and surgical masks). The company has over 89,000 employees and about 113,000 shareholders. 3M's major HSM strategies include the following:

Strong R&D focus. Approximately 6.6 percent of 3M's 1990 sales dollars were directed to R&D. 3M also has the goal of reducing by half the amount of time it takes for R&D projects to successfully hit the market. Already, nearly one-third of 3M's 1990 sales came from new products introduced during the previous five years. (See Chapters 10 and 12 for additional information.)

Aggressive goal setting. 3M sets tough goals with aggressive timelines. For example, it plans to cut manufacturing costs by 10 percent, waste by 35 percent, and energy use by 20 percent by the year 1995. Setting aggressive goals, achieving them, and then setting even more aggressive goals is one of the key foundations of HSM management. (Also review Chapters 1, 10, and 14.)

Bottom-up marketing. Creativity and innovation are strongly encouraged at 3M. For example, a 3M scientist casually created the Post-it self-stick note to mark a place in his book. Secretaries around the company started using these notes, too. This product, initially developed in 1980, turned into a $500 million line by 1990, even though initially it was never part of any formal planning process. 3M used bottom-up marketing to capitalize on this creative discovery. (See Chapters 6 and 11 for additional information.)

Commitment to investors. The 3M company stays committed to its shareholders, reflected in the fact that it has not missed a quarterly dividend since 1916. 3M received an A + + financial rating from *Value Line*. A strong commitment to investors is a driving force at all major HSM companies. (Also review Chapters 13 and 14.)

Financial Performance of 3M Company.

Annual Figures	1989	1990
Total sales ($ million)	$11,990	$13,021
Sales per share	$53.85	$59.23
Net profit ($ million)	$1,244	$1,308
Net profit margin	10.4%	10%
Earnings per share	$5.55	$5.91
Dividends paid	$2.60	$2.92
Book value per share	$24.15	$27.79

4. Sony Corporation

Sony is a leading producer of consumer and industrial electronics products. The Japanese giant has about 30 percent of its sales in Japan, 30 percent in the United States, 25 percent in Europe, and 15 percent in the rest of the world. Sony's three strongest product lines are video equipment and televisions (41 percent of 1990 sales), audio equipment (25 percent of 1990 sales), and records and movies (19 percent of 1990 sales). Sony has about 78,900 employees and over 52,000 shareholders. Sony's major HSM strategies include the following:

Strong R&D commitment. This is reflected in R&D expenditures that exceed $1 billion per year. Sony uses its R&D prowess to creatively develop many innovations, including the first transistor radio, the first transistor television, and the first home video recorder. Sony is hoping its R&D investments will also pay off with its high-definition color television efforts. When consumers think of an innovative electronics company that is constantly first to market, it typically thinks of Sony. (See Chapters 8, 10, and 11 for additional information.)

Creative products. Sony offers highly innovative, creative, and well-designed products, including some of the best-known and well-respected brand names in the world: the now-famous Walkman, the Watchman, the 8-millimeter Camcorder, and the Sony Data Discman (an electronic book). (Also review Chapters 6, 10, 11, and 12.)

Future focus. Sony took a risk by recently acquiring both CBS records and Columbia Pictures to gain control over the software (records, tapes, and films) it needs to play on its hardware. Sony expects a successful synergy with these acquisitions in the future, but knows it will take some time for the gains to fully materialize. The odds are in favor of Sony's ultimate success as we approach the age of entertainment and leisure in the early twenty-first century. Sony's acquisitions were probably more a part of its ten-, twenty-, and thirty-year plans than its three- to five-year plan. (See Chapters 3, 5, and 11 for additional information.)

Financial Performance of Sony Corporation.

Annual Figures	1989	1990
Total sales ($ million)	$16,678	$18,760
Sales per share	——	——
Net profit ($ million)	$549	$655
Net profit margin	3.3%	3.5%
Earnings per share	$1.82	$1.95
Dividends paid	$0.34	$0.34
Book value per share	$24.44	$27.44

5. Liz Claiborne, Inc.

Liz Claiborne is the largest producer of clothing and accessories for women in America. Its best-selling product lines, based on their percentage of 1990 sales, are (1) misses' sportswear (42 percent), (2) petite women's sportswear (12 percent), (3) dresses (9 percent), and (4) accessories (9 percent). Cosmetics made up 4 percent of its 1990 sales. The company has about 6,000 employees and over 12,500 shareholders. Liz Claiborne's dominant HSM strategies include the following:

Strong management. The company has well-organized management, distribution, and sales teams. It has mastered the basics of management. Management emphasizes attention to detail, quality, and a keen understanding of customers' preferences. An extremely loyal customer base has been the result. (See Chapters 1, 2, 4, and 8 for additional information.)

Fine market segmentation. Management has broken down the fashion year into six segments: holiday, pre-spring, spring one, spring two, summer, and fall. Hence, consumers can choose from new styles every two months. Such short fashion cycles put the new fashions on the shelf at the most appropriate times. (Also review Chapters 11, 12, and 13.)

Strategic use of technology. A computerized inventory tracking system allows management to quickly analyze a week's sales trends. Quicker responses to customers' demands are therefore possible. Strategic use of automation seems especially crucial in the fast-moving fashion industry. (See Chapters 2, 6, and 13 for additional information.)

Strong sales channels. Liz Claiborne has established a vast sales distribution network. Its products are sold by approximately 9,400 stores in North America alone. The company also opened its first retail stores in 1988. (Review Chapters 12 and 13 for further information.)

Financial strength. Value Line gave Liz Claiborne an A+ rating. Earnings per share are also showing solid growth. H. Skip Weitzen (1991) classified Liz Claiborne as a leading hypergrowth company. (Other relevant information can be found in Chapters 12 and 14.)

Financial Performance of Liz Claiborne, Inc.

Annual Figures	1989	1990
Total sales ($ million)	$1,411	$1,729
Sales per share	$16.00	$20.35
Net profit ($ million)	$165	$206
Net profit margin	11.7%	11.9%
Earnings per share	$1.87	$2.37
Dividends paid	$0.19	$0.24
Book value per share	$6.94	$8.40

The Silver Medalists

The five Silver Medalists are not discussed in quite as much depth as were the Gold Medalists, but readers can still gain a strong sense of their major HSM strategies. Again, chapters that shed additional light on a particular strategy are listed after the description of that strategy.

6. Wal-Mart Stores, Inc.

Wal-Mart is one of the fastest-growing and most profitable retailers in America. It overtook Sears as the largest retailer in 1990. It operates over 1,573 Wal-Mart Stores, 148 Sam's Clubs, and four Hypermarts in thirty-six states. These numbers are increasing almost daily. Wal-Mart can be characterized as a discount retailer—the only segment in which it competes. Wal-Mart has over 328,000 employees and approximately 122,420 stockholders. Its major HSM strategies include the following:

Niche focus. A leader in the discount-retailer niche, Wal-

Mart offers an extensive product selection at very low prices. When consumers think discount, they usually think of Wal-Mart. (See Chapter 11 for additional information.)

Service commitment. Wal-Mart uses friendly customer service to attract and retain buyers. Some stores even have employees who greet customers and hand them their shopping carts. This level of service has its origin in the spirit of founder Sam Walton; he never interacted with customers in any other way. (Also review Chapter 13.)

Computerized operations. This includes highly automated distribution centers that are required to continually cut shipping costs and delivery time in catchment areas. (A catchment area typically consists of 150 stores.) Computerization is also used to speed up checkouts, track inventory, and facilitate quick reordering. (See Chapters 4, 6, 12, and 13 for additional information.)

Rapid expansion. Wal-Mart is expanding at a lightning pace, opening more than 100 new stores a year and purchasing complementary businesses. Wal-Mart rapidly established a solid customer base by opening stores in remote areas of the country that had few, if any, competitors' stores. It therefore dominated the remote-area niche. Once it gained dominance in these primarily uncontested markets, it began to move with confidence toward the more saturated markets. (Review Chapter 11 for additional information.)

Financial Performance of Wal-Mart Stores, Inc.

Annual Figures	1989	1990
Total sales ($ million)	$25,811	$32,602
Sales per share	$22.80	$28.54
Net profit ($ million)	$1,076	$1,291
Net profit margin	4.2%	4%
Earnings per share	$0.95	$1.14
Dividends paid	$0.11	$0.14
Book value per share	$3.50	$4.70

7. Apple Computer, Inc.

Apple Computer is a major producer of computer systems. In 1990 Apple became the world's second largest personal computer manufacturer (behind IBM). Its main product lines include (1) computers (the Apple II and Macintosh lines), (2) software (including HyperCard, Multifinder, Pro Dos), (3) peripheral products (such as disk drives, monitors, and printers), and (4) communication products (such as file servers, networking software, and modems). The company has about 14,500 employees and approximately 32,750 stockholders. Its major HSM strategies include the following:

Strategic positioning. The selection of the name "Apple" established the company as being innovative and user-friendly in customers' minds. Strategic positioning also set Apple apart from the competition, since the name appealed to nontechnical buyers, and helped to differentiate Apple's products. (See Chapters 11 and 12 for additional information.)

Creative R&D. Apple's R&D department is funded with over eight percent of the total sales revenues. It was responsible for inventing the revolutionary Macintosh. An enhanced version of the Macintosh, the Mac Plus, was bundled with Apple's Laser Writer printer to usher in the desktop publishing revolution, with Apple leading the way. Indeed, Apple has established itself as a prime leader in desktop publishing applications. (Review Chapters 6, 8, 10, and 11 for more information.)

Timely strategic relations. Apple has formed strategic relationships with companies, to capitalize on synergies and to speed up new product offerings. For example, it recently formed a relationship with Sony to develop a notebook computer. The relationship with Sony was designed to yield a high-quality product in significantly less time than either of the two companies could achieve working on their own. (See Chapters 1, 5, and 10 for additional information.)

Event marketing. Apple excels in event marketing, which quickly and almost permanently captures the imagination of the marketplace. For example, Apple advertised its Macintosh as the computer "for the rest of us" when it challenged IBM during a 1984 Super Bowl commercial. Apple routinely uses great fanfare to announce new product releases and to make important corporate announcements to the press and the investment community. (See Chapters 9 and 11 for additional information.)

Niche selling. Apple is very much in touch with its customers' buying behaviors. It was the first to sell its computers to students in college bookstores, instead of in the more traditional retail outlets. This unusual sales and marketing strategy quickly strengthened Apple's position in the educational market. (See Chapter 12.)

Financial Performance of Apple Computer, Inc.

Annual Figures	1989	1990
Total sales ($ million)	$5,284	$5,558
Sales per share	$41.85	$48.18
Net profit ($ million)	$454	$475
Net profit margin	8.6%	8.5%
Earnings per share	$3.53	$3.77
Dividends paid	$0.40	$0.44
Book value per share	$11.77	$12.54

8. Reuters Holding PLC

Reuters, a pioneering company in the United Kingdom that helped usher in the paperless society and the Information Age, is one of the world's leading distributors of computerized information. Reuters offers international stock and bond trading systems. It provides on-line business news, stock market prices, and historical data on worldwide currencies and securities. Reuters has about 10,800 employees and approximately 17,500 shareholders. Its major HSM strategies include the following:

Global communications systems. Reuters has established a global communications network with over 200,800 terminals in nearly 130 countries. It also relies on satellite communications and cable linkups. Reuters's key competitive angle is that it provides timely news and information from around the world. (See Chapters 3, 6, and 12 for additional information.)

Commitment to the information age. Reuters is a true Information Age enterprise. It provides on-line access to a wide variety of information products and services, which made up about 80 percent of its sales in 1990; transaction and media products accounted for the remaining 20 percent. Reuters provides access to important real-time information data bases twenty-four hours a day, including stock quotes and late-breaking news. (Also review Chapters 3, 6, 12, and 13.)

Strategic relationships. In conjunction with two Chicago exchange and trading groups, Reuters has developed an international after-hours futures exchange using computer technology and satellite and cable technologies to capture a larger part of the international investment market. An important strategy is its focus on the after-hours niche to avoid head-on competition in the other time slots. (See Chapters 5, 10, and 11 for additional information.)

Financial stability. Reuters received a solid A+ financial strength rating from *Value Line*, yet it has recently been experiencing a contraction in some of its financial products markets. Therefore, it has quickly directed its attention to serious cost cutting in areas such as R&D. Such cost cutting should keep it profitable, especially as more companies begin to aggressively compete as Information Age experts. (Also review Chapter 14.)

Financial Performance of Reuters Holding PLC.

Annual Figures	1989	1990
Total sales ($ million)	$1,916	$2,640
Sales per share		
Net profit ($ million)	$292	$339
Net profit margin	15.2%	15.1%
Earnings per share	$2.11	$2.86
Dividends paid	$0.64	$0.95
Book value per share	$4.75	$7.61

9. Microsoft Corporation

Microsoft is the leading developer of software for personal computers. In fact, one of its key HSM strengths is that it does not deviate from this software niche. Its main product groups include (1) operating systems software (such as MS-DOS, Microsoft, and OS/2), (2) business applications software (including Microsoft Word and Microsoft Works), (3) systems/languages software (such as Windows 3.0, Microsoft Pascal, and Microsoft C), and (4) hardware, recreation, and CD-ROM products (for instance, Microsoft Bookshelf and Microsoft Flight Simulator).

Microsoft's MS-DOS software alone runs on over 60 million IBM and IBM-compatible personal computers. This was made possible by Microsoft's timely relationship with IBM in 1981. Microsoft has over 5,600 employees and about 8,700 shareholders. Key HSM strategies include the following:

Incremental development. Microsoft has a very strong commitment to R&D (about 15 percent of sales). The R&D unit frequently turns out award-winning software. Microsoft also seems to focus on an incremental improvement research strategy. For example, a small-scale strategic acquisition set the foundation for Microsoft's future dominance of the software industry. Microsoft was chosen by IBM to develop the operating system for its first personal computer, thus forming one of the most important alliances in Microsoft's history.

In order to meet IBM's timelines for developing the operating system, Microsoft bought a currently existing operating system for approximately $50,000 from a Seattle programmer. The existing program was then converted, using an incremental research model, to the Microsoft Disk Operating System (MS-DOS). This is a classic case of high speed management. Many incrementally improved versions of DOS for different brands of IBM-compatible computers eventually evolved, thus setting the stage for Microsoft's strong sales growth and expansion. (See Chapters 4, 5, 6, and 10 for additional information.)

User-friendly products. Microsoft continues to develop and market highly innovative, appealing, and user-friendly products. This was the case with Windows 3.0, which provides a friendly interface between users and their computers. Microsoft was able to skillfully market both the user-friendliness of Windows 3.0 (the value) and the uniqueness of the product (the cutting-edge features). (Also review Chapters 11 and 12.)

Anticipating the future. Microsoft is constantly trying to anticipate the future. Important target areas for future software applications include multimedia software, pen-based operating systems (an electronic stylus rather than a keyboard or mouse is used to interact with the computer), and advanced networking software. In fact, Microsoft's ability to accurately anticipate the future needs of the marketplace might be one of its most important corporate challenges in the 1990s. (See Chapter 3.)

Financial Performance of Microsoft Corporation.

Annual Figures	1989	1990
Total sales ($ million)	$804	$1,183
Sales per share	$4.91	$6.94
Net profit ($ million)	$171	$279
Net profit margin	21.2%	23.6%
Earnings per share	$1.01	$1.56
Dividends paid	0	0
Book value per share	$5.15	$8.08

10. Abbott Laboratories

Abbott is a leading provider of health care products worldwide. Its vast holdings of products include drugs, diagnostic tests, intravenous solutions, hospital instruments, prepared infant formulas, and nutritional products. It also produces miscellaneous agricultural and chemical products. Approximately half of Abbott's revenues come from its hospital and laboratory products, and half from its drugs and nutritional products. Abbott employs approximately 43,700 workers and has about 49,800 shareholders. Abbott's major HSM strategies are discussed in the following paragraphs.

Commitment to R&D. Abbott is highly committed to R&D, having spent approximately $567 million on research in 1990 alone (9.2 percent of sales). Abbott is targeting much of this research funding on its next generation of products (a new allergy test, a new treatment for hypertension, modernized blood gas monitors). In addition, Abbott has recently developed Hytrin, a drug treatment for prostate enlargement. This should become a very lucrative new market. (See Chapters 3, 10, and 11 for additional information.)

Strategic alliances. Abbott is the major shareholder in Amgen, a leading biotechnology company. It also owns half of one of Japan's largest pharmaceutical companies. Therefore, it is able to use strategic alliances to stay abreast of new technologies and to improve its global presence. Abbott has operations in forty-four different countries and has established a worldwide sales network. (Review Chapters 3, 10, 12, and 14 for additional information.)

Important inventions. Abbott has a history of quickly inventing effective products for very important niches. For example, it was the first company to introduce an AIDS antibody diagnostic test, thereby becoming a world leader in AIDS testing. It is also committed to constantly improving its most successful inventions. (Review Chapters 10 and 11 for additional information.)

Financial soundness. This company received an A + + financial strength rating by *Value Line.* This is reflected in its stock-price stability, price-growth persistence, and most importantly, earnings predictability. Abbott is also very cash-flow positive. (Review Chapter 14 for further information.)

Financial Performance of Abbott Laboratories.

Annual Figures	1989	1990
Total sales ($ million)	$5,380	$6,159
Sales per share	$12.16	$14.35
Net profit ($ million)	$860	$966
Net profit margin	16.0%	15.7%
Earnings per share	$1.93	$2.22
Dividends paid	$0.68	$0.81
Book value per share	$6.16	$6.60

The Bronze Medalists

The Bronze Medalists are only briefly described, and a few of their key HSM strategies are summarized.

11. Walt Disney Company

Walt Disney is a major supplier of entertainment, and includes Disneyland, Disney World, Epcot Center, Disney–MGM Studios, and Touchstone Pictures. The company recently has returned its focus to one of its strongest niches—animation. Disney has recently released animation blockbusters *The Little Mermaid* and *Beauty and the Beast.* Disney saves production time and money by continually rereleasing its classic films every few years. (See Chapters 11 and 12 for additional information.)

Disney is quickly expanding into new, global markets (such as Euro Disney in France). A theme park in Tokyo is also planned. (See Chapters 3, 4, and 12 for additional information.)

The Disney Channel on cable television, which uses the enduring popularity of Mickey Mouse and Donald Duck in all its marketing and promotional efforts, is both a revenue generator and a form of continuous advertisement. (Review Chapters 11 and 12.) Finally, Disney is nicely poised for the future, especially for the predicted Age of Leisure and Recreation that is expected early in the twenty-first century. (See Chapter 3.)

Financial Performance of Walt Disney Company.

Annual Figures	1989	1990
Total sales ($ million)	$4,594	$5,844
Sales per share	$33.95	$44.34
Net profit ($ million)	$703	$824
Net profit margin	15.3%	14.1%
Earnings per share	$5.10	$6
Dividends paid	$0.46	$0.56
Book value per share	$22.50	$26.47

12. Albertson's, Inc.

Albertson's is the nation's sixth largest retail grocery chain. Its stores are primarily located in fifteen Western states, although it has some strong stores emerging in the Sunbelt. Albertson's utilizes strategic retail site selection to maximize the market area of a given store. It also utilizes highly efficient and modernized distribution facilities to quickly service its widely dispersed store units. (See Chapters 4, 6, 11, 12, and 13 for additional information.)

Albertson's skillfully promotes its one-stop shopping advantage and utilizes "superstores" (food/drug combination stores that offer over thirty thousand items) to deliver on this promise. In fact, industry analysts point out that Albertson's has four different sized superstores (big, huge, colossal, and gargantuan), thus ensuring dominance in the superstore niche. (Review Chapter 11.) Albertson's uses professionally developed employment tests to accurately select, place, and promote management and other personnel. (Review Chapter 8.) And it continually closes its least profitable stores and opens new units in fast-growing or underserved markets. This type of muscle build-

ing continually strengthens the company's profit margins. (See
Chapters 12 and 14 for additional information.)

Financial Performance of Albertson's, Inc.

Annual Figures	1989	1990
Total sales ($ million)	$7,423	$8,219
Sales per share	$55.43	$61.42
Net profit ($ million)	$197	$234
Net profit margin	2.6%	2.8%
Earnings per share	$1.47	$1.75
Dividends paid	$0.40	$0.46
Book value per share	$6.94	$8.13

13. Nintendo Corporation, Ltd.

Nintendo is one of the leaders in the multibillion-dollar home
video game market. The company has attained 90 percent of the
Japanese video game market, 80 percent of the American market, and is now methodically entering the untapped European
market. Nintendo has the perseverance that characterizes most
HSM companies. (See Chapters 3, 11, and 12 for additional
information.) Nintendo continually promotes and benefits
from its advertising mascot, the Italian plumber Mario. Some
market researchers say that Mario has become more popular
with school-age children (Nintendo's primary customer base)
than Disney's Mickey Mouse. (Review Chapters 11 and 12, too.)
     Nintendo's commitment to innovation is exhibited in
such new products as its handheld Game Boy game system and
its new sixteen-bit Super Family Computer, which has color
graphics and sound features that are superior to the company's
original Nintendo Entertainment System (NES). (Review Chapters 3, 4, and 10.) Only the highest-quality games are offered.
Nintendo utilizes a stringent licensing and review policy for any
software developer who makes a game cartridge, thus ensuring
the highest level of game quality. (Review Chapters 4, 10 and 13
for additional information.) The company also provides outstanding customer service, offering a phone line staffed by over
two hundred game counselors to keep users from getting frustrated with a particular game. (See Chapters 6 and 13.)

Financial Performance of Nintendo.

Annual Figures	1989	1990
Total sales (billion yen)	291 yen	411 yen
Sales per share	———	———
Net profit (billion yen)	34 yen	33 yen
Net profit margin	11.8%	13.7%
Earnings per share	327 yen	314 yen
Dividends paid	33 yen	30 yen
Book value per share	1,499 yen	1,809 yen

Note: $1 = 135 yen; sales for 1990 are annualized.

14. Intel Corporation

Intel is a leading manufacturer of integrated circuits for computers and other communications and electronics equipment. The company has established itself as the third largest semiconductor manufacturer in America. Intel's 286, 386, and 486 trademarked chip designs supply the brains for approximately 80 percent of all desktop computers. In fact, PC users are increasingly migrating to Intel's 386 and 486 microprocessor chips for greater computing power. (See Chapters 10, 11, and 12 for additional information.)

Intel's strong commitment to research and development is evident in the fact that the 1990 research budget was 13 percent of sales. This commitment led to the development in 1989 of Intel's 486 chip (804486 chip), which gives portable computers the power of mainframes. For the same reason, in 1991 Intel was also able to introduce a new 100 MHz microprocessor that was twice as powerful as anything else on the market. (Review Chapters 3 and 10.)

Intel wisely and quickly trademarked its 386 and 486 chips. It announced it would sue anyone who used these trademarks, thus delaying competitors' activities in this market. Therefore, when users think "486 power," they think of Intel. (See Chapters 4 and 11 for additional information.)

Intel shows strong profit margins, compared to the industry overall. Prodigy's *Strategic Investor* showed that Intel's profit margin was over five times greater than the industry average in 1991, while its return on equity was approximately two and a half times greater than the industry average. (Review Chapter 14.)

Financial Performance of Intel Corporation.

Annual Figures	1989	1990
Total sales ($ million)	$3,127	$3,921
Sales per share	$16.95	$19.64
Net profit ($ million)	$391	$650
Net profit margin	12.5%	16.6%
Earnings per share	$2.06	$3.20
Dividends paid	0	0
Book value per share	$13.81	$17.99

15. McDonald's Corporation

McDonald's is a worldwide chain of over 11,850 fast-food and beverage restaurants built around a standardized menu of hamburgers. McDonald's is considered the inventor of the fast-food restaurant. It has rapidly evolved into the world's largest food service company. Over twenty million customers visit McDonald's restaurants each day, and the number is rapidly increasing. (See Chapters 1, 3, 5, 11, and 13 for additional information.)

McDonald's invests heavily in advertising its brands around the world. It runs creative television commercials that showcase its mascot, Ronald McDonald. One of its most successful advertising slogans is "You deserve a break today—so get up and get away to McDonald's." (Review Chapters 11 and 12.) The company quickly captured a health-conscious leadership position in the fast-food industry by improving on the nutritional and health value of its fast food. For example, it added low-fat selections to its menu, and it no longer fries in beef fat. In 1991, it introduced the McLean, a low-fat hamburger, at a national level. McDonald's displays the vitamins, nutrients, and calories in all of its food and beverage products. (See Chapters 3, 4, and 10 for additional information.)

Financial Performance of McDonald's Corporation.

Annual Figures	1989	1990
Total sales ($ million)	$6,065	$6,640
Sales per share	$16.97	$18.49
Net profit ($ million)	$727	$802

Net profit margin	12.0%	12.1%
Earnings per share	$1.95	$2.14
Dividends paid	$0.30	$0.33
Book value per share	$9.25	$11.09

Conclusion

This chapter highlighted a few of the key HSM strategies used by some of the top HSM companies in America and the world. The fifteen HSM companies described should serve as role models for all management teams that want to become time-based competitors. There are surely many more companies effectively using HSM principles. While it is fair to say that the HSM strategies are not responsible for all of these companies' successes, it seems safe to conclude that the effective utilization of HSM management is at least a contributing factor.

Becoming a High-Speed Manager

Managers and organizations ideally should take an incremental, one-step-at-a-time approach to HSM management, because a gradual accumulation of successful small steps usually evolves into a full-blown culture shift away from traditional management practices and toward HSM strategies. Trying to do too much too soon will surely lead to confusion, frustration, and the eventual elimination of HSM strategies from management's repertoire.

For example, a prospective HSM manager might first want to take a general yet contemporary management course to review essential management skills such as strategic planning, employee motivation, and leadership skills. Next, she should try to become a master of time management. After gaining full control over her time, she should then rank-order the remaining HSM skills for managers and decide which ones would be most beneficial, given her current job demands and responsibilities. A manager who is currently involved in persuading groups of people (employees, customers, alliances, investors) to respond more quickly in a favorable manner might want to focus on powerful communication and negotiation skills. A manager involved in corporate strategic planning might want to learn new ways to become more efficient at locating and accessing relevant on-line data bases using the fastest available computer workstation. She might also want to develop some reliable techniques for accurately predicting the future. Prospective HSM managers should also acquire effective coping skills for avoiding debilitating work stress, while enhancing their personal wellness.

Managers also need to realize that they personally might be ready to implement a number of different HSM strategies, but their staffs and/or superiors might need to be prepared to understand and support these new time-based initiatives. For example, a staff that is used to delegating upward to a manager will need to learn the new rules of the game. Also, the prospective HSM manager's boss might need to be convinced that a notebook-size computer with a built-in modem will truly allow the manager to be more productive and effective both on the road and at home. Also, it might take some time and some convincing to move one's superiors, peers, and subordinates from using a drawn-out decision-making process to using a decision-making model that yields faster and more accurate decisions. The prospective HSM manager must be very patient, yet continuously persevere in the face of any opposition.

Entire organizations usually become HSM corporations only under the direction of a time-oriented senior management team or chief executive officer. Organizations should adopt and successfully implement only one or two organizational-level HSM interventions at a time. For example, a company might want to quickly bolster the effectiveness of its work force by implementing a professionally developed personnel selection program along with some much-needed employee training and development programs. A company that is facing a serious sales slump might begin to immediately focus on implementing a niche marketing campaign coupled with a training program designed to help salespeople close sales significantly more quickly. A company in serious financial difficulties might take some immediate and decisive steps to contain costs and generate sufficient cash flow during tough times, while at the same time strengthening its customer service department to retain the few profitable clients in its current portfolio. A company that is always one step behind its competitors in terms of new product offerings might want to establish an effective competitor intelligence system while at the same time speeding up its product development process.

A prospective HSM manager needs to become aware of some other key issues as well. For example, becoming a successful HSM manager does not necessarily cost a lot of money. Many HSM skills (for example, time management, quicker decision making, strategic negotiating) simply require a good deal of study and practice to be perfected. The same is true for many of the organizational-level strategies. For example, niche marketing and selling could conceivably cost less than the more traditional shotgun approaches to these disciplines. Also, professionally developed employment tests, such as those discussed in Chapter Eight, are available for $8 to $12 per assessment, that allow management to quickly hire dependable and productive employees. This is much cheaper than using no selection tests and then hiring an unreliable and unproductive workforce.

Prospective HSM managers should never forget that they must do their duties faster as well as more effectively. They should not sacrifice quality for speed, nor should they do the wrong things faster. They also should avoid doing things so quickly that they become forced to outgrow their resources, growing so fast that they do not have the staff or the cash flow to support their growth.

Prospective HSM managers must also realize that fast companies can quickly slow down, stumble, and stall. Time-based companies can also quickly burn out if they make too many sudden wrong moves, or if they lose the key managers who provided the fuel, the spark, and the acceleration for their previous speed. Even some of the very best HSM companies can stall.

For example, Citicorp is a pioneering HSM company. It offers twenty-four-hour banking by phone in addition to outstanding customer service. It also pioneered the automatic teller machine (ATM), which redefined convenience in banking. These are all very admirable HSM strategies. Yet Jack Willoughby, in a 1991 *Financial World* article, revealed how some poor business decisions that led to "tons of tanked foreign and real estate loans [coupled with]. . . $10 billion in debt" (1991, p. 24) has forced Citicorp to stall, despite its many HSM technology advances. Citicorp could probably benefit from learning how to make faster and more accurate strategic decisions while better anticipating the future.

HSM strategies should be seriously considered by all turnaround companies. Alex Taylor III reports in a 1992 *Fortune* magazine article that General Motors is currently attempting to turn itself around. GM was facing slumping sales, falling productivity, shrinking profits, lost market share, and dropping stock prices at the time of Taylor's article. HSM strategies at both the managerial and the organizational level could only benefit GM. In fact, Taylor polled a number of industry consultants who were familiar with GM's predicament and they suggested that GM's chairman, Robert Stempel, should immediately adopt a lean and mean approach to management, and quickly implement some of the following strategies:

1. Speed up new-model design and prototype development
2. Improve efficiency to speed up the entire manufacturing process
3. Reorganize to improve and speed up decision making
4. Instill tough accountability standards
5. Promote only programs that solve problems *now*
6. Encourage candor to quickly get problems out in the open
7. Increase flexibility to build more models in each plant
8. Rethink all product lines to reduce redundancies
9. Drastically cut production engineering costs

10. Get tough with unions to ensure more union jobs in the long run (Adapted from Taylor, 1992)

Articles written by John Byrne and associates for a 1991 issue of *Business Week* suggest that IBM also could benefit from a variety of HSM strategies in its quest to become more competitive. And a 1991 study published by William Weitzel and Ellen Jonsson in the *Academy of Management Executive* suggests that Sears might benefit from HSM strategies as well.

HSM strategies are also useful for nonprofit organizations. For example, a 1991 *Chicago Tribune* article (Kuczka, 1991) revealed that drug-running gangs in the suburbs are using high-tech equipment to conduct surveillance on the police. The police need similar equipment in order to stop being out-maneuvered. Similarly, Rogers Worthington (1991) reports that a Minneapolis community development agency is enlisting gang members to help curb gang crime. These gang members are being used as outreach counselors, to use their contacts with the gang members to quickly curb gang violence. The agency thought that gang members could access and influence their colleagues more quickly than outsiders. This is an excellent application of an HSM strategy.

The U.S. military used HSM strategies and technologies to bring a quick end to the Gulf War, employing a brilliant strategic plan, extremely high-tech weapons systems, and effective use of the media by President Bush and his generals to win over and retain the support of most of the American people. High-level strategic negotiation skills were also used to win the support of critical allies in the Middle East. And finally, a crystal clear end goal was established (liberation of Kuwait) so that President Bush knew exactly what needed to be accomplished before he would end the war. This was excellent goal setting.

Prospective and current HSM managers must be aware of overarching societal trends that can quickly affect their ability to optimally perform their jobs. For example, businesses will need to work more closely with the American educational system to make sure students are acquiring the knowledge and skills necessary to make American companies highly competitive in the twenty-first century. U.S. businesses cannot leave this to chance. Michael Porter, in a 1990 *Harvard Business Review* article, suggested that entire countries, not just managers and organizations, need to be more competitive in the global marketplace. Better cooperation and coordination between American companies and the federal, state, and local governments is needed to reach this goal in the United States.

Finally, a manager's job as we know it today will surely become obsolete. Managers of tomorrow might be required to manage lines of knowledge and ideas, rather than groups of people. As emphasis on formal job titles is reduced, some people might be the manager for some projects, the subordinate for others. An increase in "telecommuting" could drastically reduce a company's reliance on a corporate headquarters. A manager's need for daily in-person interactions with his staff would be changed to the need for daily on-line interactions. In brief, the HSM manager must be prepared for both the predictable and the unpredictable as he enters the twenty-first century.

REFERENCES AND SUGGESTED READINGS

Introduction

Davis, S. M. (1987). *Future perfect*. Reading, MA: Addison-Wesley.

Keen, G. W. (1988). *Competing in time: Using telecommunications for competitive advantage*. Cambridge, MA: Ballinger.

Peters, T. (1987). *Thriving on chaos: Handbook for a management revolution*. New York: Knopf.

Peters, T. (1990, September). Time-obsessed competition. *Management Review*, pp. 16–20.

Peters, T. (1991, June 3). Beyond speed: We're all in the fad-and-fashion business. *Industry Week*, pp. 20–26.

Peters, T. S., & Waterman, R. H. (1982). *In search of excellence*. New York: Warner Books.

Rosenau, M. (1990). *Faster new product development: Getting the right product to market quickly.* New York: AMACOM.

Stalk, G., & Hout, T. M. (1990). *Competing against time: How time-based competition is re-shaping global markets.* New York: Free Press.

Tucker, R. B. (1991). *Managing the future: Ten driving forces of change for the '90s.* New York: Putnam.

Vesey, J. T. (1991). The new competitors: They think in terms of "speed-to-market." *Academy of Management Executives, 5*(2), 23–33.

Chapter One

Baehr, M. E. (1992). *Predicting success in higher-level positions.* Westport, CT: Quorum.

Baehr, M. E., Jones, J. W., & Nerad, A. (1991). *Psychological correlates of business ethics in executives.* Park Ridge, IL: London House Research Series.

Bennis, W. (1989). *On becoming a leader.* Reading, MA: Addison-Wesley.

Blanchard, K., & Johnson, S. (1982). *The one minute manager: The quickest way to increase your own prosperity.* New York: Berkley.

Carnegie, D., & Carnegie, D. D. (1981). *How to win friends and influence people.* New York: Simon and Schuster.

Kets de Vries, M.F.R., & Miller, D. (1984). *The neurotic organization: Diagnosing and changing counterproductive styles of management.* San Francisco: Jossey-Bass.

Kets de Vries, M.F.R., & Miller, D. (1987). *Unstable at the top: Inside the troubled organization.* New York: New American Library.

Kouzes, J. M., & Posner, B. Z. (1990, January). The credibility factor: What followers expect from their leaders. *Management Journal,* pp. 28–33.

London House, Inc. (1991). *The System for Testing and Evaluating Potential (STEP).* Rosemont, IL: London House.

McCauley, C. D., & Ruderman, M. N. (1991). Understanding executive derailment: A first step in prevention. In J. Jones, B. Steffy, & D. Bray (Eds.), *Applying psychology in business: The handbook for managers and human resources professionals.* Lexington, MA: Lexington.

Moretti, D. M., Morken, C. L., & Borkowski, J. M. (1989). *Profile of the American CEO: Comparing Inc. and Fortune executives.* Paper presented at the Annual Conference of the Academy of Management, Washington, DC.

Stoner, C. R., & Fry, F. L. (1987). *Strategic planning in the small business.* Cincinnati, OH: Southwestern.

Sculley, J., & Byrne, J. A. (1987). *Odyssey: Pepsi to Apple . . . A journey of adventure, ideas, and the future.* New York: Harper & Row.

Verespej, M. A. (1990, March 19). Why managers fail: Visible flaws go uncorrected. *Industry Week*, p. 42.

Young, E. C. (1991). *What is a world-class manager?* Chicago, IL: DePaul University School of Management. (A complete copy of this paper is available from the Center for Enterprise Development, Chicago, IL.)

Chapter Two

Lebow, M. (1980). *Practical tools and techniques for managing time.* Englewood Cliffs, NJ: Prentice Hall.

Levinson, J. C. (1990). *The ninety-minute hour.* New York: Dutton.

MacKenzie, A. (1990). *The time trap.* New York: AMACOM.

Turla, P., & Hawkins, K. L. (1983). *Time management made easy.* New York: Dutton.

Weiss, D. H. (1988). *How to delegate effectively.* New York: AMACOM.

Chapter Three

Barker, J. A. (1992). *Future edge: Discovering the new paradigms for success.* New York: Morrow.

Berkman, R. I. (1990). *Find it fast: How to uncover expert information on any subject.* New York: Harper & Row.

Burrus, D., & Thomsen, P. (1990). *Gain a strategic advantage with the new tools of technology.* Dubuque, IA: Kendall/Hunt.

Celente, G., & Milton, T. (1991). *Trend tracking: Find out how to transform trends into opportunity and profit.* New York: Warner.

Drucker, P. (1980). *Managing in turbulent times.* New York: Harper & Row.

Feather, F. (1989). *G-forces: The thirty-five global forces restructuring our future.* New York: Morrow.

Lorie, P., & Murray-Clark, S. (1989). *History of the future: A chronology.* New York: Doubleday.

Makridekis, S. G. (1990). *Forecasting, planning, and strategy for the twenty-first century.* New York: Free Press.

Naisbitt, J., (1982). *Megatrends: Ten new directions transforming our lives.* New York: Warner Books.

Naisbitt, J., & Aburdene, P. (1986). *Re-inventing the corporation: Transforming your job and your company for the new information society.* New York: Warner.

Naisbitt, J., & Aburdene, P. (1990). *Megatrends 2000: Ten new directions for the 1990's.* New York: Morrow.

Research Alert. (1991). *Future vision: The 189 most important trends of the 1990's.* Naperville, IL: Sourcebooks.

Sculley, J., & Byrne, J. A. (1987). *Odyssey: Pepsi and Apple...A journey of adventure, ideas, and the future.* New York: Harper & Row.

Toffler, A. (1980). *The third wave.* New York: Morrow.

Tucker, R. B. (1991). *Managing the future: 10 driving forces of change for the '90s.* New York: Putnam.

Chapter Four

Bourgeois, L. J., & Eisenhardt, K. (1988). Strategic decision processes in high velocity environments: Four cases in the microcomputer industry. *Management Science, 34,* 816–835.

Bransford, J. D., & Stein, B. S. *The ideal problem solver: A guide for improving thinking, learning, and creativity.* New York: Freeman.

Cosier, R. A., & Schwenk, C. R. (1990). Agreement and thinking alike: Ingredients for poor decisions. *Academy of Management Executives, 4*(1), 69–74.

Drucker, P. F. (1967). *The effective executive.* New York: Harper & Row.

Eisenhardt, K. M. (1989). Making fast strategic decisions in high-velocity environments. *Academy of Management Journal, 32*(3), 543–576.

Hiam, A. (1990). *The vest-pocket CEO: Decision-making tools for executives.* Englewood Cliffs, NJ: Prentice Hall.

Judge, W. Q., & Miller, A. (1991). Antecedents and outcomes of decision speed in different environmental contexts. *Academy of Management Journal, 34*(2), 449–463.

Pelton, W. J., Sackman, S., & Boguslaw, R. (1990). *Tough choices: The decision-making styles of America's top 50 CEO's.* Homewood, IL: Dow Jones-Irwin.

Russo, J. E., & Schoemaker, P. J. (1989). *Decision traps: The ten barriers to brilliant decision-making and how to overcome them.* New York: Doubleday.

Chapter Five

Brewer, K. C. (1990). *Personal negotiating skills.* Shawnee Mission, KS: National Press Publications.

Buskirk, R. (1989). *Frontal attack, divide and conquer, the fait accompli and 118 other tactics managers must know.* New York: Wiley.

Fisher, R., & Ury, W. (1981). *Getting to yes: Negotiating agreement without giving in.* New York: Penguin.

Fisher, R., & Brown, S. (1988). *Getting together: Building relationships as we negotiate.* New York: Penguin.

Fuller, G. (1991). *The negotiator's handbook.* Englewood Cliffs, NJ: Prentice Hall.

Glaser, R., & Glaser, C. (1991). *Negotiating style profile.* King of Prussia, PA: Organization Design and Development.

Griffin, T. J., & Daggatt, W. R. (1990). *The global negotiator: Building strong business relationships.* New York: Harper Business.

Kuhn, R. L. (1988). *The dealmaker: All the negotiating skills and secrets you need.* New York: Wiley.

Malin, S., Montgomery, D. J., & Gallagher, R. (1984). *The negotiation edge* [computer software]. Palo Alto, CA: Human Edge Software Corporation.

Nierenberg, G. I. (1990). *The Art of Negotiating Software* [computer software]. Berkeley. CA: Experience in Software.

Chapter Six

Baron, J. B., & Sternberg, R. J. (1987). *Teaching thinking skills: Theory and practice*. New York: W. H. Freeman.

Berkman, R. I. (1990). *Find it fast: How to uncover expert information on any subject*. New York: Harper & Row.

Bodin, M. (1991). *Using the telephone more effectively*. New York: Barron's Educational Series.

Bowen, C., & Peyton, D. (1989). *How to get the most out of CompuServe*. (4th ed.). New York: Bantam.

Bureau of Business Practice. (1988). How to sell your ideas. *Management Letter, 107,* 4–5.

CompuServe, Inc. (1990a). *CompuServe almanac: An off-line reference of on-line services*. Columbus, OH: Author

CompuServe, Inc. (1990b). *CompuServe navigational chart*. Columbus, OH: Author.

Dean, W., & Morgenthaler, J. (1991). *Smart drugs and nutrients: How to improve your memory and increase your intelligence using the latest discoveries in neuroscience*. Santa Cruz, CA: B & J.

DeBono, E. (1985). *DeBono's thinking course*. New York: Facts On File.

Dow Jones & Company. (1991). *Dow Jones news retrieval: Quick reference guide*. Princeton, NJ: Author.

Griffin, M. P. (1991). *Lotus 1-2-3 release 2.3 in business: Worksheet shortcuts and applications*. Carmel, IN: SAMS.

McCarthy, M. J. (1991). *Mastering the information age: A course in working smarter, thinking better, and learning faster*. Los Angeles: Tarcher.

Meyer, N. D., & Boone, M. E. (1989). *The information edge*. Homewood, IL: Dow Jones-Irwin.

Nelson, R. (1989, April). Building the CEO workstation. *Personal Computing*, pp. 70–84.

Porter, M. E., & Millar, V. E. (1985, July-August). How information gives you competitive advantage. *Harvard Business Review*, pp. 149–160.

Que Corporation. (1989). *Introduction to business software*. Carmel, IN: Que Publications.

Que Corporation. (1989). *Introduction to business software.* Carmel, IN: Que Publications.

Quinn, G. V. (1989). *The fax handbook.* Blue Ridge Summit, PA: TAB.

Sullivan, N. (1991). *Computer power for your small business.* New York: AMACOM.

Scott, C. D., & Jaffee, D. T. (1988). *How you and your organization can survive and thrive in times of change.* San Francisco: Heartworks.

Stewart, T. A. (1991, June 3). Brain power. *Fortune,* pp. 44–60.

Timeworks, Inc. (1987). *Evelyn Wood dynamic reader* [computer software]. Deerfield, IL: Author.

Weitzen, H. S. (1988). *Infopreneurs: Turning data into dollars.* New York: Wiley.

Chapter Seven

Benson, H. (1975). *The relaxation response.* New York: Morrow.

Benson, H. (1984). *Beyond the relaxation response.* New York: Time.

Diethrich, E. B. (1981). *The heart test.* New York: Cornerstone Library.

Ellis, A. (1972). *Executive leadership: A rational approach.* New York: Citadel.

Foell, E. W. (1984, June). Lee Iacocca: The man who wouldn't be president. *Executive Excellence,* pp. 5–6.

Jones, J. W. (1982). *The burnout syndrome: Current research, theory, interventions.* Rosemont, IL: London House.

Levinson, H. (1975). *Executive stress.* New York: Mentor.

Maddi, S., & Kobasa, S. (1984). *The hardy executive: Health under stress.* Homewood, IL: Dow Jones-Irwin.

Metropolitan Life Insurance. (1960). Frequency of overweight and underweight. *Statistical Bulletin, 41,* 4–7.

Selzer, M. L. (1971). The Michigan Alcoholism Screening Test: The quest for a new diagnostic instrument. *American Journal of Psychiatry, 127,* 1653–1658.

Chapter Eight

Brogden, H. E. (1949). When testing pays off. *Personnel Psychology, 2,* 171–183.

Hunter, J. E., & Schmidt, F. L. (1983). Quantifying the effects of psychological interventions on employee job performance and workforce productivity. *American Psychologist, 38,* 473–478.

Jones, J. W. (1991). *Personnel selection and corporate financial performance.* Rosemont, IL: London House.

Jones, J. W., Bray, D., & Steffy, B. (1991). *Applying psychology in business: The handbook for managers and human resource professionals.* Lexington, MA: Lexington.

London House, Inc. (1990). *Test catalog for business.* Rosemont, IL: Author. (Available from London House, Inc., 9701 West Higgins Road, Rosemont, IL 60018.)

Slora, K. B., & Boye, M. W. (1989). *Employee theft in the supermarket industry: Final report of findings.* Rosemont, IL: London House.

Steffy, B. D., & Maurer, S. D. (1988). Conceptualizing and measuring the economic effectiveness of human resource activities. *Academy of Management Review, 13,* 271–286.

Chapter Nine

Magrath, A. J. (1988). *Market smarts: Proven strategies to out-fox and out-flank your competition.* New York: Wiley.

McGonagle, J. J., & Vella, C. M. (1990). *Outsmarting the competition: Practical approaches to finding and using competitive information.* Naperville, IL: Sourcebooks.

Porter, M. E. (1980). *Competitive strategy: Techniques for analyzing industries and competitors.* New York: Free Press.

Chapter Ten

Alster, N. (1989, February 13). What flexible workers can do. *Fortune,* pp. 62–68.

Buden, R., Weber, J., Hoots, C., & Neff, R. (1991, January 15). A tighter focus for R&D: Higher costs and lower profits force more teamwork, fewer blue-sky projects. *Business Week,* pp. 170–172.

Corcoran, E. (1991, December). Rethinking research: Bell Labs seeks a new model for industrial research. *Scientific American*, pp. 136–130.

Crosby, P. B. (1984). *Quality without tears: The art of hassle-free management*. New York: New American Library.

Drucker, P. F. (1985). *Innovation and entrepreneurship: Practice and principles*. New York: Harper & Row.

Dumaine, B. (1989, February 13). How managers can succeed through speed. *Fortune*, pp. 54–59.

Port, O., Schiller, Z., & King, R. W. (1990, April 30). A smarter way to manufacture. *Business Week*, pp. 110–117.

Reiner, G. (1989, August). Winning the race for new product development. *Management Review*, pp. 52–53.

Roussel, P. A., Saad, K. N., & Erickson, T. (1991). *Third-generation R&D: Managing the link to corporate strategy*. Boston, MA: Harvard Business School.

Schaffer, R. H. (1988). *The breakthrough strategy: Using short-term successes to build the high performance organization*. New York: Harper & Row.

Stalk, G., & Hout, T. M. (1990). *Competing against time: How time-based competition is reshaping global markets*. New York: Free Press.

Takeuchi, H., & Nonaka, I. (1986). The new product development game: Stop running the relay race and take up rugby. *Harvard Business Review*, *86*(1), 137–146.

Chapter Eleven

Ames, B. C., & Hiavacek, J. D. (1989). *Market driven management*. Homewood, IL: Dow Jones-Irwin.

Bowden, M. B. (1992, February). The game of the name. *TWA Ambassador*, pp. 28–33.

Field, A. R. (1989, October). First strike: The entrepreneur's edge. *Success*, pp. 44–48.

Lenner, J. (1989, October). Seize tomorrow's markets: Eight steps to master your entrepreneurial advantage. *Success*, pp. 35–42.

McKenna, R. (1986). *The Regis touch: New marketing strategies for uncertain times*. Reading, MA: Addison-Wesley.

McKenna, R. (1989). *Who's afraid of big blue? How companies are challenging IBM—and winning.* Reading, MA: Addison-Wesley.

McKenna, R. (1991). *Relationship marketing: Successful strategies for the age of the customer.* Reading, MA: Addison-Wesley.

Rapp, S., & Collins, T. (1992). *The great marketing turnaround: The age of the individual and how to profit from it.* New York: Plume.

Ries, A., & Trout, J. (1989). *Bottom-up marketing.* New York: McGraw-Hill.

Ries, A., & Trout, J. (1991). *Horse sense: The keys to success in finding a horse to ride.* New York: McGraw-Hill.

Weitzen, H. S. (1991). *Hypergrowth: Applying the success formula of today's fastest growing companies.* New York: Wiley.

Chapter Twelve

Behrens, G. (1992). *The Sales Professional Assessment Inventory (SPAI): A research review.* Rosemont, IL: London House.

Brooks, W. T. (1992). *Niche selling: How to find your customer in a crowded market.* Homewood, IL: Business One Irwin.

Cathcart, J. (1990). *Relationship selling: The key to getting and keeping customers.* New York: Perigee.

DeRose, L. (1989). *Value selling.* New York: AMACOM.

Gellerman, S. W. (1990, May/June). The test of a good salesperson. *Harvard Business Review,* pp. 64–69.

Hanan, M. (1985). *Consultative selling.* New York: AMACOM.

Henry, P. (1987). *Secrets of the master sellers.* New York: AMACOM.

Johnson, S., & Wilson, L. (1984). *The one minute sales person.* New York: Avon.

London House, Inc. (1991). *The Telemarketing Applicant Inventory.* Rosemont, IL: London House.

London House, Inc. (1992). *The Sales Professional Assessment Inventory.* Rosemont, IL: London House.

Magrath, A. J. (1990). *The revolution in sales and marketing.* New York: AMACOM.

Miller, R. B., Heiman, S. E., & Tuleja, T. (1987). *Conceptual selling.* New York: Warner.

Nierenberg, G. I. (1992). *Negotiating the big sale.* Homewood, IL: Business One Irwin.

Porter, M. E. (1985). *Competitive advantage: Creating and sustaining superior performance.* New York: Free Press.

Sandler, C., & Otte, P. (1991, June). Contact management software: Ten top "memory management" programs you'll never forget. *Mobil Office,* pp. 64–86.

Smith, H. B. (1988). *Selling through negotiation: The handbook of sales negotiation.* New York: AMACOM.

Taylor, T. C. (1991, July). Laptop fever grips marketers. *Sales and Marketing Management,* pp. 68–69.

Taylor, T. C., & Companelli, M. (1991, December). Directory of PC-based sales and marketing applications software. *Sales and Marketing Management,* pp. 51–100.

Weitzen, H. S. (1988). *Infopreneurs: Turning data into dollars.* New York: Wiley.

Chapter Thirteen

Albrecht, K., & Zemke, R. (1985). *Service America: Doing Business in the New Economy.* Homewood, IL: Irwin.

Bowen, D. E., Chase, R. B., & Cummings, T. G. (Eds.) (1990). *Service management effectiveness: Balancing strategy, organization and human resources, operations, and marketing.* San Francisco: Jossey-Bass.

Cleary, J. (1991). *Customer service: Making the vision a reality.* Rosemont, IL: London House.

Jones, J. W., & Werner, S. H. (1988). *The Account Retention Index: A construct validity study.* Rosemont, IL: London House.

Liswood, L. A. (1990). *Serving them right: Innovative and powerful customer retention strategies.* New York: Harper Business.

Martin, W. B. (1989). *Managing quality customer service.* Los Altos, CA: Crisp.

Peters, T. (1987). *Thriving on chaos: Handbook for a management revolution.* New York: Warner Books.

Chapter Fourteen

Gill, J. O. (1990). *Understanding financial statements: A primer of useful information.* Los Altos, CA: Crisp.

Shim, J. K., & Siegel, J. G. (1986). *Theory and problems of managerial finance*. New York: McGraw-Hill.

Siegal, J. G., & Shim, J. K. (1990). *Thinking finance: Everything managers need to know about finance and accounting*. New York: Harper Business.

Spurga, R. C. (1986). *Balance sheet basics: Financial management for nonfinancial managers*. New York: Mentor.

Stoner, C. R., & Fry, F. L. (1987). *Strategic planning in the small business*. Cincinnati: Southwestern.

Tracy, J. A. (1989). *How to read a financial report: Wringing cash flow and other vital signs out of the numbers*. New York: Wiley.

Chapter Fifteen

Ballen, K. (1992, February 10). America's most admired corporations. *Fortune*, pp. 40–72.

Hoover, G., Campbell, A., & Spain, P. J. (1991). *Hoover's handbook of American business — 1992*. Austin, TX: Reference Press.

Hoover, G., Campbell, A., Chai, A., & Spain, P. J. (1991). *Hoover's handbook of world business — 1992*. Austin, TX: Reference Press.

Prodigy Services Company. (1992, January). *The Strategic Investor*. White Plains, NY: Author.

Value Line Publishing. (1991 Editions). *The Value Line Investment Survey*. New York: Author.

Walden, G. (1991). *The 100 best stocks to own in the world*. Chicago, IL: Dearborn Financial.

Weitzen, H. S. (1991). *Hypergrowth: Applying the success formula of today's fastest growing companies*. New York: Wiley.

Conclusion

Byrne, J. A., Dapke, D. A., Verity, J. W., Neff, R., Levine, J. B., & Forest, S. A. (1991, June 17). IBM: As markets and technology change, can Big Blue remake its culture? *Business Week*, pp. 24–32.

Dreyfus, J. (1989, August 14). Reinventing IBM. *Fortune*, pp. 30–39.

Kuczka, S. (1991, November 28). County police want to regain high-tech advantage on gangs. *Chicago Tribune*, section 2, p. 3.

Porter, M. E. (1990). The competitive advantage of nations. *Harvard Business Review, 68*(2), 73–93.

Taylor III, A. (1992, January 13). Can GM remodel itself? *Fortune*, pp. 26–34.

Waller, D., & Barry, J. (1992, January 20). The day we stopped the war. *Newsweek*, pp. 16–25.

Weitzel, W., & Jonsson, E. (1991). Reversing the downward spiral: Lessons from W. T. Grant and Sears Roebuck. *The Academy of Management Executives, 5*(3), 7–22.

Willoughby, J. (1991, August 20). Too big to fail: How Citicorp's leverage tricks have produced a big headache for Washington. *Financial World*, pp. 24–27.

Worthington, R. (1991, December 15). Minneapolis enlists gang members: City joins trend to stem violence. *Chicago Tribune*, section 1, p. 29.

INDEX